Icons of Aviation History 1900-1945

Significant and Historic Aircraft And the Stories Behind Them

by Lenny Flank

Red and Black Publishers, Florida

Contents

Montgolfier Balloon

When the Wright Brothers left the ground at Kitty Hawk in 1903, people had already been flying for over a century. In fact, the first manned flights were launched in front of huge crowds in Paris, just a few years before the French Revolution. But they did not happen in airplanes.

For thousands of years, the Chinese had been making "Konming Lanterns". These were paper bags attached to a small wooden frame which held a candle. The warm air from the candle gathered in the bag, causing the lantern to float off into the sky. Although used primarily for religious festivals, they were also used on the battlefield as signaling devices. When a Brazilian priest living in Lisbon, Father Bartolomeu de Gusmão, used the heat from a candle to float a small paper bag at the court of King John V in 1709, he had probably gotten the idea from descriptions given to him by fellow Portuguese clergymen who had been to China.

The ancient Chinese probably did have the technological capability of constructing a larger version of the Konming Lantern — big enough to carry a human aloft — but there is no indication that they ever tried it. Renaissance Europe almost certainly knew of the Chinese lanterns, but also never did anything with the idea.

In 1782, a pair of brothers in Paris, Jacques-Etienne and Joseph-Michael Montgolfier, began their own experiments. They owned a paper-making shop, and one day one of the brothers had happened to see a paper bag, filled with hot air from the machinery, float off the floor. With bigger bags, they found that they could lift objects into the air — and the idea came that if they made their *balon* bag large enough, they could lift a person into the air. They could fly.

Using taffeta cloth that was glued over with strips of paper, the brothers had a material that was sufficiently light, strong and airtight to make large bags, which they heated up with a straw-fueled fire built underneath. Not realizing that it was the less-dense hot air that was producing the buoyancy needed for flight, the brothers thought they had found a new type of gas that was lighter than air, which they referred to, immodestly, as "Montgolfier Gas".

Confident in their new gadget, the Montgolfiers announced that they would make a public flight of their balloon on June 4, 1783. The 33-foot bag was inflated by hot air from a fire on the ground at the Anonnay Marketplace and was then released. Unmanned and unguided, the balloon rose steadily, climbing quickly to an estimated 5-6,000 feet, and floated off on the wind. With no fire on board, the air inside the bag began to cool, causing the balloon to steadily descend. It stayed aloft for 10 minutes before settling back on the ground, covering a distance of over a mile.

The "hot-air balloon" had been born. But it already had competition.

In 1766, almost 20 years before the Montgolfier brothers thought they had discovered a new gas, the English chemist Henry Cavendish had in fact discovered the gaseous element hydrogen and studied its properties. One immediately obvious characteristic was that hydrogen gas was lighter than air, and floated upwards. Years later, an experimenter in Paris named Jacques-Alexandre Charles came upon Cavendish's work and immediately grasped what this meant: if he could fill a large gas-tight bag with hydrogen, it could produce enough lifting power to carry a human.

Making enough hydrogen gas for such a device was the easy part. By mixing iron and sulfuric acid, he produced a chemical reaction that released pure hydrogen gas. The hard part was constructing a large durable bag that was sufficiently gas-tight to be inflated. After a series of experiments, Charles found a workable method: he sewed pieces of silk to form a bag and coated this with a solution of rubber dissolved in turpentine, which sealed all the seams and prevented the hydrogen from passing through the cloth.

By August 1783, Charles was ready for a demonstration flight of his gas balloon. The bag he built was about 12 feet wide, and had lift sufficient to carry about 20 pounds. On August 27, after filling his *balon* with hydrogen gas in front of a large crowd of Parisians at the Champ du Mars, he released it. The American ambassador to France, Benjamin Franklin, was among the spectators who watched as the balloon lifted into the sky, reaching a height of several hundred feet and drifting northwards with the wind. As people on horseback followed along, it flew for 45 minutes before landing in the little village of Gonesse. The experiment then ended ignominiously, as the terrified peasants of Gonesse, thinking that any large thing that had drifted silently down from the sky must be demonic, attacked the balloon and tore it apart with their pitchforks.

The next logical step was a manned flight, and both Charles and the Montgolfiers made their plans. The brothers were ready first. Louis XVI, the King of France, had heard about the earlier flights and was interested, and invited them to make their next flight from the grounds at the Royal Palace. Their new balloon, made with the help of local wallpaper manufacturer Jean-Baptiste Reveillon, was 30 feet in diameter and was decorated with zodiacal signs and suns, in honor of the French "Sun Kings".

Since nobody knew anything at all about how the human body would react to the cold thin air at high altitudes, it was decided that a test flight would be made first. King Louis helpfully offered to provide a couple of condemned criminals as test subjects to be sent aloft, but the Montgolfier brothers decided on a more scientific selection of passengers: they would send a sheep, a duck, and a rooster. The sheep, they concluded, was a good stand-in for a human, being about the same in size and lung capacity. The duck and rooster would be the "controls" in the experiment; since ducks often fly at high altitude it was expected that the balloon ride would not affect it at all, and the rooster, being a bird that did not fly to high altitudes, provided an additional check on the flight's effects. To hold the passengers, a woven wicker basket was attached at the bottom, hanging below the balloon.

All was ready within a month, and on September 19, 1783, the first air passengers lifted off. Eight minutes later, they were back on the ground, and all were happy and healthy. It was the human's turn now.

Once again, the Montgolfiers politely turned down Louis's offer of some prisoners as human guinea pigs, and instead selected a Paris professor named Jean-François Pilâtre de Rozier and a French military officer named Francois Laurent Marquis d'Arlanders as the first air travelers. The balloon, now named the *Aerostat Reveillon*, was modified: the bag was almost 50 feet wide, and the wicker basket was replaced with a circular wooden platform where the passengers stood. To give a longer flight, they would carry a fire along with them in an iron tray slung in the center of the platform. The balloon bag was fireproofed by coating it with alum. In October a final test was made by raising the tethered balloon to a height of several hundred feet with Pilâtre de Rozier aboard, and when he showed no ill effects from the altitude, the flight was ready.

On November 21, 1783, the *Aerostat Reveillon* lifted off from the Bois de Boulogne, in front of a cheering crowd that included King Louis XVI, his wife Queen Marie Antoinette, and US ambassador Benjamin Franklin. Franklin later wrote, "We observed it lift off in the most majestic manner. When it reached around 250 feet in altitude, the intrepid voyagers lowered their hats to salute the spectators. We could not help feeling a certain mixture of awe and admiration." Reaching an altitude of around 500 feet, the balloon covered a little over five miles in 25 minutes. The fire had enough straw fuel aboard for at least another hour; however the pair became concerned when sparks began smoldering on the alum-coated paper envelope, and decided to land. But for the first time in history, humans had flown.

The "Montgolfier Balloon" became a sensation. In one of the first examples of "merchandising", commemorative dinnerware was produced with depictions of the flight; clocks were made in the shape of a balloon. The brothers became the most famous people in Paris. By January 1784, just two months later, larger versions of their hot-air balloon were carrying groups of up to seven people and reaching altitudes over 3000 feet.

But the future of flight did not belong to them. When Jacques-Alexandre Charles finally got his new hydrogen gas balloon ready on December 1, 1783, ten days after the Montgolfier balloon's flight, he conclusively demonstrated that his was the superior flying apparatus. The hydrogen balloon did not need a fire or fuel, its gas bag could carry it higher and further, and with sandbags as ballast it could be raised and lowered at will. The first manned flight of a hydrogen balloon, piloted by Charles and one of his partners, Nicolas-Louis Robert, took off from the Royal Garden at the Tuileries in front of a crowd of 400,000 Parisians, including the King, Queen, much of the French nobility, and, once again, Benjamin Franklin. Also on hand to watch was Joseph-Michael Montgolfier. The gas balloon reached an altitude of 1800 feet (Charles was carrying a barometer and a thermometer with him to take measurements), and flew over two hours, at one point landing and taking off again, before setting down at dusk, 25 miles away.

The age of flight had begun.

Blanchard Balloon

After the successes of the Montgolfiers and Charles, interest in balloons quickly spread across Europe, and the race was on to reach the next technical milestone: to fly between France and Britain over the English Channel.

The history of aviation is full of colorful figures, but Jean-Pierre Blanchard may be one of the most colorful. Born into a poor family in Normandy, Blanchard was largely self-educated. As a young man, he had developed an interest in science and mechanics, and had built his own form of velocipede, an early bicycle, and then designed a new hydraulic pumping system. By the 1770's, Blanchard had already turned to the problems of powered flight and was working on building a pedaled bicycle with flapping wings, steered by paddle-like oars. Although it never had any chance of actually getting off the ground, Blanchard was, to put it bluntly, a self-promoting BS artist, and he loudly claimed to have made several flights with his contraption. No one believed him.

After the successes of the Montgolfiers and Charles, however, Blanchard was quick to adopt something that really *could* fly, and he built his own hydrogen balloon in March 1784. Hoping to improve upon the design, he began to fit his balloon with a variety of flapping wings, aerial screws, and paddle-oars that he had earlier tried out on his "flying bicycle". And to finance and promote his experiments, he moved to London and began carrying paying passengers for rides. Here, Blanchard got himself into trouble when a wealthy doctor named Sheldon hired him to carry a barometer and other weather instruments aloft, and Blanchard threw them overboard during the flight to lighten the ballast.

One of the Londoners who paid for a trip in Blanchard's balloon was Dr John Jeffries. Born in Boston, Jeffries had served as a surgeon in the British Navy during the American Revolution, and had fled to England after Independence. After a balloon flight together, the American expat and the mercurial French aeronaut became unlikely friends, and together they decided to attempt a feat that they knew would guarantee a place in the history books — they would fly across the English Channel.

They were not the first ones with that goal in mind. Jean-François Pilâtre de Rozier, who had piloted the first manned balloon flight in Paris, made an attempt to fly from France to England in January 1875. The balloon caught fire on the way, and Rozier and his partner were both killed when they crashed into the Channel. Blanchard and Jeffries, after three weeks of waiting for favorable winds, would take off just a few days later, on January 7.

They almost didn't get off the ground. As part of Blanchard's experiments, the balloon had been fitted with silk-covered paddles and a rudder along with a hand-cranked propeller, and was seriously overweight. But the oddest part of all was that Blanchard, ever the shameless self-promoter, had hatched a scheme to keep Jeffries (who was financing the entire adventure) on the ground and enable himself to make the flight alone and get all the glory. While the balloon was being inflated, Blanchard barricaded himself into a room at Dover Castle and locked Jeffries out, hoping he'd leave. It took an intervention by the castle's governor to talk Blanchard out. Then, when the inflated balloon was tested for lift and refused to rise, Blanchard calmly announced that the balloon was already too loaded to carry Jeffries' weight, and helpfully offered to make the flight anyway, alone. Jeffries, with what must have been amazing patience, searched the Frenchman, and found he was wearing a leather pouch-belt filled with lead shot.

Once they took off and headed out over the water, however, the pair found that their balloon really *was* too heavy and was unable to climb to a safe altitude. As they skimmed just above the waves, they began throwing out all of their ballast weights. When that didn't work, they broke off and tossed all of the gondola's wooden decorations, then the useless paddle and propeller gadgets, and finally all the ropes and other loose equipment. As they approached the French coastline, they desperately tried to lighten the load even more, first by relieving themselves over the side of the gondola, then by disrobing and tossing their clothes into the Channel. One wonders if, had worse come to worst, Blanchard would have attempted to throw Jeffries overboard as well. Fortunately, things never got to that point, and the balloon barely cleared the trees and reached France. Blanchard and Jeffries had landed clad only in their underwear, but they had made it.

After their flight, the two men, now world-famous, went their separate ways. Jeffries returned to Boston and worked as a doctor until his death in 1819. Blanchard toured Europe giving balloon rides, was granted a Royal Pension by the King of France, then went back to London and formed a ballooning school. There, he apparently went back to his old BS-ing ways, and after one flight he proclaimed that he had landed at the exact spot that he had taken off from—an impressive feat of navigation. Alas, it didn't take long for people to discover that he had actually landed miles away, and had a team of horses carry his balloon back to the starting point.

When his "Aeronautical Academy" in London failed, Blanchard went back to Paris. After the French Revolution broke out in 1789, he was arrested in Austria for printing revolutionary pamphlets, and escaped to the United States. Here, in 1793, he made the first balloon flight in the US, then began a series of early experiments with parachutes, tying cloth prototypes onto cats and dropping them out of balloons. He also claimed to have made several successful parachute jumps himself, but, unable to substantiate his feat or duplicate it publicly, he lost all credibility and returned to Europe. In 1808, during preparations for a balloon flight in Holland, Blanchard suffered a heart attack and fell some 50 feet from the gondola, causing injuries that left him mostly bed-ridden until his death in March 1809.

Today, the barometer that Blanchard and Jeffries carried with them on their cross-Channel flight is on display at the Smithsonian's Udar-Hazy Center, and the International Balloon Museum in Albuquerque NM has a full-scale replica model of their balloon gondola.

For the next 125 years after these achievements, lighter-than-air balloons remained the only method of flight, and they steadily became bigger and more sophisticated. When lightweight gasoline engines became available in the 1890's, steerable "airships", which used hydrogen bags for lift and engine-driven propellers for thrust and steering, began to appear. Airships were used for a variety of civilian and military uses until the 1930s, when airplanes became cheaper, faster and safer.

Wright 1902 Glider

By the closing years of the 19th century, balloons and airships had become fairly commonplace, and attention turned to the possibility of flight using machines that did not depend upon buoyancy for their lifting ability.

One of the most important of these early aerial researchers was Otto Lilienthal. During the 1890s, Lilienthal built a number of crude gliders, big enough to carry a man, that he flew by jumping off hills into the wind. Through careful measurement, and by testing several potential wing sizes and shapes, he was able to publish data on such basic matters as lift and drag. In 1896, Lilienthal was killed in a crash of his "flying machine".

In America, the publicity surrounding Lilienthal's death caught the attention of two brothers in Ohio. Orville and Wilbur Wright ran a bicycle shop in Dayton. They had both a mechanical bent and an interest in flight, and now they decided to continue where Lilienthal had left off. After scouring the local libraries for information, they somewhat naively wrote to the Smithsonian Institution in 1899 asking for any information they might have about "aeronautics", assuming that it could all be worked out in just a short time. (They knew that a number of other people in Europe and the US were also looking into the problem.) Instead, it was the beginning of a multi-year project in which the Wright brothers demonstrated their genius by not only solving all the problems of flight, but by designing and building all the testing equipment they would need to do it.

Almost immediately, they recognized that the real difficulty that needed to be solved in heavier-than-air flight was the problem of flight control—how to both keep the "aeroplane" steady while at the same time allowing for movement in three different axes ("pitch" for up-and-down, "roll" for spinning, and "yaw" for side-to-side). Nearly all of the other people working on the matter were trying to produce a design that was inherently stable and would automatically fly itself in a straight line. The Wright brothers, however, influenced by their work in designing bicycles, realized that a flying machine had to be inherently *un*-stable: rather than being something in which the occupant passively rode, it would have to be actively controlled by its operator, like a bicycle. This is what Lilienthal had done: his machines were steered by shifting one's body weight around, similar to a modern hang-glider. But the Wrights decided that this method was too difficult and dangerous, and they sought a mechanical method of controlling their machine. At first, they experimented with a system of gears and levers to do this, but they quickly determined that this would make their machine too heavy to get off the ground. They needed a better way.

The answer came one day in the bicycle shop as Wilbur was talking with a customer and absent-mindedly twisting an empty cardboard box from an inner tube. As he twisted the box, the shape remained rigid, but one corner rose higher than the other—which in the air would, he quickly realized, produce more lift on one side and turn the aeroplane. The concept became known as "wing-warping".

In July 1899, in their first actual experiments, the Wrights built a working model, five feet wide, from balsa and cloth, which they flew as a kite. The kite's biplane wings were based on an 1896 design by researchers Chanute and Herring. The upper and lower wings were attached to each other by struts to form a rectangular box structure, and four cables were attached to the wing edges and ran down to control levers held by the operator. And it worked. As the kite rode on the wind, the brothers found that they were able to turn and bank it at will using the control levers. It was a revolutionary breakthrough, and it put the Wrights far ahead of everyone else. (Though nobody else knew it: the brothers, afraid that someone would see and steal their designs, were obsessed with secrecy, did all their testing out of the public eye, and did not publish any of their results.)

The next step was to build a model that was large enough to carry a person. Their first glider was finished in 1900. It used a bigger version of the biplane wing-warping system to control roll, and a small flat elevator at the front to control pitch. To keep the plane from side-slipping, it had a fixed vertical rudder. Testing the design required stronger and steadier winds than were available in Dayton, so, after an inquiry to the US Meteorological Service, the Wrights took their new glider to Kitty Hawk NC. Here, it was first flown a few times as a giant kite, then was launched from the top of nearby Kill-Devil Hill, piloted by one of the brothers. In 1901, after making a few changes, the Wrights built a second glider and made a number of flights with it.

The 1900-1901 experiments showed the brothers that they now had a workable control system. But there were still two big problems. The gliders proved to be unsteady in yaw: occasionally the aircraft would unexpectedly veer in the opposite direction and crash. After some thought, the brothers decided that this could be solved by making the rudder moveable and connecting it to the wing-warping controls to push the nose into a turn.

A bigger problem involved the plane's lifting ability. They had based their wing design on the data published by Lilienthal, but in the actual tests the wings produced far less lift than expected. Now the Wright's true genius came into play: they concluded that Lilienthal's data was simply wrong and, to calculate it correctly, they designed and built their own wind tunnel at their bicycle shop, testing various wing shapes and measuring their lift and drag. After determining the best wing shape, they built a new glider in 1902 and took it to Kitty Hawk for testing.

The first tests, in which the 32-foot-wide glider was flown as a kite, showed a drastic improvement. In September and October 1902, the brothers made almost 1,000 flights from the top of Kill-Devil Hill (hauling the 100-pound glider back up the hill after each one), some of them lasting over 25 seconds and covering over 600 feet. The design proved to be fully controllable in all three axes. In effect, they had built an airplane. Since the 1902 Glider did not have an engine, the first powered flight would not happen for another year, but all of the basic systems of flight control had now been demonstrated, and when the Wright Brothers eventually got their patent for a heavier-than-air flying machine, it was based on the 1902 Glider.

After finishing their flight tests in 1902, the Glider was stored in a wooden shed at Kitty Hawk. When the Wrights returned in September 1903 with their powered Flyer, they first refreshed their piloting skills by reassembling the 1902 Glider and making over 1,000 flights with it. By December they were ready to try out the new Flyer.

After 1903 the Glider was unceremoniously abandoned at Kitty Hawk and deteriorated in the weather. Today, the only remaining original piece is a small section of wingtip, on display at the Smithsonian Air and Space Museum. A number of replicas were made later, some of them under the direct supervision of Orville Wright himself. One of these is on display inside the Wright Cycle Company Museum in Dayton OH, and another is on display at the Kitty Hawk National Monument in North Carolina.

Langley Aerodrome A

The Wrights were not alone in their quest to fly. A number of people were experimenting in Europe, and in the US one of the most famous scientists in the country, with generous government financing, was also attempting to get into the air. His last attempt was on December 8, 1903 — just a few days before the Wright Brothers.

In 1886, Samuel Pierpont Langley attended a lecture on the possibility of manned flight. By this time, balloons had already carried people into the air, and a small but enthusiastic group of dreamers had begun to explore the idea of a controllable heavier-than-air craft that could carry people aloft. But unlike most of these dreamers, Langley had the resources available to make a serious attempt at building such a machine—he was the Secretary of the Smithsonian Institution in Washington DC, and he had access to government funding and to the best scientific minds in the country.

Langley, who had been an astronomer at the University of Pittsburgh before working for the Smithsonian, began a systematic study of heavier-than-air flight. His first small models were powered by a wound-up rubber band. He then spent several years attempting to build small but powerful engines, experimenting with electric motors, gasoline internal-combustion engines, and even with motors that used gunpowder as fuel, before settling on a steam engine. In 1896, Langley fit a small gasoline-fueled steam engine to a 16-foot unmanned model that he called the "Aerodrome". The Aerodrome had tandem wings—one in front of the other—which were dihedral, bent into a shallow V-shape for stability. In May 1896, he launched his Aerodrome Model Number 5, using a catapult, from a houseboat in the Potomac River. It was a complete success—the model flew in a straight and steady path, covering 3,300 feet in 90 seconds. In a second test flight in November, the modified Aerodrome Number Six flew 4,200 feet at a speed of 30 miles per hour. He had proven that a powered heavier-than-air flying machine was possible.

With these successful tests, Langley now assumed that he could simply scale up his small models and add a more powerful engine to produce a "Great Aerodrome" that would be capable of carrying a pilot.

When the Spanish-American War broke out in 1898, Langley told the US War Department about his flying machine experiments. The Assistant Secretary of the Navy, Theodore Roosevelt, expressed interest and a willingness to fund further work, and the project was given the green light by President McKinley. The War Department eventually spent over $50,000 financing Langley's experiments. Langley hired an assistant, Charles Matthew Manly, an engineer who had just graduated from Cornell University. Manly was in charge of producing the engine for Langley's flying machine, and would also be the pilot.

By this time, internal-combustion engines had been improved remarkably in power and reliability, and Langley decided to use a gasoline engine in his Aerodrome. Under Manly's supervision, the Smithsonian contracted with Stephen Marius Balzer, a Hungarian living in New York, to design and build a lightweight yet powerful "aero engine". Balzer had already built one of the first automobiles in the US, powered by a three-cylinder internal combustion engine. He now began work on a five-cylinder version, and in anticipation, Langley began building his full-scale Aerodrome A from wood and canvas, in a work shed behind the Smithsonian Castle on the National Mall.

Balzer, however, ran into a series of problems. His designs were for a rotary engine, in which the entire motor spun around on its axis, spinning the propeller along with it. The design had worked well for his automobile, but enlarging it for an aeroplane presented a whole new series of challenges, and by the summer of 1900, he had still not produced a workable design.

After a trip together to Europe to examine new developments being made there in gasoline engine technology, Langley and Manly abandoned Balzer's rotary design, and focused on a water-cooled radial engine instead, in which the fixed-position cylinders would rotate a crankshaft to spin the propeller. By September 1900, Manly had made a working model capable of producing 12 horsepower, and reached 18 horsepower by March 1901. In a quest for more power and less weight, Manly continued to modify the engine, increasing the size of the cylinders and making them of lighter materials. By March 1903, Manly triumphantly wrote to Langley, "The engine proper weighs 120 lbs., and develops on test 52 brake horsepower.... I am prepared to risk myself with it in actual flight." That summer, Langley carried out a final flight test with a one-quarter scale model of his Aerodrome A, then decided he was ready for a manned flight. Like the models, the Aerodrome A would be launched by catapult from a houseboat anchored in the Potomac River. Charles Manly would be the pilot. The 69-year-old Samuel Langley had been working towards this point for 17 years.

On October 7, 1903, Manly climbed into the cockpit of the Aerodrome A as a small flotilla of press reporters and photographers looked on. The engine was started, the twin propellers whirled, the catapult was released — and the Aerodrome dropped ignominiously into the water. Much of its structure was broken by the impact; Manly struggled out of the wreckage and swam to the boat. The derisive press reported that Langley's Aerodrome had flown "like a handful of mortar".

Upon investigation, Langley and Manly concluded that the plane was too nose-heavy, and modified the design to move the balance point further back. Manly explained to the press, "The balancing, upon which depends the success of a flight, was based upon the tests of the models and proved to be incorrect, but only an actual test of the full-sized machine could determine this."

On December 8, Langley and Manly were ready for another try. Once again, Manly climbed aboard, once again the engine was started, once again the catapult was triggered—and once again, the Aerodrome dropped into the water. This time, the tail got tangled in part of the catapult, and both wings broke away as the plane accelerated down the catapult. Manly fished himself from the freezing water and swore intensely as the press once again jeered.

Where had Langley gone wrong? He had been on the right track; his engine designs were far more advanced than anyone else's. Balzer's original rotary engine concept would power most of the early "aeroplanes" used in the First World War, while Manly's radial engine concept would later power many of the aircraft used in the Second World War. Langley's mistake was in assuming that he could simply scale up his small aero models to produce a flyable airframe. Unlike the Wright Brothers, who had done extensive (but secretive) experiments with full-scale gliders, Langley had never tested a full-size version of his design, and was therefore unaware that the exponentially-increased drag and stresses of flight in a full-scale plane required that the airframe be very much stronger, proportionately, than any small-scale model. His airframe was far too weak to withstand the stresses of flight.

A more serious problem, though, was that his propeller was all wrong, and his flat cloth-covered paddle-shaped blades were not capable of producing thrust. Langley had also neglected another crucial area of aeronautics—flight control. His Aerodrome had nothing akin to the Wright Brothers' "wing-warping" system. Even had Langley's plane been capable of achieving flight, it would have traveled only in a straight line, and would not have been capable of maneuvering.

Samuel Langley died in 1906, a broken man who was mocked and laughed at by the press and public. Despite his failure to make a successful manned flight, though, the US Navy did not forget his role as an aviation pioneer—when the first American aircraft carrier was built in 1920, it was christened the USS *Langley* in honor of the Smithsonian Secretary and his Potomac houseboat.

Langley's almost-airplane is now on display at the Smithsonian's Udvar-Hazy Center.

Wright 1903 Flyer

On a December day in 1903, the Wrights changed the world with a 12-second flight.

After the success of their 1902 Glider, the Wright Brothers realized that they now had a suitable wing design and an effective flight control system. All they still needed for powered flight was a means to produce forward thrust, and this consisted of two components: a propeller and an engine. And so they began planning for an engine-driven version of their Glider, which they referred to as "The Flyer".

When Wilbur and Orville first began to think about a propeller for their powered flyer, they assumed, as had Langley and all the other aeronauts before them, that in theory an aircraft propeller was much the same thing as a marine propeller, and that it worked by pushing itself against the air in the same way that a ship's "screw" pushed against the water. In reality, though, despite several attempts by people around the world, no one could get this concept to actually work.

It was now that the Wrights once again demonstrated their genius. Looking at the data which they had gathered from their wind tunnel experiments, they realized that everyone had been approaching the problem in a way that was completely wrong: an aerial propeller was *not*, they realized, an analogue of a ship's propeller, but was instead an aerodynamic wing that sat on its side and turned in the air to produce "lift" at its front surface — thrust — which pulled the aircraft forward in the same manner that the lift on a wing pulled it upward.

Once that remarkable insight was grasped, the rest fell into place. Looking again at their wind tunnel data, they selected a curved shape labeled "Number Nine" which seemed to produce the best results, and based their propeller blade on it. However, they realized that a propeller, unlike a fixed wing, turned through the air in a constant spiral, and that some modifications needed to be made in its shape to account for that. Using some complicated math, they figured out what the best theoretical curved and slightly twisted shape would be, then hand-carved a series of wooden models to those measurements and tested them using a gasoline engine in the shop. To their relief, the measured thrust came within 1% of their mathematically-calculated values. The final propeller shape they settled on, carved from several layers of spruce glued together, had a measured efficiency of at least 75% — that is, it converted about three-fourths of all the energy from the engine into thrust. This achievement, made with paper, pencil, and hand tools, is all the more amazing when one considers that even the best computer-designed wooden propellers made today have a top efficiency of around 85%.

After some more calculations and testing, the brothers decided that the best configuration for a flying machine would use two slowly-turning propellers, which gave better thrust than would one larger rapidly-turning set of blades. To avoid creating air turbulence over the wings, which would interfere with lift, the two propellers would be mounted at the back of the plane, in what is today known as a "pusher" design. The Wrights also understood that the spinning propellers would create a gyroscope effect that would tend to rotate the relatively lightweight aircraft in the direction opposite to that of the turning blades, and this would interfere with aerodynamic control in flight: to counteract this, they mounted the drive chains (made from bicycle parts) so that each propeller turned in the opposite direction to counterbalance the torque produced by the other. It is the same counter-rotating principle used in modern multi-engine airplanes.

The amazingly efficient propeller design also allowed Orville and Wilbur to solve another problem that had defeated every other potential flyer—the engine. With their non-aerodynamic paddle-shaped propellers, all the other aeronauts were forced to try to make up for that inherent inefficiency through sheer brute power, using high-horsepower engines that were, of necessity, big and heavy. It was an impossible task, which is why none of them ever got off the ground. But the Wrights, with their unique thrust-producing propeller design, could get by with a much smaller engine. It was a breakthrough of immense significance.

But it was still no easy task. After many calculations and tests, the brothers concluded that they needed an engine of at least 8 horsepower to generate sufficient thrust in the propellers to keep the flyer airborne, and that it could not weigh more than 200 pounds. No such engine existed at that time—even the smallest and lightest gasoline-powered automobile engines were far too heavy. So, once again, the Wrights went off in their own direction, and decided that if no such engine existed, they would design and build it themselves.

Recruiting a mechanic from their bicycle shop named Charlie Taylor, the brothers went to work. Their first innovation came after they learned of two automobile makers in Europe—named Benz and Daimler—who were successfully making automobile engines out of a new material, aluminum. This had the advantage of being much lighter than steel, although it was also much more expensive. After making several different test versions, Taylor and the Wrights began casting their engine blocks from an alloy of 92% aluminum and 8% copper, which gave the best balance of strength, weight, and heat resistance.

The first of the Wright engines was powered up in February 1903. The next day, during a bench test, it overheated and seized up, destroying itself. Improvements were made and new tests carried out, and by July a workable and reliable engine was ready.

The engine was unsophisticated, even by 1903 standards. There were four cylinders, in a horizontal straight-line configuration. The fuel tank held just 22 ounces and was mounted on one of the wing struts, where the gasoline was gravity-fed into the engine. There was no throttle—once turned on, the engine ran at full speed. There was also no battery—the engine was started by priming each cylinder with a bit of gasoline, closing the switch on a pack of dry cells on the ground, and igniting the gasoline by manually turning both props. A magneto then took over. The ignition sparks came from two contacts inside the cylinders. And there was no radiator: instead, water from a small tank mounted on the wing drained into a jacket around the engine block to keep it cool.

But the finished powerplant weighed just 180 pounds and produced 12 horsepower. It would, the Wrights calculated, be more than enough to get them into the air.

The control system on the Flyer was essentially the same as the 1902 Glider. As in the Glider, the wing-warping and rudder systems were both connected by cables to a wooden cradle at the pilot's hips, which he operated by moving his body from side to side. A small wooden lever operated the elevators at the front of the Flyer. Since the sandy soil at Kitty Hawk was unsuited for wheels, the brothers planned to launch the Flyer from a 60-foot long steel-topped wooden rail that would be half-buried in the ground. Once the engine started, the plane was held back by a rope connected to a metal clip near the pilot, which was then released for takeoff.

By September 1903, the Wrights were ready to put their Flyer to the test, and transported themselves and the crated machine to Kitty Hawk NC. After some test flights in their 1902 Glider to re-familiarize themselves with the controls, they assembled the Flyer, fixed a few minor problems with the transmission chains, and prepared for their first flight. Supremely confident in their calculations, they had already cabled their father back in Ohio that "Success is certain".

The first attempt was made on December 14, when the two brothers tossed a coin to see who would go first. Wilbur won, and climbed into the control cradle. But as he rolled down the takeoff rail something went wrong and the Flyer tumbled off, causing some minor damage to the frame.

Three days later on December 17 they were ready to try again, and this time it was Orville's turn. At 10:35am, he lifted off into the air and traveled 120 feet in the next 12 seconds. The distance he covered was less than the wingspan of a modern passenger jet, but it changed the world.

For the rest of the day, the two brothers took turns piloting the Flyer. Their second and third flights each covered around 200 feet, and the fourth flight, with Wilbur as pilot, lasted an incredible 59 seconds and covered 852 feet.

By this time, the winds had begun to pick up, and as Orville and Wilbur discussed whether they should try a fifth flight, a sudden gust blew the flimsy little Flyer onto its back, breaking the wings and cracking the aluminum engine block. The world's first airplane would never fly again. The Wrights packed it into a crate and returned to Ohio.

Still crated, the Flyer was stored behind a shed at the Wright Bicycle Shop, and left there for the next 13 years. At one point it was covered with water and mud for almost two weeks during a flood. In 1916 the Flyer was re-assembled with a new engine and exhibited at various places over the next several years.

In 1925 Orville Wright (Wilbur had died in 1912) found himself in a controversy with the Smithsonian Institution. When the Smithsonian exhibited Langley's Aerodrome as the first airplane "capable of flight", Orville took offense, and instead of donating the historic 1903 Flyer to the Smithsonian, he sent it on loan to the London Science Museum in 1928. It remained there until 1948 when, after the Smithsonian formally apologized and acknowledged that the Wrights had been first, the aircraft was shipped back to DC. It was displayed in the Smithsonian Arts and Industries Building until 1975, when the new Air and Space Museum opened. In 1985 the Flyer underwent a restoration, and in 2003 it was relocated to its own gallery in the museum titled "The Wright Brothers and the Invention of the Aerial Age".

Wright Flyer III

The Wright Flyer III has been called "the first practical airplane". Indeed, Orville Wright himself declared that "it was in the Flyer III that I really learned how to fly."

After returning to Ohio from their historic 1903 flight at Kitty Hawk, the Wrights decided not to repair their wrecked Flyer, but to build a new version from scratch, with a larger engine. Although they had successfully gotten into the air, they knew there was much work to be done before their machine would be practical, and many modifications and test flights would need to be made.

To test their Flyer II, the Wrights obtained permission to use a cow pasture just outside of Dayton known as Huffman Prairie. Over the next year, Wilbur and Orville made over 100 flights with the new machine, testing modifications to the wing shape, propeller length, and control surfaces. Without the strong winds that had helped them at Kitty Hawk, the brothers designed and built their own catapult, using a 20-foot wooden tower and several hundred pounds of metal weights to pull their Flyer along the launch rail and into the air. Their flights lengthened to 1000 feet, then half a mile. As the controls were improved, there were 90-degree turns, then 180 degrees. In September 1904, the Flyer II made a full 360-degree aerial circle.

Although they were still secretive about the details of how their flying machine worked, the Wrights contacted newspapers across the country, offering to allow them to witness the test flights on condition that they did not publish any photographs of the Flyer II. Only one person, the editor of a local bee-keeping magazine, took them seriously, and so the first published description of the Wrights' test flights at Huffman Prairie was published not in the *New York Times* or the *Chicago Tribune* or the *Philadelphia Inquirer*, but in *Gleanings in Bee Culture*. By the end of 1904, the Flyer II was making flights up to five minutes long, circling the field three or four times.

In January 1905, the Wrights dismantled the Flyer II and re-used all the metal parts to construct the Flyer III. This had a more powerful 25-horsepower engine, though it still required the use of a catapult to get into the air. They added a bigger gas tank and an improved radiator system. But the new design was unstable and difficult to control. In July, Orville made a hard crash-landing that wrecked the Flyer and prompted the brothers to make some changes.

The most important modifications were in the control surfaces: the elevators and rudders were enlarged by 50% and were also extended forward by over five feet, and the rudder control was removed from the hip cradle which operated the wing warping and given its own independent hand control. With these changes, the Flyer III was a vast improvement over the earlier versions: the stability was greatly enhanced, and the pilot now not only had complete control over pitch, roll and yaw, but could turn the airplane in any direction, make circles and S-turns, could change altitude at will, and make smooth controlled landings. In October 1905, with Wilbur at the controls, the Flyer III stayed aloft for slightly over 39 minutes and covered a distance of 24 miles—longer than all of their previous flights put together—landing only because he ran out of gas.

By this time, word had gotten around from some of the locals about the feats being accomplished by the brothers, and newspaper reporters at last began to show an interest. But now the Wrights, afraid that detailed descriptions and photos of their machine would lead to someone stealing their designs, dismantled the Flyer III and halted their flights, determined not to give away their secrets until they had confirmed their patent rights and had signed a contract for commercial production. They would not fly again until 1908, when the Flyer III was taken to Kitty Hawk, reassembled, and fitted with a larger engine. With the pilot now sitting upright, there was room for an extra chair, and it became the first aircraft to carry a passenger when both Wilbur and Orville each took one of their mechanics, Charlie Furnas, aloft. Later that same day, Wilbur made a hard landing and damaged the front elevator. The Flyer III was disassembled and sat crated in a museum in Massachusetts for the next four decades.

In 1947, after the Wright Brothers had become world famous, the city of Dayton opened Carillon Historical Park, a series of exhibits containing samples from local industry. Part of the park would celebrate the Wright Brothers and their achievements, and Orville was asked to provide a suitable display. So, working with a team of mechanics, he gathered almost 85% of the original wooden frame and metal parts from the Flyer III, including the actual 1905 engine, and reconstructed it. Today, the rebuilt Wright Flyer III remains on display at Carillon Park, where it is maintained by the National Park Service.

Wright 1909 Military Flyer

When the US Army bought its first airplane, it wasn't really sure what to do with it. But within just a few years, the Signal Corps was experimenting with different ways to utilize air platforms.

With the success of the Flyer III, the Wrights decided that they were ready to begin offering a commercial version of their flying machines. And naturally they presumed that their best customer would be the US Army.

In January 1905, the brothers contacted their local Congressman, Robert Nevin, who agreed to submit a proposal from them to the US Secretary of War, William Howard Taft, describing the capabilities of their aircraft and offering it for the Army's consideration at a proposed price of $25,000 per machine. Their Flyer, they noted, had now made over 150 flights, in straight paths and circles and in various wind conditions, and would, they thought, be of great use to the military in "scouting and carrying messages in time of war". Nevin submitted the letter to the War Department, who in turn passed it to the Army Ordnance Board.

In response, however, the Wrights received the standard form letter that was sent to all of the dozens of requests that the Army received asking for funding to build a flying machine, declining to provide any money until a particular design had reached "practical operation". Puzzled, Wilbur wrote again, explaining that they were not asking for money to build a flying machine—they already *had* one, and were offering it for sale. In reply, they once again received another form letter.

It's not clear today whether this snub was due to reluctance on the Army's part to become involved again with a "flying machine" so soon after Langley's spectacular and expensive failure, or to bureaucratic inertia and bungling, or simply to a disbelief that the Wright's machine could actually do what they said it could do. In any case, the brothers, exasperated, in essence decided that the US had its chance and had blown it, and now approached the European countries instead. By 1906, serious talks had begun with the French, British, and Germans.

But when the US Government got wind of this, however, it decided that it didn't want to miss the boat, and negotiations soon began. In December 1907, the Army Signal Corps formally issued Specification Number 486, a request for proposals for a "heavier-than-air flying machine". The Army specified that the machine had to be capable of carrying two people (a pilot and observer) with a combined weight of 350 pounds, have a flight range of at least 125 miles and a speed of 40mph for at least one hour, that it be able to take off and land from unprepared ground, and that it could be disassembled for transport in a standard Army wagon. The purchase price was set at $25,000 per plane, with a bonus of 10% for every average mile per hour over 40 and a 10% penalty for every mile per hour under.

Although the War Department received a total of 41 proposals, only one of them had actually built and flown a flying machine, and the Wrights were the only ones to bring an aircraft to Fort Myers VA in 1908 for evaluation. Basically a modified Flyer III with a bigger engine, the "Military Flyer" met all the Army's specifications, and by exceeding the 40mph requirement by 2mph, it earned the Wrights a $5,000 bonus.

But during the test flights, tragedy struck: one of the propeller blades broke and the Flyer plunged to the ground. Orville Wright, who was piloting the craft, suffered a broken hip. His observer/passenger, Army Lieutenant Thomas Selfridge, was killed. The Wrights took the engine from the crashed aircraft and built a new frame, with a modified rudder and some changes to the wire rigging. Testing resumed in June 1909. At one point, William H Taft, now the President of the US, went to observe some of the flights.

On August 2, 1909, the Army Signal Corps formally accepted delivery of "Aeroplane Number 1". The Wrights were retained under contract to train three Army volunteers as pilots: Lieutenants Benjamin Foulois, Frank Lahm, and Frederic Humphries. In February 1910, Aeroplane Number 1 and its new pilots arrived at Fort Sam Houston in Texas. It remained the Army's only aircraft for almost another year, and was crashed and repaired several times.

Other nations soon joined in the field of military aeronautics. In Europe, armies began purchasing planes designed by Voisin, Farman, and Blériot, who were making important technical advances. In Mexico, Alberto Braniff was flying a Voisin biplane which he had brought back from France. In the US, the Signal Corps soon obtained a number of Wright Model B aeroplanes and began experimenting with light machine guns: meanwhile, pilots in the Balkans War of 1912 were dropping grenades out of airplanes. One of the first conflicts in which both sides had military aircraft was the Mexican Revolution, when guerrillas under Pancho Villa flew Martin and Curtiss aeroplanes that they had captured from the Madero Government. In early 1914, one of the Mexican biplanes dropped a number of small bombs onto a rival gunship, the first known air attack on a ship at sea. Despite some ill-informed resistance (one US congressman famously remarked, "What's all this talk about aeroplanes—I thought the Army already has one?"), the airplane was finding its place as a weapon of war.

By 1911, the US Signal Corp's Aeroplane Number 1 was retired from active service. In March 1911 it was donated to the Smithsonian. Today, the original 1909 Military Flyer is on display at the Smithsonian's Air and Space Museum. There is also a reproduction on display at the Udvar-Hazy Center, and another replica is exhibited at the US Air Force Museum in Dayton OH.

Wright Model B

The Model B was the first aircraft to be mass-produced on a commercial scale. But the Wright brothers proved to be far worse businessmen than they were engineers, and within a few short years they would be out of the airplane business completely.

In 1904, the Wright brothers had an absolute monopoly on powered flight. Their 1903 Wright Flyer was the first workable airplane in the world, their 1904 and 1905 Flyers had made flights over half an hour long, with complete maneuvering capability — and they were the only two people who knew how to fly them. By any rational measure, the Wright brothers should have monopolized the entire aviation industry for the foreseeable future. Instead, in just over ten years they were out of the aircraft business entirely, the company they had founded would be floundering, and others would dominate the aviation industry.

When the Wright brothers made their historic flights in December 1903, they had done so in almost complete secrecy, making only a brief announcement to the press that was largely ignored (and flatly disbelieved by many). After their flight at Kitty Hawk, the Wrights retreated back to Ohio where, in a field near Dayton that was chosen specifically for its isolation, they began to modify and improve their designs. The 1903 Flyer had made only short hops in a straight line; by 1905 the new Flyer III was capable of carrying two people for distances up to 50 miles, and could maneuver easily in three dimensions.

By 1906, others had also developed workable airplanes, particularly in France. Albert Santos-Dumont was making demonstration flights in public, covering distances up to 700 feet. In 1908, the Voisin brothers and Louis Blériot were building and flying their own aircraft, and Henri Farman made a circling demonstration flight of over one kilometer.

But once again, the Wright's penchant for secrecy crippled them. The Wright's latest Flyer, the 1907 Model A, was superior to all of these, but nobody knew it. Obsessed with preventing others from stealing their secrets, the Wrights made no demonstration flights. The brothers approached military officials in the US and Europe, but steadfastly refused to demonstrate their Flyer in action, or even show a good photograph of it — to do so, they wrote to a friend, "we would have to expose our machine more or less, and that might interfere with the sale of our secrets." The business strategy of the Wright brothers was brutally simple — they wanted to cash in. As Wilbur wrote to a friend in 1907, "I want the business built up so as to get the greatest amount of money with as little work. Sell few machines at a big profit, so that we can close out." The Wrights decided to simply keep their technology secret so nobody could steal it. When they approached potential military customers, the brothers expected them to accept their word that the aircraft did what they said it could do, and helpfully offered to refund the money if it didn't. Not surprisingly, nobody took them seriously. Some

Europeans even began to doubt that the Wright brothers had ever actually flown at all.

Only one customer decided to take the chance—the US Army. In November 1908, the Army agreed to pay $25,000 for the Wright Military Flyer. On the strength of that contract, a band of New York financiers (including Cornelius Vanderbilt) approached the Wright brothers to make a deal, and the Wright Company was formed with $1 million in financing. The two brothers split $100,000 and were given one-third of the company's stock. They finally got the big payout that they wanted.

With their need for secrecy now gone, the Wrights went to Europe in 1908 and finally made some public demonstration flights. The Europeans were stunned by what they saw. While the early French aircraft flew unsteadily in mostly straight lines, the fast and maneuverable Wright Model A could literally fly circles around them. A French newspaper reporter breathlessly declared, "Not one of the former detractors of the Wrights dare question, today, the previous experiments of the men who were truly the first to fly."

But this technological superiority did not last for long. Once again, the Wright brothers, thinking themselves secure in their economic payoff, made a bad decision, by stubbornly refusing to modify their designs. The flight control system used by the Wright planes was still based on "wing-warping". The pilot used three separate levers to move a series of cables that pulled the edges of the wings up or down to control the aircraft's flight. It was a clumsy system that was difficult to learn, but the Wrights saw no need to improve it—a gap that was quickly filled by others. A whole slew of new aircraft designs appeared, most of them in France, which quickly caught up to and then surpassed the Wright design. Even today, most of the technical terms in aviation, such as "fuselage", "canard", "nacelle" and "aileron", date from this period of European innovation.

One of these new designers was an American named Glenn Curtiss, who had gotten his start in aviation with the "Aerial Experiment Association" formed by inventor Alexander Graham Bell. By 1909, Curtiss was building and flying his own airplane designs. One important innovation pioneered by Curtiss was the "aileron", a flight-control mechanism that changed the airplane's flight path by manipulating a small flap at the trailing edge of the wing instead of the whole wing itself. This was quickly integrated into a French system in which a single control stick operated the ailerons and the elevators, while a foot bar operated the rudder. It was a simpler and more elegant solution. When Louis Blériot crossed the English Channel in his homebuilt monoplane in July 1909, he was using the aileron-based single-stick system, and it was quickly adopted by virtually every other aircraft builder.

Except for the Wrights. Wilbur and Orville had patented the flight-control system for their Flyers, and they considered that all of the European systems were simple variations of their own patented "wing-warping" mechanism. So rather than using improved technology to keep ahead of the European designers, the Wrights decided to use the legal system — in a series of court filings that became known as "The Patent Wars", the brothers filed a series of infringement lawsuits against virtually every other airplane manufacturer in the world, seeking 20% of all their revenues.

Some airplane companies paid up. Others decided to fight — and the most prominent of these was Glenn Curtiss. In a series of court filings, Curtiss argued that his aileron system was fundamentally different than the Wright's wing-warping, and filed for patents of his own. And anyway, Curtiss declared, the Wrights hadn't produced the first workable airplane after all — Langley's pre-Kitty Hawk design, he claimed, was capable of flying even though it had crashed during its tests. (Curtiss even went so far as to borrow Langley's Aerodrome, modify it a bit, and "fly" it for short five-second hops.)

At around the same time, the Wrights began to realize that they needed a new airplane design. The Model A was handmade, one at a time. What the Wright Company needed was a simpler model that could be produced on a much larger scale. The result was the Model B, first introduced in 1910. To improve their design, the Wrights removed the front elevator on the Model A and moved it to the end of the tail, behind the rudder, which made the plane more controllable. They also shortened the landing skids and added wheels to them, allowing the plane to land on virtually any flat surface. And finally, a new more powerful 40-horsepower four-cylinder engine removed the need for a catapult at launching — the plane could now take off on its own from any flat surface. The Model B could carry a pilot and one passenger at speeds up to 44 mph. The price tag was $5,000 per airplane.

From 1910 to 1914, about 100 Model B's were built, reaching a rate of four planes per month. Most of these went to the US Army's Signal Corps, which wanted them for aerial reconnaissance but also did a series of experiments by fitting its Model B's with Lewis machine guns, aerial bombs and bombsights, and radio telegraphs. The Navy also purchased a few Model B's and some other designs, using them as seaplanes (after modifying the landing gear by adding floats).

But the Wright Model B was already obsolete. Newer planes were far superior to it in performance and technology, and the Curtiss Aircraft Company was now the largest manufacturer in the

US. As President of the Wright Company, Wilbur Wright put all his energy into pursuing his patent lawsuits, which dragged on for years and continued after Wilbur died of typhoid fever in 1912 and was replaced as President by Orville. Shortly before his death, Wilbur, realizing that his dogged pursuit of the patent suits at the expense of technological innovation had ultimately allowed others to surpass him, had written wistfully to a friend, "We have been compelled to spend our time on business matters during the past five years. When we think what we might have accomplished if we had been able to devote this time to experiments, we feel very sad." By the time the US Courts awarded the Wright Company victory in its patent suit against Curtiss in 1914, it no longer mattered. The Wright designs had stagnated technologically and were no longer relevant. In October 1915, Orville sold the Wright Company to a group of financiers for $1.5 million. In 1929, the Wright Company was bought by its arch-rival, Curtiss, and became Curtiss-Wright.

Today, only a handful of original Wright Model B airplanes still exist. One of these is held by the Air Force Museum in Dayton, Ohio. Another is a restored 1911 Model B on display at the Franklin Institute museum in Philadelphia. This plane was originally purchased in 1912 by early aviator Grover Cleveland Bergdoll, and was abandoned when Bergdoll fled to Europe to avoid prosecution for evading the draft during World War One. The Model B was donated to the Franklin Institute in 1936 and remained in storage until 2001, when it was restored and placed on display.

Blériot XI

In 1909, Frenchman Louis Blériot, in his homemade single-wing design, proved the long-range capabilities of the airplane.

In 1901, a French engineer named Louis Blériot was making a comfortable living manufacturing automobile headlights when he became interested in the challenges of heavier-than-air flight and decided to try his hand at it. His first design had moveable wings that were supposed to flap like those of a bird (a model known as an "ornithopter"). It was an unworkable concept.

By the time the Wright Brothers flew at the end of 1903, France was an active center of aeronautical research, and the news that somebody in America had made a successful flight spurred them to catch up. The first European to successfully fly was Albert Santos-Dumont, whose "14-bis" aeroplane made a 200-foot flight in October 1906. Blériot, in the meantime, had produced a number of designs, each more sophisticated than the last, but had no success until 1908, when his Model VIII got into the air.

Each success was celebrated in the press, but when the Wrights arrived in Paris in 1908 to make a series of demonstration flights, the Europeans were dumbstruck by how far behind they actually were. Over the next year, French designers struggled frantically to produce better and more capable aircraft.

And one of these was Blériot. Working together with Raymond Saulnier, Blériot began work on an improved version of his newest Model X. Dubbed the Model XI, it was, like its predecessor, a mono-wing with the engine mounted at the front and a box-like fuselage made from a canvas-covered wooden frame. The 7-cylinder engine produced 35-horsepower. The Blériot XI made its first flight in January 1909.

Then Blériot made three improvements which were crucial. Inspired by the Wright's successful ability to maneuver in the air, Blériot fitted the Model XI with his own version of "wing-warping", using a series of control cables that attached above the cockpit. He also abandoned the flat wooden paddle propeller blades that were being used in Europe and adopted an aerodynamic two-bladed propeller made by Chauvière Intégrale. Although not as efficient as the Wright's, the new propeller allowed Blériot to get by with a smaller and much more reliable 3-cylinder 25-horsepower engine designed by motorcycle racer Alessandro Azani. By the summer of 1909 Blériot's Model XI was making flights lasting over half an hour and covering distances of almost 30 miles.

When the London *Daily Mail* newspaper announced in July a prize of £1,000 for the first successful flight across the English Channel, Blériot found himself one of three pilots who gathered at Calais, on the French coast, vying for the honor: Hubert Latham had brought an Antoinette mono-plane, and the Count de Lambert was equipped with two Wright Model B's. For several days, bad weather prevented everyone from flying. When the rain finally cleared on the early morning of July 25, Blériot was the first into the air.

Without a compass, Blériot simply pointed his aeroplane towards England, 25 miles away, and set off. Fighting against rough winds, he was blown steadily off-course, but after 36 minutes he came into sight of the chalk cliffs. He landed hard and broke a propeller blade, but he had made it.

Several others had already made longer and further flights, but Blériot's Channel crossing caught the imagination of the public and became a sensation. His Model XI aeroplane was placed on display in London, then in Paris, and finally found a home in the Paris Museum of Arts and Science, where it remains on exhibit today.

The military implications of Blériot's flight were also not unnoticed. For centuries England had depended upon her Royal Navy for protection. Now, Blériot had demonstrated that a potential enemy did not need to go through the seas: he could go over them. "Britain", concluded one newspaper headline, "is no longer an island."

With the success of the cross-Channel flight, the Model XI became the most widely-produced airplane of the time. Before the end of 1909 Blériot had already sold over 100 copies, and opened up a chain of flight schools across Europe and America (flight lessons were free with the purchase of a Model XI).

New versions were produced. The outdated wing-warping system was replaced by ailerons. The "trainer" version had shortened wings to specifically prevent it from taking off. Student pilots would begin their instruction by running the aeroplanes across the grass without leaving the ground. Once they had mastered the ability to control the aircraft with the rudder pedals and keep it in a straight line, they moved to the full-powered flight version and learned how to perform controlled turns. It typically took between two and six weeks to learn how to fly a Model XI.

The military also took an interest, and was provided with an enlarged two-seat version for a pilot and observer. The French Army began using Blériots in 1910 as artillery spotters and scouts, and a few Model XIs found their way to Mexico. In 1911 Italian pilots in North Africa began dropping grenades out of the cockpits of their Blériot spotters, in what may be the first examples of aerial bombardment. In Britain, the Royal Flying Corps purchased several Model XIs in 1912. A naval seaplane version known as the Blériot XI-2 followed. As more powerful engines like the 70-horsepower Gnome became available, they were fitted to the Model XI airframe. When the stresses caused by the bigger engines and faster speeds proved to be too much, causing a number of fatal accidents, Blériot modified the design by strengthening the wing spars and adding stronger bracing wires.

The Blériot factory produced and sold Model XI's right up to the start of the First World War, and several hundred more were produced from factory plans by amateur builders. Today, over a dozen original Blériot XIs survive in museums in the US, France, England, Canada, Sweden, Argentina, and Spain. The aeroplane exhibited in the Smithsonian Air and Space Museum was flown in air shows by John Domenjoz, an instructor at one of Blériot's flight schools. It was built in 1914 and has a 50-horsepower engine. In England a Model XI, built in 1909 with a 3-cylinder Azani engine, is believed to be the oldest-known aircraft still in flyable condition. In New York, the Old Rhinebeck Aerodrome has two Model XIs, both flyable, one of which was built just a couple weeks after the one in England. One of the Rhinebeck Blériots still makes regular demonstration flights.

Curtiss A-1 Triad

The US Navy carried out a number of crucial early experiments with aircraft, using a specially-designed seaplane from Glenn Curtiss. Ultimately, this led to the aircraft carrier, which has dominated naval warfare for decades.

The first military airplane, the 1909 Wright Military Flyer, was used by the US Army as an aerial observer for reconnaissance and as an artillery spotter. Various navies around the world, however, recognized that the airplane might be useful in fleet engagements too, both to scout for enemy ships and to correct the aim of naval gunfire on targets over the horizon.

In March 1910, the French Navy modified a number of Fabre monoplanes by replacing their landing wheels with pontoon floats, and produced a plane that could take off and land on water—they called it the Hydravion ("sea plane"). It was the birth of naval aviation.

In the United States, the leading researcher into seaplanes was Glenn Curtiss. In February 1911, Curtiss began testing on a new Model E seaplane, which was a modification of his earlier Model D biplane. The new design was revolutionary. It used a central air pontoon and two smaller wingtip floats to allow the plane to act as a "flying boat". The flight controls used a set of ailerons, located between the two wing planes, which were manipulated through a shoulder harness worn by the pilot. The elevators and rudder were combined in the tail at the rear, and the propeller was mounted behind the pilot in a pusher configuration. More importantly, the aircraft had a set of wheels next to the pontoon which could be cranked up and down, allowing the pilot to land on either water or ground. Since it could operate on land, sea and air, Curtiss dubbed it the "Triad".

The US Navy took interest and requested that some modifications be made. Curtiss complied, and the new Model E-8-75 was capable of carrying two people aloft for two hours. The Navy purchased fourteen of the seaplanes (at around $4,000 each), designating it the A series. Curtiss was also hired to train a number of pilots for the Navy, and in June 1911 Theodore "Spuds" Ellyson successfully flew a Triad from Keuka Lake in New York, becoming the first certified US naval aviator. Soon Triads with extra fuel tanks were staying aloft as long as ten hours.

The next step was to take the airplane to sea. In December 1911, the French Navy commissioned a ship, the *Foudre*, that was specially-built as a seaplane carrier. She stored four Fabre seaplanes (later replaced by more-capable Voisin flying boats) in a hangar on deck, which were lowered into the water by a crane, flew off for their missions, then landed in the water alongside the carrier to be winched back aboard. By 1913, the British Royal Navy and the US Navy had seaplane carriers of their own, the HMS *Hermes* and the USS *Mississippi*. In the Pacific, the Japanese, who were quickly becoming a naval military power, had purchased three of Curtiss's Triads and were also experimenting with seaplane carriers.

When World War One broke out in August 1914, the seaplane carrier finally got its chance for action. In September, the Japanese navy, fighting for the Entente allies, launched the first naval air strike in history: four Japanese copies of French Farman seaplanes were lowered from the seaplane carrier IJN *Wakamiya*, flew off to bomb a German base in Tsingtao, China, and returned to their ship to be recovered. Three months later, on Christmas morning, the British launched a more ambitious attack: a fleet of three seaplane carriers, HMS *Engadine, Riviera* and *Empress*, launched a group of nine Short seaplanes loaded with bombs to attack the German Zeppelin base at Nordholz, and damaged several of the airship sheds.

But the seaplane carriers presented some crippling problems. The ships were slow and unable to keep up with the fleet. The seaplanes could not take off in rough seas and were useful only in good weather conditions. And winching the planes off and on the ship was a time-consuming task. It was quickly realized that naval airplanes would be much more useful if they could take off and land directly onto a fast-moving ship.

The first experiments took place in the US. In November 1910, a modified Curtiss Model E took off from a flat wooden platform that had been built over the forward turrets of the cruiser USS *Birmingham*, and landed on shore. Two months later, the same pilot took off from land, flew to the battleship USS *Pennsylvania* anchored offshore, and landed on a flat wooden deck built over the aft section of the ship. To stop within the short landing distance, the plane used a metal hook hanging from its tail to snag a series of ropes stretched across the deck and weighted down with sandbags. The concept of the aircraft carrier had been born.

The British Royal Navy took a passenger ship that was in the process of construction, added a flat wooden flight deck that ran the length of the ship, and launched her in December 1917 as the HMS *Argus*. She carried up to 18 Sopwith Pups and Sopwith Ship Strutters. The first American aircraft carrier, a converted coal-carrier, was commissioned as the USS *Langley* in 1922. She carried 36 biplanes, and was used mostly to test various operations procedures. In 1927, the first American fleet carriers were commissioned, the *Lexington* and the *Saratoga*. They carried a mix of 78 fighters, dive bombers and torpedo bombers.

Today, a replica A-1 Triad is on display at the Museum of Naval Aviation in Pensacola FL. This was built by engineers from the Navy and the aircraft companies Ryan and Convair in the 1960's for the 50th anniversary of naval aviation, using photographs and original drawings.

Benoist XIV

The first regularly-scheduled passenger air service was established not in New York, London, or Paris — but in Florida.

In 1913, the Tampa Bay region was a little-known backwater in Florida, noted, if at all, for its cigars, phosphate fertilizers, and oranges. The area's two largest cities, St Petersburg and Tampa, were on opposite shores of Tampa Bay. Only 21 miles of open water separated them, but no bridge was capable of crossing the Bay, and traveling from one "sister city" to the other required either a 2.5-hour steamboat ferry ride, or a 4-hour railroad trip completely around the Tampa Bay shoreline.

Enter St Petersburg resident Percival Elliott Fansler. Fansler sold boat engines for a living, but his interest in mechanics also led him to pay close attention to the new field of aviation. The Wright Brothers had flown ten years earlier, but by 1913 "aeroplanes" were still viewed by the public as novelties, something thrilling to watch (or, for the most daring, to take a short hop in over some fields as a passenger), but not really of much practical use.

In 1912, pilot Tony Jannus made the newspapers by flying, with a passenger, 250 miles along the Mississippi River from Paducah, KY to St Louis, in a Benoist "flying boat"—an airplane designed to take off and land on water. Jannus was already famous—he had piloted the airplane from which the first successful parachute jump was made, and already held several distance records for seaplanes. Intrigued by Jannus's latest feat, Fansler began corresponding with the aircraft's manufacturer Tom Benoist (pronounced "ben-wah"), and broached the idea of using a flying boat to ferry paying passengers across Tampa Bay. Benoist agreed to provide two seaplanes for the venture, and Tony Jannus as pilot, if Fansler could arrange funding for it. When the city of Tampa turned him down, Fansler went to the city of St Petersburg, which agreed to fund 50% of the needed $3,000 and to construct a hangar for the airplanes (at the spot where Albert Whitted Airport stands today). Eleven local businessmen together put up the rest of the money. The new "St Petersburg-Tampa Airboat Line" contracted with Benoist and the city of St Pete on December 17, 1913—ten years to the day after the Wright brother's first flight—for two planes and pilots to make twice-daily flights six days a week from January to March 1914. The commercial airline was born.

The first Benoist Model XIV seaplane, Number 43, arrived in St Petersburg by train on December 12, 1913, some two weeks before its scheduled debut. Built of wood and canvas, the biplane had a wingspan of 44 feet and was 26 feet long. It weighed about 1250 pounds. Its Roberts six-cylinder inline engine produced 75 horsepower, enough to move the plane at a top speed of 64 mph. The engine was located in the lower part of the airplane, but the propeller was mounted at the rear of the cockpit in a "pusher" configuration. The cockpit had room for two—the pilot and one passenger—but on some flights two small passengers were crammed into one space. In addition to the regularly-scheduled flights to Tampa, charter trips could also be booked to Clearwater, Sarasota, Bradenton, Tarpon Springs, or Safety Harbor.

The local newspaper, the *St Petersburg Times*, promoted the upcoming flight extensively, and on the morning of January 1, 1914, a crowd of at least 3,000 people (almost half the entire city's population) had gathered at the St Pete Municipal Pier along the waterfront to watch the spectacle, as a band played, speeches were made (Benoist himself had traveled from St Louis to Florida for the occasion), and ceremonial photos were shot. (One person in the crowd was the humorist Will Rogers, who was performing in St Pete at the time.) Although the regular price of a round-trip passenger ticket was $10 (about $200 in today's money), an auction was held for the honor of taking the first flight. Former St Pete mayor Abram Pheil won with a bid of $400, which the airline donated to the city government to help pay for installing harbor lights. Pheil climbed in, he and pilot Jannus waved to the crowd, and they took off. To save fuel and avoid winds, the plane flew just above the waves at an altitude of less than 50 feet (although, the advertising declared, the plane could go up to 1,000 feet "at the passenger's request"). Partway through the 20-minute flight, the plane developed minor engine trouble—the drive chain that connected the engine to the propeller was slipping on its sprockets. Jannus landed on the surface of Tampa Bay, climbed out and adjusted the chain, and took off again. When they landed in Tampa at the mouth of the Hillsborough River, a crowd of 3,500 was there to greet them. After more speeches, Jannus and Pheil climbed into their plane once more, and were back in St Pete before lunchtime.

The St Petersburg-Tampa Airboat Line continued to operate until May 5, five weeks after its contract had expired. The airline's two Benoist XIV planes (the second plane, Number 45, was piloted by Tony Jannus's brother Roger. It was a little larger than Number 43 and could carry two passengers comfortably) made 172 scheduled flights, a large number of privately-chartered flights, and carried a total of 1205 passengers. In a publicity stunt, the *St Pete Times* booked cargo space for morning delivery of its newspapers to Tampa, while an enterprising florist in Tampa flew fresh flowers every day to customers in St Pete. The Port of Tampa required Jannus to obtain a "commercial pilot's license", which was issued by the US Department of Commerce in February. On the license, the word "steamboat" was crossed out, and "aeroplane" written in.

By May, most of St Petersburg's "snowbird" residents and tourists had returned north for the summer, and passenger bookings dwindled. When the city's contracted subsidy ran out, the Airboat

Line continued another five weeks on a schedule of chartered flights, then ceased operations. Benoist planned to return later with a larger seaplane capable of carrying twelve passengers. Just three months later, however, World War One broke out. Tony Jannus was killed in 1916 while training new pilots in Russia, when his Curtiss Jenny crashed into the Black Sea. His brother Roger was killed over France in a DH-4 spotter in 1918.

After the airline folded, the two Benoist aircraft were taken on tours of the US, giving airshows and taking passengers for rides. Number 45 crashed into the ocean during a flight in San Diego in 1915, and was destroyed. The original airliner, Number 43, crashed on a lake in Pennsylvania, was rebuilt, and returned to do airshows in St Petersburg in 1915, where it crashed in the Bay after losing a wing and was rebuilt again. In November 1916, Number 43 was crated for storage by the Benoist Company, and was never seen again.

In the early 1980's, members of the Florida Aviation Historical Society began building a replica of the Benoist XIV Number 43, painstakingly recreating the plane from photos since no original engineering drawings could be found. Because no Roberts engines still existed, the replica had to use a 6-cylinder inline Chevrolet engine instead. On January 1, 1984, 70 years after Jannus's first commercial passenger flight, the replica Benoist flew from St Petersburg to Tampa and back again. After being filmed for an IMAX movie that was shown at the Smithsonian Air and Space Museum, the replica Benoist was donated to the St Petersburg Museum of History, where it remains on display.

In 2013, another flying replica of the Benoist was built to celebrate the January 2014 100th anniversary of the first airline. This time the Fantasy of Flight museum was able to find original drawings of a Roberts engine and build a working reproduction. Although bad weather and FAA paperwork prevented the plane from flying, it was placed on display at Jannus Landing for the anniversary celebrations.

Rumpler Taube

As the First World War began in 1914, aviation was still in its infancy. But several pre-war designs were rushed into military service, even though it was not yet clear what battlefield role they would serve.

While the US Army experimented with the Wright Military Flyer and the Model B, similar testing was being done in Europe. In Austria, Igo Etrich had developed a design based on some of Lilienthal's monoplane gliders, but also incorporating the Wrights' idea of wing-warping and even some design features from a native tree seed pod. Etrich's aeroplane was large enough to carry two people. To strengthen the wings, Etrich used a series of riblike radiating struts which gave the aircraft an elegantly graceful curved appearance. It first flew in 1910. Etrich called it the Taube ("Dove").

Etrich formed an aeroplane company with partner Edmund Rumpler to manufacture the plane, but after a dispute Etrich dropped out, abandoned his patents, and left Rumpler to himself. With the patents effectively dead, at least a dozen other companies began producing knock-offs, but Rumpler's product was of superior workmanship and quality, and within a year most of the aeroplanes being made in Germany were Rumpler Taubes.

It didn't take long for the military to take an interest. By the end of 1911 the German, Austrian and Italian armies were all flying Taubes, a few copies were made in Japan, and even the British Army obtained one of the aircraft. During the conflict in Libya in November 1911, an Italian Taube carried out what may be the first aerial bombing mission in history, with the rear-seat observer carefully dropping 4-pound grenades over the side of the plane at ground targets. By the time of the 1912 Balkans war, Taubes were being used for reconnaissance, for aerial bombing, for artillery spotting, and as trainers for new pilots.

When the First World War broke out in August 1914, everyone assumed it would be over quickly. By September, German troops were within thirty miles of Paris, and it seemed as if the defeat of France was imminent. On September 6, however, French reconnaissance airplanes detected a gap between two German armies, and, in the "Miracle of the Marne", French and British troops poured in and drove the Germans back over forty miles. Paris was saved. Within weeks, both sides dug themselves in, constructing a string of defensive trenches that stretched, unbroken, from the Swiss border all the way across Europe to the English Channel.

Meanwhile, German Taube aeroplanes were being used for reconnaissance on the Russian front, playing an important role in the Battle of Tannenburg. When the Great War had broken out, the German Army already had almost 250 aeroplanes—over half of them Taubes. By September 1914, daring aircrews were flying over Paris and dropping seven-pound bombs onto the streets. Before the end of the year Taubes were also accompanying Zeppelin airships across the English Channel to bomb London.

They soon played a more vital role. The generals on both sides needed all the help they could get to blast a way through the tangle of trenches. The best weapon they had for this was artillery. The new field guns, however, had such long ranges that the gunners often could not see where their shells were landing, making it impossible for them to adjust their aim for greater accuracy.

It was the European expertise in aeronautics that helped solve the problem, and the earliest stage of aerial warfare centered around reconnaissance and artillery spotting. Unarmed two-seater airplanes began to regularly fly over enemy trenches—the observer in the rear seat would photograph them and provide critical information for planning ground assaults, as well as giving advance warning of enemy troop movements and imminent attacks. Observation planes were also used as aerial artillery spotters, watching the shells fall and, using a wireless Morse code transmitter, advising gunners on corrections to their aim, allowing intense and accurate bombardments of enemy positions with pinpoint accuracy.

The rapid increase in technological know-how spurred by the war, however, soon left the Taube obsolete and vulnerable to anti-aircraft machine guns and then to newer armed scout airplanes. The "Dove" was removed from frontline service by early 1915, though it continued to serve the Germans throughout the war as a trainer for new pilots.

Only a tiny number of Taubes survived the war. One pre-war model is in the Technisches Museum Wien in Germany, and another Taube is on display in Norway. The Owl's Head Transportation Museum in Maine produced a full-size reproduction in 1990 with a modern engine, which is on display there and still flies. In the late 1990s a pair of hobbyists in Missouri constructed a half-scale replica of a Rumpler Taube and flew it at air shows. This plane was donated to the Combat Air Museum in Topeka in 2006, where it is on display.

Morane-Saulnier Model N

The first military "fighter plane" was a crude and improvised affair, cobbled together quickly to meet the challenge of the First World War trenches.

At first, WW1 aerial observation was a tranquil, almost gentlemanly affair. Opposing pilots would often wave to each other as they passed by, each on the way to photograph the other's trenches. It quickly became apparent, however, that it was a huge military advantage to prevent the other side from observing one's fortifications. Rear-seat observers soon began carrying pistols and rifles to take potshots at each other, and it wasn't long before light machine guns (like the British Lewis gun) were mounted at the rear of the plane for the observer to use against enemy reconnaissance flights. By 1915, both sides began designing single-seat "scout" planes, which were specifically intended to seek out and shoot down enemy observation planes and to defend their own spotters from enemy scouts.

Before an effective aerial fighter plane could be produced, however, a puzzle had to be solved. The simplest way for a solitary pilot to aim his gun was to mount it in line with the fuselage of his airplane, thus allowing him to aim the gun accurately simply by pointing the airplane's nose at the target. And since machine guns were prone to jamming and also held a limited amount of ammunition, they had to be physically within the pilot's reach so they could be reloaded and, if necessary, unjammed. The best location for this was on the cowling directly in front of the cockpit.

This, however, presented an awkward problem – it put the machine gun directly in line with the whirring propeller, and any pilot who aimed and fired his machine gun at an enemy would be virtually certain to shoot off his own propeller.

The first pilot to come up with an effective solution was the Frenchman Roland Garros, who had been a famous air racer before the war. Garros attached a light Hotchkiss machine gun to the front of his Morane-Saulnier Model L "Parasol" monoplane, and, to prevent it from shooting off his own propeller, he bolted two steel wedges to the back of the blades, deflecting any bullets that might hit them as he was firing. On April 1, 1915, Garros successfully shot down a German observation plane over British trenches. Later that day, another French pilot with a modified Morane, Jean Lavarre, also shot down a spotter plane.

Over the next week, Garros refined his tactics. Since his Morane airplane was slower than the German biplanes he was chasing, he learned to loiter above the altitude normally taken by the spotters, then, when they passed below him, dive on them from behind to attack before they could speed away. On April 11, Garros intercepted two German spotter planes and shot them both down. They were his fourth and fifth claimed aerial victories, making Garros the first fighter ace in history (though this is now disputed, as some researchers have Navarre reaching "ace" status first and others conclude that Garros only had three actual air victories).

Less than a week later, though, Garros developed engine trouble while flying over German trenches and was forced to land. He was held as a POW until he escaped in early 1918 and made his way back to France. After a refresher training to learn to handle the newer French fighters, Garros returned to combat. He was shot down and killed in October 1918, just a month before the war ended.

The French military, meanwhile, carried on with Garros's idea by equipping a number of Morane-Saulnier Model N scout planes with forward-firing machine guns. Although it had been designed before the war as a civilian air machine, the Type N was surprisingly modern-looking: a low-wing monoplane, it had a cone-shaped aerodynamic fairing built into the propeller hub, giving it the nickname "The Bullet". The British armed it with the Lewis light machine gun, while the Russians built their own versions. A later variant known as the Model I had a more powerful engine and a larger Vickers machine gun. The Saulnier company had already been working on a synchronizer gear which would time the bullets from a machine gun so they would not hit the prop blade, but the ammunition of the period was unreliable and the system never worked.

With the Germans now successfully flying their synchronized Fokker Eindekkers, the Entente needed a quick solution, and the modified Morane-Saulnier provided it. The Bullet remained the Allies' primary fighter plane until early 1916, when newer designs began to replace it.

There are no surviving wartime Morane-Saulnier aircraft. The Western North Carolina Air Museum, in Hendersonville, has a full-scale replica of an N1 "Bullet" on display.

Fokker Eindekker

The first purpose-built fighter plane came from the Germans, and made the name "Fokker" a part of aviation history.

Roland Garros's captured Morane L monoplane was turned over to Anthony Fokker. Fokker was a Dutch mechanical engineer with an interest in aviation. At the outbreak of the war, he had offered to design airplanes for the Entente, but the British and French generals did not view the flimsy little craft as important, and they turned him down. In response, Fokker offered his services to the Germans instead.

When Fokker examined the steel wedges that Garros had attached to his propeller blades, he knew that they enabled the plane to fire through the propeller, but Fokker was already working on a better system. His "interrupter gear" used a pronged cam attached to the propeller shaft to push a metal rod attached to the machine gun mechanism, which inactivated the gun whenever a propeller blade was directly in front of the barrel. Although the pilot could fire the machine gun continuously, the cam would interrupt the fire whenever the propeller was in the way.

The interrupter gear system was incorporated into one of Fokker's new "scout" models, the A-3. Though it still used the outmoded "wing warping" method of control instead of ailerons, this was an advanced design for its time, with a low mono-wing configuration and a body frame made of steel tube instead of wooden spars. The armed version became known as the Eindekker, officially designated the E-1. Although faster than the Morane, the Eindekker was still slow (top speed about 85mph) and not very maneuverable, but its fixed forward-firing machine gun made it superior to anything the Entente could put into the air.

The first confirmed aerial victory with an Eindekker was in July 1915, when Kurt Wintgens, flying one of the prototypes, shot down a French Morane L Parasol. Once production began on the E-1, one Eindekker was assigned to each air observation squadron to serve as a protective escort. Among the first pilots to fly the new fighter planes were Max Immelman and Oswald von Boelcke. On August 1, 1915, a flight of British BE2c bomber/observer planes attacked the German airfield at Douai, and Immelman and Boelcke took off in their Fokkers to intercept. Boelcke's gun jammed and he was forced to land, but Immelman shot down one of the BE2c's and damaged another.

For the rest of 1915, Immelman and Boelcke carried on a friendly rivalry, with each matching the other's score. By October, both had scored five aerial victories and reached "ace" status. On January 12, 1916, both aces scored their eighth victories, and both were awarded the *Pour le Merite*, the coveted military medal known informally as "The Blue Max". Immelman was killed in June 1916, after scoring a total of 15 aerial victories—he was shot down in combat with a number of British Fe2b's. Boelcke was killed not long afterwards in an air collision while flying an Albatros—he had 40 air victories.

Although Immelman received most of the attention from the German press (he was known as "The Eagle of Lille"), it was Boelcke who made the most lasting contribution to aerial combat. A skilled tactician, Boelcke was also a masterful organizer and, more importantly, an instructor (one of his students was Manfred von Richthofen). His observations on aerial combat and organization, known as "Boelcke's Dicta", are still taught today to modern jet fighter pilots. They were:

"1. Each pilot must know about the construction of his aircraft, and the strengths and weaknesses, so that he can get the best out of his machine and avoid getting into situations in which his opponent can exploit the weaknesses of design.

"2. He must know as much as possible about the strengths and weaknesses of any enemy aircraft he will likely encounter.

"3. The pilot must be fully at home in his aircraft as a result of training and familiarization flights, so that the machine can be exploited fully without conscious thought, the full spectrum of aerial maneuvering being second nature to the pilot.

"4. The pilot must know all about his armament, so that the right range and deflection can be easily selected, and jams and stoppages cleared quickly and without taking his attention away from more pressing matters.

"5. The pilot must develop the knack of seeing enemy aircraft without himself being seen, developing this knack of spotting opposing aircraft at a considerable range by constant practice in knowing how to search the sky and what to look for.

"6. The pilot must acquire the habit of 'taking in' unconsciously the general progress of the whole multi-aircraft dogfight going on around the individual combat in which the pilot will become involved, so that a third party entering the duel can be spotted and allowed for, and no time wasted in assessment of the general situation after the end of an individual combat.

"7. The pilot should become accustomed to flying in a regular position in the formation, so that teamwork will improve and each man will get used to flying with the same companions.

"8. The pilot must memorize a number of rendezvous points in the area, so that if the formation is split up, lost pilots can pick up the formation again by circling over the rendezvous point just under the clouds (aircraft over clouds being very easy to spot) until rejoined by others of the formation.

"9. Formation is to be kept at all times, leaving the leader to spot the opposition while the others cover his and each others' tail by constant vigilance, unless another pilot spots the opposition first and signals the leader by moving ahead and waggling his wings before turning in the direction of the opposition.

"10. The leader will signal the best method of attack, using all the advantages of sun, cloud, haze, and rain, but always attacks will be from above where possible.

"11. Once combat has been joined in a dogfight, it is every man for himself, but it is essential to keep a cool head and courting disaster to try to evade the attacker by the execution of copybook aerobatics such as loops and half-rolls.

"12. The use of smooth executed, predictable maneuvers in combat is futile. One should always turn into the attacker so that a circling combat will ensue; here it is essential to turn as tight as possible to try to close up on the attacker and dispatch him with an accurate burst of machine-gun fire.

"13. It is senseless to run from a fight with an aircraft of equal performance, unless some tactical consideration gives the pursued a considerable advantage.

"14. To be avoided at all costs are jinking maneuvers, for the pursuer can always cut across the corner so formed and make up the necessary distance on the pursued aircraft."

Improved models of the Eindekker soon appeared. The E-2 had a larger engine but its smaller wing area made it more difficult to fly. The most widely-produced version was the E-3, introduced in September 1915. The final version, the E-4, carried two machine guns. A little over 450 Eindekkers were built during the war, of which over half were the E-3 model. In all, 11 early Fokker pilots became aces, and the Eindekkers were shooting down so many Entente spotter planes that French and British fliers referred to the period as "The Fokker Scourge".

Only two Eindekker fighter planes survived the war. One of these was E-1 model serial number E.13/15, flown by Immelman himself. It was housed in a museum in Dresden, where it was destroyed during a World War II bombing raid. Another Eindekker, an E-3 model flown by a rookie pilot, was captured in April 1916 when it mistakenly landed on a British airfield in a fog. It was returned to England for evaluation, and is now on display in the London Science Museum.

A full-scale replica of an Eindekker E-4 is on display at the Combat Air Museum in Topeka KS. Another replica is exhibited at the San Diego Air and Space Museum, and the Military Aviation Museum in Virginia Beach VA also has a replica Eindekker on exhibit.

Voisin 8

One of the first purpose-built bombers, the Voisin 8 quickly adapted to a number of roles, including night-bombing.

While the impetus for the first military aircraft came from the need for reconnaissance (and to prevent enemy air reconnaissance), with the outbreak of the First World War the potential usefulness of the aeroplane as an offensive weapon was also clear. There had already been experiments with dropping explosive bombs from the air, during conflicts in the Balkans and in Mexico, but it was in the first years of the Great War that the "bomber" took its place in warfare.

The pioneer in this field was the Frenchman Gabriel Voisin. Voisin's interest in aviation pre-dated the Wright Brothers' first flight: in 1902, as the Wrights were testing out their Glider, Voisin was already building gliders in France. In 1905, Voisin formed an airplane-manufacturing company with Louis Blériot, but they did not get along very well, and a year later Voisin bought out Blériot's share of the company and gave it to his brother Charles, and "*Les Freres Voisin*" became Europe's leading airplane designers. When Henri Farman won the 50,000-franc prize for the first flight of over one kilometer, he was flying a Voisin.

By 1912, the French military purchased a number of Voisins, modified with an 80-horsepower engine, as observation platforms. This "Type 1" was a pusher design, with the engine mounted at the rear along with elevators and rudders in the tail, and a pilot and observer sitting together in a nacelle at the front. The landing gear consisted of a four-wheel carriage. The Voisins were by nature cautious and conservative designers, and although the French Army turned to them for more powerful versions during the War, they never changed the basic configuration. Although deployed for reconnaissance and artillery spotting, the Type 1 was sturdy and stable, and observers soon doubled as bombardiers, by dropping hand grenades or small finned bombs over the side onto ground targets. Within a short time, crude improvised bomb racks were being jerry-rigged that could carry up to 125 pounds of bombs.

By 1915, newer Voisin Model 3 planes with 120-horsepower engines were being fitted with factory-made bomb racks on the wings which could carry a 330-pound load to a range of 125 miles. A year later, the first dedicated bomber units were formed. The Voisin Type 5 and Type 6, with 155-horsepower engines, were sent on air raids against targets as far away as Germany. But their design was already becoming obsolete and they were vulnerable to German fighters and anti-aircraft fire.

So when the Voisin 8 appeared in November 1916, it was assigned to a new role—as a night bomber. The new bomber was originally planned to have a 300-horsepower Hispano-Suiza engine to give it more range and speed, but the Entente was unable to produce enough of these, so the Voisin was fitted with 225-

horsepower 8-cylinder in-line Peugeot engines instead. The Model 8 became the standard Allied night bomber for most of the war, capable of delivering almost 400 pounds of bombs in an internal bomb rack, and also attacking ground targets with its 37mm cannon.

In all, the French, British and Russians produced a little over 1000 Model 8 Voisins. The British fitted a series of sand filters on the engine and used it during fighting in the Middle East, while the Russians replaced the landing wheels with skis for use on ice and snow. Just as the war ended, the Model 8 was being replaced by the Model 10, with a bigger engine and a 600-pound bomb load.

Before the United States entered the war in 1917, the Army obtained a Voisin 8 from France for "technical evaluation". But by this time the design was already outdated. The US, when it entered the war, instead produced its own versions of the DH-4, and the War Department's Voisin 8 was given to the Smithsonian Institution (without an engine). In 1989, while being restored, the aircraft was fitted with an original Peugeot engine, and went on display at the Air and Space Museum. It is the only surviving Voisin Model 8.

Airco DH2

Although the British were technologically far behind the Germans in the early months of aerial warfare, they were soon able to field an effective response to the "Fokker Scourge", and win air superiority through a completely different approach to fighter design.

When the Fokker Eindekkers with synchronized machine gun appeared in the summer of 1915, the Entente had to field a response, and do it quickly. And since neither British nor French aircraft designers yet knew how to make an interrupter gear, they had to seek a different solution.

The answer came from English designer Geoffrey de Havilland, the chief designer for the Airco company. De Havilland had already produced a two-seat scout plane called the DH-1, which used a "pusher" configuration with the engine mounted at the back of the fuselage and the propeller facing backwards. This left the front of the plane open and avoided the entire problem of "how to shoot through the propeller". By modifying this design—reducing the size to hold just one person and adding a machine gun to the front—De Havilland offered a fighter that would be capable of taking on the German Fokkers.

The DH-2 was designed from the start with input from British fighter pilots, particularly Major Lanoe Hawker of the Royal Flying Corps, who had already scored seven air victories over France. The open-cockpit nacelle on the new De Havilland gave maximum all-around visibility for the pilot. The French-made 9-cylinder Gnome Monosoupape engine could reach a speed of just under 100mph, giving it better performance than the Eindekker. Armament consisted of a single .303-caliber Lewis light machine gun, fed from 47-round drum magazines.

When the first DH-2s reached the front in June 1915, however, they ran into trouble. These early versions had three flexible mounting points for the Lewis gun, which could be manually moved from one attachment point to the other by the pilot. It was awkward to use and proved ineffective. In addition, pilots reported difficulty in keeping the aircraft steady while firing the machine gun. Trainees, moreover, had trouble controlling the DH-2 on landing and takeoff, and after a number of accidents it gained the moniker "Spinning Incinerator".

So De Havilland modified the design to make it more stable, and replaced the two-blade propeller with a narrower four-blade version. Hawker, meanwhile, concluded that it was easier and more effective to have the machine gun fixed in place, and to aim it by pointing the entire airplane at the target. After designing a metal clip that locked the machine gun into position, Hawker added a round fixed gunsight that allowed accurate aiming.

The new DH-2s were supplied to frontline squadrons in April 1916, and soon proved their worth. The first shootdown of a German Eindekker happened on April 25, and a string of victories followed: during the fierce fighting at the Battle of the Somme, DH-2s destroyed almost 50 German machines. Major Hawker himself was given command of RFC 24 Squadron, the first unit in British service to be dedicated solely to single-seat purpose-built fighters, and in time six other British squadrons were equipped with DH-2s. In all, around 450 of them were produced. Along with the new French Nieuport 11, the De Havilland won back air superiority for the Entente and ended the "Fokker Scourge".

But even before the end of 1916, the DH-2 was outclassed by newer German fighters like the Albatros D2. On November 23, 1916, Major Hawker found himself in a dogfight with German ace Manfred von Richthofen and, although both pilots were highly skilled and maneuvered around each other for almost an hour, in the end Richthofen's Albatros was superior to Hawker's DH-2. Hawker was shot down and killed. By this time, the DH-2 was already being withdrawn from frontline service in France, and was first transferred to lesser theaters like Palestine, then relegated to the "trainer" role. No DH-2 aircraft survived the war.

In 2015, aviation enthusiasts Dick and Sharon Starks built an 80%-scale replica DH-2 using photographs and some original plans, and donated it to the Combat Air Museum in Topeka KS. A month later, a university professor drew up a set of CAD plans for the engine and produced a plastic model at 80% scale, using a 3d printer. In 2016, this model engine was fitted to the replica DH-2 airframe. It is still on display at the Museum.

Caudron G.4

The introduction of the Caudron multi-engined bomber began the development of air power as a weapon with long-range offensive capabilities and potential strategic power.

In pre-war France, one of the most active aeroplane designers were the Caudron brothers Gaston and René. By 1910, the Caudrons had established an aircraft factory and a flight school, and were producing six different models.

In 1912, they introduced a new design, known as the Caudron G. It was intended as a trainer for their flight school, but when the First World War broke out, the single-engine biplane was adopted by the French military as well. By 1915, the latest G3 model was also being used for air reconnaissance and artillery spotting, and experiments were being carried out by slinging small bombs under the wings.

Although the Caudron G3 was a reliable air platform that was easy to fly, it was still primitive in some ways (it still used wired wing-warping instead of ailerons), and was not powerful enough to carry sufficient defensive weaponry or an effective bomb load, and by 1915, as the aerial bombing role became more and more important, the Caudrons decided to make radical improvements. Adapting the same basic nacelle and tail-boom design of the G3, the new plane was bigger with a wider wingspan and four tail fins instead of two. It was designated the Caudron G4.

More importantly, the G4 was one of the first combat aircraft designs to have two engines, giving it increased range and also allowing it to carry substantially more weight. In early versions, the plane was fitted with two 80-horsepower Gnome rotary engines: these both rotated in the same direction and caused trouble with torque. In later versions, two 90-horsepower Anzani radial engines were fitted instead and these were counter-rotating to eliminate torque. In front, the pilot had a fixed machine gun for defense. In early versions, the observer had a rear-facing machine gun fixed to the upper wing, but this arrangement proved to be awkward and was dropped. If necessary, the observer would simply carry a light Lewis or Hotchkiss gun with him on a rack inside his cockpit.

The most useful improvement, however, would be the bomb racks in the fuselage, capable of carrying 100 kilograms (220 pounds) of bombs made from modified artillery shells. With two engines and enough fuel for 3.5 hours of flight, the Caudron was capable of reaching targets deep behind enemy lines—it had enough range to carry out raids into Germany itself. A frequent target for bomber raids were the zeppelin pens in Belgium; another was the poison-gas factory at Ludwigshaven.

With the Caudron, the RAF was able to begin the process of learning how to organize and launch large-scale strategic air raids using multi-engine heavy bombers. As bombers became more effective, both sides developed dedicated anti-aircraft guns (the British referred to this as "Archie"). At first, individual bombers would make their own way to the target and bomb as they arrived.

This, however, led to heavy losses, and it was found that it was better to have a large group of bombers all arrive at once as a formation, which forced the Archie gunners to spread their fire.

In all, some 1400 Caudron G4s were built during the war, reaching the front lines in 1916. It quickly became the standard long-range bomber for the French, British, Italian, and Russian air services. Unarmed versions were also produced for training and for artillery spotting. They remained in service until replaced in 1917 by the much larger and more-capable Handley-Page bombers.

In 1917, the US Army purchased ten Caudron G4s from France for testing and evaluation, and these were transferred to a US base near Tours for use as trainers. By this time, however, the G4 was already becoming obsolete, and the US never adopted it for combat.

That same year, another Caudron, serial number C4263, an armored air reconnaissance version manufactured in December 1916, was transferred to the US mainland, where it was donated to the Smithsonian in 1918. Today this aircraft is on display at the Udvar-Hazy Center. One of only two remaining Caudron G4s (the other is in the Musee de l'Aire museum in France), it is the oldest multi-engine bomber on display in the US.

Albatros D5a

The Albatros D series was one of the most widely-produced German aircraft of the First World War, serving for the entire second half of the conflict. Nearly all of Germany's top air aces scored the majority of their victories in Albatros D fighters.

In early 1916, the Germans were beginning to lose air superiority on the Western Front. The French had introduced the Nieuport 11 and the British were flying DeHavilland DH-2 "pushers". Both of these outclassed the Fokker Eindekker monoplanes that equipped the German squadrons.

In response, in August the Albatros Werke aircraft company introduced a revolutionary new design. Called the D1, the new Albatros had a plywood body, replacing the frame-and-canvas fuselage on the Eindekker. The D1's biplane wings provided more lift, enabling it to carry two Spandau machine guns mounted in front of the cockpit. The new fighter was one of the first to use an inline engine instead of a rotary, producing 160 horsepower, and the propeller hub was streamlined into the fuselage to make it more aerodynamic. It was superior to the Entente fighters in speed, climb rate, and firepower.

Even as D1's were being sent to frontline squadrons, an improved version was already in the works. Designated the D2, it had an upper wing that was slightly moved to give better visibility to the pilot, and also relocated the radiator unit from the front of the fuselage and mounted it flush in the upper wing plane. By the end of 1916, around 50 D1's and 200 D2's were in service, and they quickly established their superiority over the Entente Nieuports and DH-2's.

Just a few months later, the Albatros D3 appeared. This new model had a narrower lower wing, which improved the pilot's visibility. It also used the same type of V-struts on the wings that the Nieuport 11 did. The radiator was moved from under the center of the wing, where it had a tendency to spray boiling water onto the pilot when it was hit by gunfire, off to one side. The new Albatros became Germany's standard fighter, and served until mid-1918.

But the D3 had a dangerous flaw. One of the first squadrons to be equipped with the new fighter was Jasta 11, commanded by Manfred von Richthofen, the "Red Baron", who had already scored dozens of air victories in Albatros aircraft. On one of his flights in the new D3, Richthofen was forced to make an emergency landing when his wings cracked. Over the next few weeks, others reported the same problem, and a number of pilots were killed when their wings broke away. The D3's lower wings were supported by only a single spar and it was too weak. Under the stresses of a high-speed dive the spar would sometimes bend, allowing the V-struts to twist and break, tearing the wings from the body. Some attempts were made to strengthen the spars with braces, but they never worked, and pilots were instructed to avoid high-speed dives in the Albatros.

An effort was also made to address the problem in the next design model, the D4, which went back to a wider lower wing. The D4 also had a rounded plywood fuselage rather than the straight-sides used in the earlier models, which saved about 75 pounds of weight. (Furniture-makers were hired at the factory to assemble the fuselages.) The D4 was intended to use an experimental new engine that could run in different gears, but this never worked, and the D4 design was dropped. Instead, the new rounded fuselage was fitted with the narrower lower wing used in the D3, with more bracing, and was designated the Albatros D5. The lighter airframe, combined with a more powerful 180-horsepower engine, produced better speed and climb than the D3.

The D5 entered service in June 1917. It was quickly discovered, however, that not only were the lower wing braces still too weak, but the upper wing spar was also subject to cracking under stress. Several pilots were killed when their wings broke during violent maneuvers. In response, a number of metal braces were added to strengthen both wings. The new version was known as the Albatros D5a. This solved the problem (mostly), but the added weight now dropped the top speed of the D5a to 105mph, about the same as the earlier D3. Von Richthofen, who test-flew one of the first production D5a models, said it was obsolete and inferior. Nevertheless, the Germans had no better fighter plane available, and the Albatros D5a served from October 1917 until the end of the war. Richthofen's Jasta 11 flew D5a's until they were replaced in 1918 with Fokker Dr1 triplanes—but 60 of the Red Baron's 80 victories were made in Albatros D fighters.

In all, some 4800 Albatros D models were built during the war, about 1600 of them D5a's. They kept air superiority for the Germans until late in 1917, when the Entente introduced the SPAD 13, SE5a, and Sopwith Camel.

Only two Albatros fighters survived after the war, both of them model D5a's. One is in the War Memorial Museum in Australia, and the other is in the Smithsonian in Washington DC. The Smithsonian Albatros was one of the last to be manufactured during the war, in April 1918. From the markings, it appears to have been assigned to the Jasta 46 squadron. It had been repaired several times, using parts from several earlier aircraft, and at some point was hit by a bullet that punctured its secondary fuel tank and lodged in one of its magnetos. Since the damage was never repaired, this must have happened near the end of the war.

As best as can be determined, this Albatros was held by the French Government after the armistice and was then given in 1919 to US Congressman Julius Kahn, who donated it to the De Young Museum in California. In 1947 the plane was sold to a private collector, and the Smithsonian obtained it in 1949. The D5a remained crated in storage until 1977, when a two-year restoration project was begun. The aircraft is now on display in the World War One Gallery at the Air and Space Museum.

Fokker Dr1

The Fokker Dr1 Triplane is one of the most famous airplanes to come out of the First World War, mostly because of its association with the Red Baron Manfred von Richthofen. But in reality, the Fokker was plagued by problems, was made only in small numbers, and served for only a short time.

In April 1917, the British naval air corps introduced a new fighter over the Western Front. The Sopwith Triplane was the first three-winged aircraft to play a serious role in the war, and it quickly proved to be a formidable weapon against Germany's biplane Albatros D fighters.

The Germans were impressed with the design, and wanted a triplane of their own. The task fell to Anthony Fokker. Fokker's team was already working on a new biplane dubbed the Fokker D6, and he now modified this design into a triplane. The first prototype was test-flown by German ace Werner Voss in July, and advice was also sought from Manfred von Richthofen. The German Army turned over a Sopwith Triplane that had crashed behind its lines: Fokker personally flew the repaired British plane and incorporated some of its design features, but the German triplane also differed significantly from the Sopwith. The Fokker had two synchronized machine guns firing from the engine cowl, in contrast to the single machine gun carried by the Sopwith. The Sopwith Triplane had ailerons on all three wings, but Fokker's design placed control surfaces only on the top wing. The bottom two wings were attached to the fuselage, and the top wing was supported by steel-tube V-struts. There was no tail-wheel: the Fokker used a steel-tipped wooden skid instead. The axle between the main landing gear wheels was covered with a short airfoil that acted as a sort of half-wing, adding lift.

The triplane was fitted with a 110-horsepower Oberursel 9-cylinder rotary engine. This underpowered engine, combined with the high-drag three-wing design, gave it a significantly lower speed (about 115 mph) than the British fighters, but the three wings combined with its relatively small size gave the German triplane a phenomenal rate of climb as well as superb maneuverability — traits which had been strongly emphasized by Richthofen and Voss during the design process.

In August 1917 the prototype was completed, and was designated the Fokker Dr1 Dreidecker. On August 31 Voss took one of the first production models on a combat patrol and shot down a British fighter. On September 1 von Richthofen took another Dr1 on a combat mission and shot down an English RE8, his 60th air victory and his first in the aircraft that would forever be associated with his name. He shot down another British fighter the next day.

The first batch of Dr1's to be manufactured were assigned to Voss's Jasta 10 and Richthofen's Jasta 11 squadrons. These were elite hand-picked units with experienced pilots, most of whom were already high-scoring aces. In their hands, the Dreidecker proved to be a lethal weapon, capable of defeating even the new British Sopwith Camel and SE5a. Within four weeks, Voss had shot down

20 Entente aircraft. (Just a short time later, Voss was shot down and killed when he single-handedly took on a flight of five SE5a fighters, all of them flown by British aces.)

But there were problems. The Dr1 was not an easy plane for rookie pilots to fly: the handling was very touchy, particularly during landings. It also had a limited gasoline supply, which allowed it to stay in the air for only 80 minutes. The rotary engines used castor oil as their lubricant, and by 1918 this was in short supply and was replaced by several different inferior substitutes, leading to an epidemic of engine failures.

Almost immediately after their introduction, in two separate incidents, two Dr1's had crashed after their top wing broke off during flight. All of the Dr1's were immediately grounded for a month while the crashes were investigated. Fokker declared that the problem was the result of poor workmanship during assembly and immediately designed stronger attachment points, but the accidents continued. (In March 1918, while in combat with British Sopwith Camels, the Dr1 flown by Lothar von Richthofen, the Red Baron's brother and himself a high-scoring ace, was crippled when the leading edge of the upper wing broke off: Richthofen was seriously injured in the crash.)

These incidents tarnished the Dreidecker's reputation and the German air service began searching for a replacement. Only 318 Fokker Dr1's were produced, and no more than 170 were ever in service at one time, serving in 14 different squadrons. By June 1918, the Dr1 was being replaced by the Fokker D7 biplane.

Nevertheless, the Dr1 gained a fearsome reputation, mostly because it was flown by some of the best combat pilots of the First World War. In addition to Voss (60 air victories) and Richthofen (80 victories), the Dr1 was flown by aces Ernst Udet (63 victories), Joseph Jacobs (47 victories), Paul Baumer (43 victories), Lothar von Richthofen (40 victories), Karl Bolle (36 victories), and Karl Allmenroeder (30 victories). From the factory, the Dr1 was painted in a streaked olive-brown scheme, but the members of Richthofen's elite Jasta 11 squadron customized their personal aircraft with individualized paintjobs so they could easily recognize each other in the air. The often-gaudy colors led their British opponents to refer to the Germans as "The Flying Circus".

In the end, the Fokker Dr1's wing troubles and slow speed doomed it to obsolescence. As it was replaced by the Fokker D7, the Dreidekker was sent to rear units and used for training. After the war ended in November 1918, a number of Dreideckers were taken to France and England for flight testing. But within a few years, only a few Dr1's are known to have still been in flying condition. One of these, serial number 528/17, was used as a test plane by the German

Army and was used during the filming of at least two 1920's war movies, but it disappears from records in the early 1930s and was likely destroyed in a crash. Serial number 152/17, one of the personal Dr1's used by Manfred von Richthofen, was on display at a Berlin air museum. It was destroyed during a World War Two bombing raid. There are stories which have another von Richthofen plane, serial number 425/17, being moved from Berlin to safety in the countryside, only to have been chopped up for firewood by war refugees. In 1932, Anthony Fokker assembled a complete Dr1 from existing spare parts; it was displayed by another Berlin museum and was also destroyed in a bombing raid.

Today, no authentic wartime Fokker Dr1's exist. However, copies of the original factory blueprints still survive, and a number of replicas have been built from these plans. Those that are intended to fly are usually built with small radial engines instead of the original rotaries, and have modern avionics in the cockpit. In 1966, however, Twentieth Century Fox built two Fokker Dr1's, fitted with vintage LeRhone rotary engines, for its George Peppard movie "The Blue Max".

In 1994, the US Air Force Museum in Dayton OH placed a replica Fokker Dr1, built from factory drawings, on display. It is painted in the livery of Arthur Rahn, a 6-victory German ace.

Nieuport 28

Light and highly maneuverable, the Nieuport 28C was rejected by the French air service, but found a place with the first American fighter squadrons to be deployed in World War One.

The French aeroplane manufacturer *Société Anonyme des Establissements Nieuport* was founded in 1909 by two brothers who were both killed in accidents before the war. But when the Great War broke out, designer Gustave Delage provided the French air service with its first notable scout biplane, the Nieuport 11. Nicknamed *"Le Bebe"* ("The Baby") because of its small size, it was highly maneuverable and became a very effective fighter, helping to end the Fokker Scourge.

In late 1917, Nieuport attempted to follow up on the success of *Le Bebe* with a newer model, the Nieuport 28C. Like the Model 11, it was lightly built and very maneuverable, though it had a bigger engine and was faster. The ailerons were moved from the upper wing plane to the lower. The new fighter was also more heavily armed: the *Bebe* had carried a single machine gun mounted on the upper wing which fired over the arc of the propeller, but the new Model 28 had two synchronized guns, one on the engine cowling and another on the left side of the fuselage.

Unfortunately for Nieuport, the SPAD XIII had also just been introduced, and it was a better airplane. The French adopted the SPAD as their new frontline fighter and began deploying it to the trenches in the beginning of 1918.

In the meantime, though, the Great War had received a new combatant. After years of neutrality, the United States declared war on Germany in April 1917. Both the Entente and the Central Powers knew that eventually America's industrial capacity and fresh manpower would be decisive. But at this early point, the US was completely unprepared for war. It had no trained men, only obsolete weapons, and, although volunteer pilots of the famed Lafayette Escadrille had been flying in combat with the French for several years now, the American Expeditionary Force had no battle-ready aeroplanes of its own.

Since the new American forces would be trained largely by the French, it was assumed that they would be equipped with French aircraft. But there was a supply crunch for the Hispano-Suiza engines that powered the SPADs, and French frontline squadrons were barely getting enough for themselves. The Americans would have to use something else. And in stepped the Nieuport 28C. Although it was inferior to the SPAD, it was still a serviceable fighter, and it was immediately available for rapid production. The US placed an order for 297 of them.

There would be four American squadrons which were to be equipped with the French fighters as soon as possible, the 27th, 94th, 95th and 147th. None of them had been trained yet. In February 1918, when Nieuports began arriving at the American aerodromes, they didn't have any armament: the US was not yet able to produce its own machine guns, and the French and British couldn't keep up.

Finally, by April 1918, the first of the American squadrons—the 94th "Hat in the Ring"—was ready. On its second patrol, on April 14, Lt Alan Winslow and Lt Douglas Campbell each shot down a German plane to score the first official American air victories of the war. (The Lafayette Squadron of course had already shot down dozens and had several aces, but they were officially flying for the French.) The 27th and 147th Aero Squadrons began combat flights in June.

But although the Nieuport 28 was easy to fly and maneuverable, it had serious issues. The landing gear was weak and had to be reinforced. The rotary engine was prone to fires. Most serious, the upper wing had a fragile structure, and several pilots while diving ripped the leading edge free and pulled off most of their wing cloth.

By July 1918, there were finally enough SPAD XIIIs available to begin equipping the American squadrons, and the Nieuports were pulled from frontline service and used as trainers.

After the war, 88 Nieuport 28Cs were taken back to the United States, where they served for a time as trainers and scouts, and were then sold off as surplus. The Navy obtained 12 of the planes and used them, along with some Sopwiths, to test various ideas for launching aircraft from ships. In a series of experiments, the Nieuports were sent aloft from wooden platforms that had been built on top of gun turrets aboard several Navy ships, including the new battleship USS *Arizona*. Meanwhile some small countries like Guatemala and Switzerland flew newer Nieuports, manufactured in France after the war, until the late 1920s. In 1930 four of the remaining Nieuport 28Cs were used to film the Hollywood movie "Dawn Patrol" starring Douglas Fairbanks Jr, and then its remake in 1938.

From 1958 to 1972, the Old Rhinebeck Aerodrome in New York was flying a restored Nieuport in its air shows. This plane, a mixture of parts from at least four different postwar airframes, was put on exhibit at the USS *Intrepid* in New York and then obtained by the Smithsonian, where it is now displayed at the Udvar-Hazy Center. The Naval Aviation Museum in Florida has one of the Navy's modified test versions on display. Two more original Nieuports are in museums in Europe.

Curtiss JN4 Jenny

The Curtiss Jenny was one of the primary contributions made by the United States to World War One aviation. After the war, the Jenny became famous as a barnstormer and spurred civilian interest in flight.

While the American aircraft manufacturer Glenn Curtiss was traveling in England in 1914, he met an engineer at Sopwith named B Douglas Thomas, and hired him as a designer. Curtiss had just produced a new 90-horsepower OX-5 engine, and, recognizing that his previous "pusher" designs with the engine located behind the cockpit were now obsolete, he was looking for a two-seat spotter plane that would place the new engine in front of the cockpit in a "tractor" configuration. Thomas was hired for the task.

In the end, the Curtiss company submitted two new designs to the US Army, a Model N from Thomas and a Model J from Curtiss himself. The Army placed an order for Model J's, but requested some changes in the design. Curtiss responded by incorporating some of the features from Thomas's Model N, and dubbed the result the Curtiss Model JN. It quickly became dubbed the "Jenny".

The first version of the Jenny, the JN-2, had two wing planes of equal length, and incorporated the Curtiss flight control system in which a shoulder yoke was used to manipulate the wing control surfaces. A number of these were delivered to the US Army Signal Corps for reconnaissance work, and when the 1st Aero Squadron went to Mexico in 1916 in pursuit of the Mexican rebel Pancho Villa, they took some of their Jennies with them. It was the first combat use of aeroplanes by the US Army.

The pilots, however, didn't like the performance of the unstable JN-2, especially the outdated shoulder yoke system, so Curtiss introduced the JN-3. This version had a single control wheel for the ailerons, a rudder bar, and wings of unequal length for better maneuverability. As well as being sold to the US Signal Service, the new Jenny became a favorite with civilian flying schools.

With the First World War raging in Europe, the British were now interested in the Jenny as a trainer and spotter, and after making some more changes to improve performance—including replacing the control wheel with the now-standard control stick—Curtiss introduced the JN-4 Jenny. A factory was set up in Canada to manufacture the new plane, and the US Army also adopted it as a trainer. In June 1917, after the United States entered World War One, the JN-4D model appeared, which became the iconic Jenny. The US Army and Navy placed large orders, as did several Entente nations. To keep up with production, Curtiss had to license the design to six other aircraft manufacturers. Over 6,000 Jennies were built during the war, many of them fitted with 180 horsepower Hispano-Suiza engines. Nearly all of the American pilots who flew in the war, and many of the Allied pilots as well, learned to fly in a Curtiss Jenny. Most new pilots received about 50 hours of basic training in a JN-4 over a period of six to eight weeks, before moving on to other aircraft.

When the war ended in 1918, the US Army still had around 3000 Jennies in service, which it declared "surplus" and put up for sale. Seeing an opportunity, Curtiss bought most of them himself, refurbished them, and sold them on the civilian market. The Canadian-built version, known as the "Canuck", was also readily available. War surplus Jennies initially sold for around $4000, but eventually the price dropped to less than $100. It became known as the "Model T of the sky".

Reliable and easy to fly, the Jenny became a staple of "barnstormers"—daredevil pilots, many of them former wartime fliers, who traveled around the country doing airshows featuring acrobatics, death-defying stunts such as "wing-walking", and rides for paying audience members. It also became the preferred trainer for flight schools. Both Charles Lindbergh and Amelia Earhart learned to fly in a Curtiss JN-4D.

The Jenny's heyday lasted until 1927, when the US Government introduced regulations specifying safety requirements for any aircraft that carried passengers. The now-obsolete Jenny could not meet these standards, and barnstormers turned to newer designs. Most Jennies ended their lives rotting away in a barn somewhere.

Today, about 50 original Curtiss Jennies of various models can be seen on display. The Smithsonian Air and Space Museum has a JN-4D which was manufactured under license by the Springfield Aircraft Corporation. The Chicago Museum of Science and Industry also has a JN-4D, exhibited as a "barnstormer"—upside down and with a wing-walker. The Old Rhinebeck Aerodrome in New York has a flyable JN-4D, while the US Air Force Museum in Dayton has a JN-4 and the postwar J-1 model. The Naval Aviation Museum in Pensacola has an N-9 naval version of the JN-4.

SPAD 13

The SPAD 13 was one of the best Entente fighters produced during the war, and was flown by some of the top French and American aces, including Rene Fonck, Raoul Lufbery, and Eddie Rickenbacker.

In 1915, the French company SPAD (*Société Pour l'Aviation et ses Dérives*) introduced an important innovation. Until then, most aircraft were powered by air-cooled rotary engines. SPAD was one of the first to take advantage of a new liquid-cooled V-8 engine: the Hispano-Suiza V-8 with 150 horsepower. In 1916, the SPAD 7 fighter was introduced into French service, and did very well against German Albatros D models. In all, some 5500 SPAD 7s flew in the war.

By early 1917, SPAD was working on an improved version. A larger and more powerful Hispano-Suiza V-8 of 200 horsepower had just become available, and the new fighter was designed around it. The new design was bigger, faster, and carried two cowl-mounted machine guns. It was christened the SPAD 13. The first prototype entered flight testing in April 1917.

It turned out to be a superior fighter, particularly the later versions with even more powerful Hispano-Suiza engines. The rounded fuselage reduced drag, so at 135mph it was faster than the Germans, while its twin Vickers machine guns gave it equal firepower. The wings had no dihedral, however, which made it less stable, and it had a tendency to stall at low speeds. The early V-8 engines also had reliability issues (and unlike the SE5a, which could be landed with the power turned off, the SPAD fell like a rock if the engine went out). Though the heavier SPAD was less nimble than the German Albatros, it had a higher rate of climb and could also outdive them to get away from trouble. SPAD pilots learned that the best strategy was to avoid a turning dogfight, and to use their superior vertical performance to dive down on the Germans, make an attack, then dive away to climb for another attack.

The first SPADs began reaching the front in June, and once production difficulties with the Hispano-Suiza engine were solved, the French began churning it out in large numbers. Before the end of 1917, eight different companies were manufacturing the new fighters under license, most French fighter squadrons had been equipped with SPAD 13s, and the aircraft had also been adopted by Belgium, Italy and Russia—even the British flew several squadrons of SPADs. When the US began deploying substantial forces in France, they were at first given Nieuport fighters, but by 1918 these were replaced with SPADs. Because of shortages, the Americans also substituted their French-made 30-caliber Vickers machine guns with American-made Martin 30-06 versions. In total, 893 SPAD 13s were flown by the Americans, equipping all but one of the 16 aero squadrons. By the end of the war, a new version with a 300-horsepower engine, known as the SPAD 20, was in the works.

The SPAD 13 became the preferred plane of some of the war's best fighter pilots. Georges Guynemer, Rene Fonck and Eddie

Rickenbacker all scored most of their victories in SPADs. Guynemer had become an ace flying SPAD 7s and continued with SPAD 13s, ending with a score of 54. Rickenbacker became the highest-scoring ace on the American side, with 26 victories. French pilot Rene Fonck, with 75 victories, finished the war as the highest-scoring surviving ace: only the Red Baron Manfred von Richthofen, killed in 1918, scored higher.

In all, some 8500 SPAD 13s were produced during the war. Today, only six examples remain. One of these is in the collection of the Smithsonian Air and Space Museum and is displayed in the World War One gallery. This aircraft was made in August 1918 at the Kellner Brothers Piano Company (woodworkers and cabinet-makers were often pressed into service as airplane manufacturers) and was assigned to the American 22nd Aero Squadron. It is painted in the markings of six-victory air ace Ray Brooks, who scored one of his victories while flying this particular plane. At the end of the war the SPAD went on tour as part of a war bond drive, and was given to the Smithsonian in December 1919. It was completely restored in 1985. The SPAD 13 on exhibit at the Air Force Museum in Dayton was also built by the Kellner Brothers, in October 1918, but it entered service too late to see combat. Instead it went to San Diego, had its engine replaced with an American 150-horsepower Wright version of the Hispano-Suiza, and served as a patrol craft and trainer. It is displayed in the markings of Eddie Rickenbacker's "Hat-in-the-Ring" squadron. The Sky Harbor International Airport in Phoenix AZ has a SPAD 13 that was pieced together from at least three different aircraft.

The Musee de l'Air in Paris has a SPAD on display, as does the Royal Museum of the Armed Forces in Brussels. The Memorial Flight Association in Paris also has a wartime SPAD 13, the oldest one still in existence. Serial number 4377 was produced in February 1918 by Kellner Brothers: it was found in pieces in an attic in France in 1970. Restored, it is today the only airworthy SPAD 13.

Airco De Havilland DH4

Flown as an observation plane and as a bomber, the DH4 was the only American-manufactured aircraft to enter combat during the war.

When the United States finally entered the First World War in April 1917, it was completely unprepared. The US Signal Corps had only 132 airplanes used for reconnaissance and artillery spotting, and all of them were hopelessly obsolete.

But the French and British allies were eager to take advantage of America's vast production capability as quickly as possible, and a commission was set up to decide which Entente aircraft designs could be produced in US factories. After considering the French SPAD 13 fighter, the Italian Caproni bomber, and the British SE5a fighter, they settled on the Airco De Havilland DH4 bomber, which had the simplest structure, would be the easiest to mass-produce, and could use the newly-developed American V-12 Liberty engine (designed and tested in just six weeks).

The De Havilland DH4 had been introduced in 1916, when the need became clear for a better-defended spotter/reconnaissance plane that could also deliver a useful bomb load. Powered by the Rolls-Royce Eagle engine, the DH4 carried 460 pounds of bombs under the wings, a single Vickers machine gun that was fired forward through the propeller by the pilot, and twin Lewis guns mounted on a moveable ring that was fired by the rear observer. The observer could also carry a large-format camera for photo-reconnaissance, using a wireless telegraph set to send corrections directly to artillery batteries on the ground. British squadrons equipped with DH4s also pioneered many bomber tactics, including wedge-shaped formations that would bomb en masse at the flight leader's signal, and which used interlocking fields of machine gun fire to defend the formation against enemy fighters.

The DH4 was, however, always hampered by a shortage of Eagle engines, and although the British tried substituting more readily-available engines like the BHP, the Siddeley Puma and the Fiat, none of these were as good as the Rolls-Royce. So when the US entered the war and the Liberty engine, manufactured by the Packard automobile company, became readily available, the British pushed to move production of the DH4 to the United States.

The US began production of the DH4 "Liberty Plane" in November 1917. Three companies manufactured the plane under license from Airco—the Wright Company in Dayton OH, the General Motors Fisher Body Plant in Cleveland, and the Standard Aircraft Corporation in Paterson NJ. The American versions carried 322 pounds of bombs and were armed with two 30-06 caliber Marlin machine guns in front and two .303-caliber Lewis guns in the rear. They had a speed of 125mph and a range of 400 miles.

One difficulty that was never really solved lay with the DH4's fuel system. The gas tank, which lay between the pilot and the observer, was pressurized and had rubber fuel lines, and it tended to explode if hit. Pilots in France dubbed it "The Flaming Coffin". The British replaced their pressurized tanks with wind-driven pumps, but the Americans, not wanting to alter their manufacturing process and slow production, stayed with the older design.

The United States produced about 9,500 DH4s, but only 1,885 of these actually reached France before the war ended; they began flying combat missions in August 1918. The American DH4s saw service with the French and British (the British also continued to produce their own versions equipped with Rolls-Royce Eagle engines) as well as with the American Expeditionary Force: DH4s flew with eight US Army reconnaissance squadrons and five bomber squadrons, as well as four Navy patrol units. By 1918, plans were being made for the DH9, an improved version, but this proved to be inferior to the DH4 and was never given priority with the Entente during the war.

After the war, most of the European nations switched over to newer improved DH9-A designs. (The Russians, who had been supplied with some DH4s during the war, produced their own post-war copy made by the Soviet Polikarpov design bureau.) But the United States, with limited military budgets and with a large number of undelivered stocks on hand, stayed with the DH4, flying it operationally until the 1930s. The large number of DH4s that remained in France at the end of the war were considered "surplus", and rather than go to the expense of returning them to the United States, the Army decided to destroy them all—which came to be known as "The Billion-Dollar Bonfire".

Some DH4s were modified by the Army for use in post-war experiments in air-to-air refueling. The Army also sent a number of DH4s to New Mexico and Texas as part of the Border Air Patrol, to prevent any cross-border raids by Mexican bandits and revolutionaries. Civilian versions of the DH4 were adapted by the US Post Office for use as airmail carriers, replacing the front cockpit with a cargo compartment. Some were also used by the Interior Department to patrol for forest fires, and when "surplus" DH4s became available to civilians, they were used as passenger planes, crop dusters, and barnstormers. A few models of the DH4 were fitted with radial Wright R-1 engines.

Today, there are only around a dozen surviving DH4s left. The National Air and Space Museum displays the original prototype American-built DH4, with a Packard Liberty engine, made in October 1917. It was used as a test plane for various configurations until April 1919 when it was retired and turned over to the Smithsonian. It is exhibited in combat configuration, with a bomb load and with wireless transmitter and aerial cameras used for photo-reconnaissance missions. The US Air Force Museum has a

DH4-B model that was manufactured by GM in Cleveland. And the National Postal Museum in Washington DC also has a B model on display.

Royal Aircraft Factory SE5a

One of the best fighters of the war, the SE5a was the favored plane of many of Britain's top-scoring aces.

At the same time that the French SPAD company was producing its new Model 7 fighter around the 150-horsepower Hispano-Suiza engine, the British decided that they liked the engine too. Designers at the Royal Aircraft Factory were looking for a new fighter that would replace the Sopwith Pup but would, unlike the F.1 Camel then also being designed, use the new inline water-cooled V-8 instead of an air-cooled rotary engine. The project became known as the SE5 (for Scout Experimental Model 5).

As originally designed, the SE5 was intended to be sturdy but easy to manufacture, and also stable but easy for new pilot trainees to fly. The forward part of the fuselage was made from plywood, and the rear was canvas-covered wood frame. The square-tipped equal-spanned biplane wings gave good performance at low speed, making it safer at takeoff and landing, though the long nose made forward vision difficult. The inline engine had far less torque than rotaries, and the slimmer nose was more aerodynamic and gave more speed. It was armed with a synchronized .303-caliber Vickers machine gun mounted on the left side of the engine cowling, and a .303 Lewis gun on a rail atop the wing, where it fired over the propeller arc. The rail allowed the pilot to pivot the gun down to change an empty or jammed magazine, and also allowed him to fire the gun at a target that was above him. The wings were fitted with racks to carry four external bombs, allowing the plane to function as a light bomber.

Three prototypes began testing in November 1916 and immediately ran into difficulties. The wings proved to be too weak, and two of the prototypes crashed, killing the chief test pilot. The wings were strengthened and shortened, and the first combat models began reaching the front in March 1917—just when the German Albatros was sweeping the skies of older British fighters.

Most pilots, however, didn't like the SE5. The first Royal Flying Corps unit to be equipped with the new fighter was the Number 56 Squadron: they thought the "birdcage" windscreen was too big and the seat was too high, which was dangerous in a crash landing—and most of all they thought the plane was underpowered. There were also serious mechanical issues with the gearbox that connected the propeller to the engine. Britain's most famous ace of the time, Albert Ball, dismissed it as "a dud" and "a rotten machine".

In the spring of 1917, the Wolseley Motors Company began producing its own licensed version of the Hispano-Suiza V-8 engine that it called the W4A Viper. Modified to run at a higher compression and dropping the problematic gearbox, the Wolseley Viper was capable of 200 horsepower, and when it was mated with the new British design to become the SE5a, it proved to be exactly what was needed.

Many consider the SE5a to be the best Entente fighter of the war. Compared to its contemporary Sopwith Camel rival, the SE5a was not as maneuverable, especially at lower altitudes, and had slightly less effective firepower, but it was faster and, above all, with its inline engine it was much easier and safer to fly, especially for novice pilots, than the rotary-engined Camel and its formidable torque. (While almost 400 Camel pilots died in noncombat crashes, only around 80 SE5a pilots were killed in accidents.) The SE5a also had better performance at high altitudes than the Sopwith. And with its larger fuel tank the SE5a could loiter longer at altitude and wait for German planes to pass below.

Many of Britain's best aces scored some or all of their air victories in the SE5a. These included Mick Mannock (73 victories), Albert Ball (44 victories), James McCudden (57 victories), Canadian Billy Bishop (72 victories), and South African Anthony Beauchamp Proctor (54 victories). Ball, like many of the others, modified his airplane in ways that he particularly preferred: he removed the Lewis gun from the top of the wing, took off the windscreen, and lowered the seat by eight inches—all in an effort to reduce drag and increase the speed.

By the summer of 1917, six British companies were manufacturing SE5as, and the fighter remained in production till the end of the war. Plans were made for the Curtiss Company to produce the plane in the United States using licensed American-built engines, but the war ended before they could begin. The French were also intended to have SE5a squadrons, but shortages of engines delayed this until late 1918.

In all, some 5300 SE5s were made during the war. Only six still survive. Three are in England, one is in Australia, and one in South Africa. The only example in the US is an SE5e version, built in the US too late for the war. It served as a trainer, then was refitted with a Wright engine and converted to SE5e specifications. It was sold as surplus to Lt. Col. William C. Lambert, who had scored 21.5 air victories during WW1 in an SE5a.

Sopwith F.1 Camel

Perhaps the most famous fighter plane of World War One, the Sopwith Camel shot down more enemy planes than any other model. But with its tricky handling characteristics, it also killed more inexperienced trainee pilots than any other.

In the early autumn of 1916, Sopwith Aviation Company introduced a single-seat fighter armed with a Vickers machine gun and an 80-horsepower LeRhone rotary engine. Although officially designated the "Sopwith Scout", the plane was universally known as the "Pup". It quickly became a favorite with pilots, appreciated for its gentle handling characteristics and maneuverability.

But the Pup quickly became outclassed by newer German fighters, and by the end of the year the Sopwith Company was already working on an improved version. The new plane, designated the F.1, was much larger than the diminutive "Pup". Fitted with two .303 Vickers mounted side by side in front of the cockpit, it had far superior firepower, and its large 130-horsepower engine could push it at over 100mph. While the upper wing of the biplane was flat, the lower wings slanted upwards in a dihedral, and ailerons on both wing surfaces gave superb maneuverability. The machine guns were modified to have an ejection port on each side so the empty casings would be ejected away from each other. In order to prevent the machine gun breeches from freezing in the wind, they were covered with a metal cowling which produced a distinct "hump" in front of the cockpit—leading pilots to christen it the "Camel". The F.1 would be more than a match for the newest German Albatros and Fokker machines.

But when the prototype took to the air in December 1916, it was quickly apparent that this was no "Pup". The Camel had been designed with nearly all its weight at the front end: the engine, gas tank, guns and pilot were all within seven feet of the propeller, covered with sheet metal and plywood, while the rest of the fuselage was lightweight wood and canvas.

On top of this, the big Clerget rotary engine produced an enormous amount of gyroscopic torque, constantly trying to spin the plane to the left. When combined with the forward-of-center balance point, this made the Camel inherently unstable.

When the plane entered combat in the summer of 1917, it was enthusiastically praised by experienced pilots. The superb maneuverability combined with the improved firepower of two machine guns made it a lethal weapon in the hands of a good pilot. The first air victory came in June 1917, when a Camel flown by Canadian ace Alexander Shook shot down a Gotha bomber. Remaining in service till the end of the war, the Camel was credited with shooting down 1,294 German aircraft—more than any other model.

But there was a deadly downside to the Camel. While experienced pilots were able to take advantage of its maneuverability and power, inexperienced trainees found it a very difficult plane to fly. The fearsome engine torque meant that pilots had to apply full rudder on their takeoff run to avoid a lethal ground loop; landings were equally dangerous, as the Sopwith had a strong tendency to spin if it stalled. The Clerget engines required a specific fuel mixture, and often sputtered out when inexperienced pilots forgot to adjust their settings. In combat, pilots quickly learned that making a right-hand turn in the Camel, against the gyroscopic force of the rotary engine, was painfully slow and made one a sitting duck—experienced pilots would instead turn left through a full 270 degrees, which was faster than trying to bank to the right.

As a result, the Camel gained a formidable reputation as a difficult aircraft that was just as dangerous to fly even if there was no enemy around. In the final 18 months of the war, 413 Sopwith pilots died in combat—while 385 died in accidents and training mishaps. Veteran pilots joked that flying a Camel would get you either a wooden cross, a Red Cross, or a Victoria Cross.

Nevertheless, almost 5500 Sopwith Camels were produced during the War, serving with virtually every Entente air force, including Italy and Belgium. (While the Americans flew mostly French Spad 13's and Nieuport 28's, two US Aero Squadrons, the 17th and 148th, flew British Camels.) Sopwith was unable to keep up with the demand, and licensed versions were manufactured by the Nieuport and Fairey aviation companies.

As the war went on, new variants were introduced. In one version, the cockpit was moved back a short distance and the cowl-mounted Vickers machine guns were replaced with two wing-mounted Lewis guns and racks of Le Prieur air-to-air rockets to serve as a night fighter, called the "Comic". Several Comic squadrons in England were assigned to defend London against raids by German Zeppelins and Gotha bombers, and one American squadron, the 185th, was equipped with night fighter versions for use on the French front. Another version of the Camel was fitted with racks of 25-pound bombs on the wings and steel plate armor in the cockpit: dubbed the TF.2 "Salamander", it was used for ground attack and trench strafing. The Royal Navy, which had already begun experimenting with aircraft carriers using Sopwith Pups, now replaced them with more powerful Camels fitted with better engines and landing hooks. As the war ended and the Camel became outclassed by the new German Fokker D7, an improved Sopwith fighter known as the Snipe was already in the works.

After World War One, the Camel continued to serve with some smaller countries such as Belgium, Poland, Canada, and Greece. When the US Navy wanted to carry out some experiments with ship-launched airplanes, using a wooden platform built on the battleship USS *Texas*, they obtained a number of modified Sopwith Camels from the British for this.

Today, only a handful of original World War One vintage Sopwith Camels remain in existence. One of these is in private hands in California. Two are in London, and others are in Canada, New Zealand, Belgium, and Poland.

A number of full-scale replica Camels, however, have been built from the original factory drawings. The US Naval Aviation Museum in Pensacola has a replica naval version on display, in markings used by the test aircraft on the USS *Texas* after the war. The Air Force Museum in Dayton has another replica, built in 1974, which is exhibited in the markings of American ace Lt George Vaugh, and the US Army Aviation Museum at Fort Rucker AL also has a replica Camel on display. An airworthy replica constructed with period instrument panel and an original Gnome rotary engine is on display at the Cavanaugh Air Museum in Dallas. The Old Rhinebeck Aerodrome has a flyable replica Camel fitted with a period 160-horsepower Gnome.

Fokker D7

In April 1918, just six months before the end of the First World War, Germany introduced what would be the best fighter plane of the war. Although it came too late to prevent Germany's defeat, the Fokker D7 was test-flown by top ace Manfred von Richthofen, and at the end of the war became the subject of its own special provision in the peace treaty.

By the beginning of 1918, air superiority in the First World War, which had been swinging back and forth for the past three years, was turning in favor of England and France. The SPAD 13, SE5a and Sopwith Camel were dominating the German Fokker Dr1's and Albatross D5a's, and the German air service was looking for a replacement. Over 30 new designs were submitted.

One of these was from the Fokker company. Dutch aircraft designer Anthony Fokker had produced the famed Dr1 triplane. His new design, from chief engineer Reinhold Platz, was basically a biplane version of the triplane, with the same fuselage and tail assembly, but it was extensively modified. The lower wing was made shorter and thicker, and while the top surface was flat, a dihedral effect was produced by tapering the wing's thickness towards the tips. Like the Dr1, the new design had a small airfoil between the wheels, acting as a mini-wing. Unlike most aircraft of the time, which had wooden frameworks, the new airframe was made of metal tube.

To solve the problem of structural weakness in the wings, which had plagued the earlier Albatros fighters, Fokker strengthened the wing spars and, instead of using a network of wing bracing wires, replaced them with V-shaped wing struts made from metal tubes, reducing drag. However, when Germany's leading air ace, Manfred von Richthofen, was invited to test-fly the new airplane in January 1918, he reported that while it was highly maneuverable, it was dangerously unstable, especially in a dive. Working quickly, Fokker lengthened the fuselage, added a stabilizing fin, and enlarged the tail rudder. With these modifications, Richthofen became an enthusiastic fan of the aircraft, and in February, the new design was selected for production as Germany's new frontline fighter. It was designated the Fokker D7.

The D7s began reaching combat units in April 1918, with some of the first going to Richthofen's squadron, Jasta 11. (Richthofen flew the D7 on a few missions, but was killed in his Dr1 triplane later in April.) The initial production D7s were fitted with a 160-horsepower inline Mercedes D.3 engine. This, however, allowed the Entente SE5a's and Sopwith Camels to outclimb the Fokker, and to correct this problem the 185-horsepower 6-cylinder inline D3a engine from BMW was rushed into production. With that change, the D7 became the best all-around fighter to fly in the war. It was faster and more maneuverable than Entente fighters, and its higher ceiling and climb rate allowed German pilots to gain the advantage of height. The powerful engine also allowed the D7 to climb nearly vertically without stalling, allowing it to attack enemy planes from below, unseen by the opposing pilot. The production model D7's were fitted with two .30 caliber machine guns, but some experimental models were fitted with a single .50-caliber (intended as a ground-attack weapon against tanks).

The Fokker plant was unable to produce the D7 quickly enough, and the Germans licensed the design to the Albatros and AEG companies. But materials shortages caused by the Entente's naval blockade crippled production, and in all, only 1,000 D7's were built during the last six months of the war; at war's end, about 770 of them were flying with around 40 German squadrons. Most of these used the smaller 165-horsepower engine.

The D7 quickly established its superiority to anything that the Entente could put up against it. In the month of August 1918 alone, the Fokkers shot down 565 British, French and American aircraft.

But while the German air forces were dominating the sky, the German army on the ground was collapsing. The summer offensive that was intended to win the war had failed, and as fresh American troops began to enter the trenches, the German army began to be pushed back. In November 1918, Germany asked for an armistice.

In the surrender treaty, Germany was forced to give up or destroy much of its military equipment, including its submarines and battleships. And in one particular provision, the treaty specified that "all machines of the Fokker D7 type" be turned over to the Allies.

As it turned out, Anthony Fokker was able to save enough spare parts for 120 D7's by smuggling them aboard a train into his native Holland. After the war, Fokker was able to re-start production and sell D7's to the air forces of several countries, including Holland, Belgium, Poland, Italy, Spain, Sweden, and Switzerland. Many of these nations were still flying D7's in the 1930's.

The United States shipped 142 captured D7's back to the US, where they were first test-flown for evaluation and then used as trainers (and some found their way into post-war Hollywood movies). Many of the D7's design features were incorporated into the US Navy's new carrier-based Boeing FB-1 fighter introduced in 1925.

One of the Fokker D7's brought to the US had been captured just two days before the war ended, when German pilot Lieutenant Heinz Freiherr von Beaulieu-Marconnay mistakenly landed at an American airfield near Verdun. This was an Albatros-built version, which was shipped back to the US, test-flown a few times, and given to the Smithsonian Institution in 1920. It was restored in 1961, and remains on display in the Air and Space Museum. Another Fokker D7 is on display at the US Air Force Museum in Dayton OH.

MB-2 Bomber

The Martin MB-2 was the first American-built bomber to be mass-produced. It is most famous as the airplane that was used in General Billy Mitchell's bombing tests against battleships.

During the First World War, the US had virtually no capacity to produce military aircraft. Other than the Jenny trainer and some American-made copies of the British DH-4, the fledgling US Air Service was equipped with French fighters and a handful of Handley-Paige and Caproni bombers from England and Italy.

In 1918, as the war was ending, the Army put out a design requirement for a long-range bomber. One of the responses was the MB-1, designed by Glenn Martin. Martin built a prototype and flew it, unscheduled, to an Army airfield in Dayton OH in September, where he was promptly arrested by military police who thought he was a German. Once it was all straightened out, the Army tested the MB-1, liked it, and ordered production, but none reached the front before the war ended two months later.

By 1920, Martin had redesigned his bomber, with the express purpose of giving it the biggest possible bomb load. Now designated the MB-2, it featured two engine nacelles with V-12 Liberty engines. Although slower than the MB-1, it could carry a larger load of 2,000 pounds of bombs, with a range of about 500 miles. Five Lewis machine guns provided defense against enemy fighters. A new innovation introduced with the MB-2 was folding wings: since the bomber was so big, it would not fit into standard airplane hangars, so a hinge was added to each wing, just outside the engine nacelle, that allowed them to be folded backwards. The concept was quickly adapted for Navy carrier planes.

The Army approved Martin's new design to replace the MB-1, and assigned it to night-bombing, under the designation NBS-1. Over the next few years, about 110 MB-2's were built. Martin made the first production batch, and after that three other companies were given contracts to produce the design. Eight squadrons of MB-2's were deployed in the US, Hawaii, and the Philippines, where they remained in frontline service until 1929.

The last batch of MB-2's to be manufactured came from the Curtiss company and used an experimental supercharger that pulled compressed air into the engine to give it greater power. The improvement in performance was spectacular, allowing the plane to reach a then-incredible 25,000 feet in altitude. But in the end the experiment was a failure—the superchargers were mechanically unreliable. There would be no successful supercharged airplanes until the Second World War broke out in 1939.

As the MB-2 went into production in 1920, however, a furious debate was going on in the US military. General Billy Mitchell, a colorful, brash and opinionated figure, was convinced that air power would be the decisive factor in any future conflict, and that large fleets of Navy ships were particularly vulnerable to air attack and were now virtually obsolete. Naturally, this is something the Navy did not want to hear. They argued that no airplane could deliver enough firepower to seriously damage a modern armored battleship. So, after much bluster and heat, it was decided to set up a series of experiments using some captured German leftovers from the war. Both Army and Navy aviators were invited to participate. It became known as Project B.

The first test was on June 21. A captured German submarine, the *U-117*, was attacked by a squadron of Navy airplanes. She was sunk by the first wave. On July 12, the Army got its turn: a wave of SE5e fighter-bombers and MB-2 heavy bombers with 300-pound bombs attacked the old German destroyer *G-102*. The destroyer was sunk. On July 18, MB-2's with 600-pound bombs sunk the German cruiser *Frankfurt*. And then on July 20, in the biggest test of all, the MB-2's were sent against the German battleship *Ostfreisland*, a modern "dreadnought" which naval experts believed to be virtually unsinkable. This time the flight of six MB-2's used 2,000-pound bombs. Twenty minutes and two bomb hits later, the *Ostfreisland* was at the bottom of the sea.

Mitchell was right—the days of the big battleship were over. But the Navy continued to resist, arguing that Mitchell's test was invalid because the battleship had been unmanned and had no anti-aircraft defenses. The debate over the effectiveness of aircraft versus battleships came to an abrupt end on December 7, 1941, and airpower would come to dominate the next World War. Unfortunately for Mitchell, though, his constant verbal attacks in the press on the US military for being "unprepared" and "irresponsible" eventually led to a court-martial (for "insubordination") and his resignation.

Of the 110 MB-2 bombers manufactured after the First World War, none survive today. In the 1990's, the US Air Force Museum began producing an exact replica from original factory drawings, which was completed in 2002. It is currently on display.

The MB-2 bomber also played a role in Hollywood movie history. In 1927 Paramount released the silent movie "Wings", a story about World War One air combat. Some of the scenes were shot from airplanes, including simulated dogfights. In one scene, an MB-2, painted in German markings to depict a Gotha bomber, is shown in its hangar undergoing an attack from the air. "Wings" was the first motion picture to win an Academy Award for Best Picture.

NC-4

In 1919, the US Navy seaplane NC-4 became the first aircraft to fly across the Atlantic Ocean, in a multi-plane mission that very nearly became a disaster.

In 1913, the London *Daily Mail* offered a prize of 10,000 pounds to the first airplane pilot to fly from North America to Europe, within 72 hours, across the Atlantic. At this time, it had only been ten years since the Wright brothers flew for 120 feet, and a trans-Atlantic flight was not even remotely possible.

But the outbreak of the First World War in 1914 provoked rapid advancements in aircraft technology. By 1916, multi-engine bombers were routinely traveling between Germany and England. In 1917, the United States entered the war, and the US Navy began drawing up plans for a number of "flying boats", large aircraft that used floats to take off and land on water, which would be capable of flying all the way across the Atlantic to search for German U-boats and protect the supply convoys sailing for England. These would be built by the Curtiss Aircraft Company, which already had experience producing seaplanes for the Navy; they were designated NC (for "Navy/Curtiss") 1, 2, 3 and 4, but were christened "Nancys" by those who worked with them. As designed, they were to have a crew of six, a hull measuring 45 feet long at the waterline, a wingspan of 126 feet, and would be powered by three 400-horsepower V-12 Liberty engines, mounted on a network of struts just above the wing, behind the cockpit. NC-1 made her first flight on October 4, 1918. A month later, on November 11, Germany surrendered and the First World War ended.

But the NC project was continued, motivated now by a proposal submitted by US Navy Commander John Towers, suggesting that the seaplanes be used to achieve the first trans-Atlantic flight as a way of winning prestige for the United States (the flight would not be able to win the *Daily Mail's* prize because the flying boats were too slow to cover the distance within 72 hours). A prominent supporter of the plan was Assistant Secretary of the Navy (and future US President) Franklin Delano Roosevelt. The project was designated "NC-TA". On November 25, the newly-completed NC-1 made a test flight in which she carried 51 people inside her hull, the largest payload carried by any aircraft up to that time. But, the Navy decided, she was underpowered for a reliable trans-Atlantic flight, and the NC-TA project was put on hold until a fourth Liberty engine could be added. This was mounted with a series of braces behind the other three engines, facing backwards in a "pusher" configuration. This arrangement was able to drive the NC-1 at a top speed of about 90mph; at cruising speed of 75mph, the seaplane could fly for some 15 hours. The same change was made to NC-3 and NC-4, which were still undergoing construction. As an experiment, NC-2, also still being built, was modified to have all four engines facing forward, in two pairs above the wings.

All four NCs were finished by the end of April 1919, and plans were made to launch them across the Atlantic in May. Initial flight tests, however, immediately demonstrated that the "four up front" engine configuration in the NC-2 caused problems with balance, and when the NC-1 suffered some damage during a hangar fire on May 5, it was decided to ground the NC-2 and cannibalize her for repair parts.

On May 8, 1919, the three remaining NC's, now designated "Seaplane Squadron One", were ready to go, and they lifted off from the Navy base at Rockaway NY en route to their staging area in Halifax, Canada. NC-1 was piloted by Lt Commander Patrick Bellinger; NC-3 was piloted by Commander John Towers, who had originally suggested the project and who was also in command of the Squadron; NC-4 was piloted by Lt Commander Albert Read.

On the way, the NC-4 had engine trouble and had to land on the sea and cruise to the Navy base in Chatham MA for repairs. The NC-1 and NC-3, meanwhile, both suffered cracked propellers and had to spend a day in Halifax replacing them. By May 10, the NC-1 and NC-3 were in Trepassey, Newfoundland, where the official trans-Atlantic flight was to begin. The NC-4 was still in Massachusetts having her engines repaired. The Navy had arranged for a string of 21 destroyers, 50 miles apart, to stretch all the way across the Atlantic along the planned flight path, both as navigational aids and to rescue any planes that had to ditch. The "Nancys" were to fly all the way to the Azores, stop for refueling, and then go on to Portugal. But now the flight was delayed by bad weather. By the time it cleared, the NC-4 had rejoined the others in Trepassy. All three seaplanes took off across the Atlantic on May 16, launching just before nightfall so they could reach the Azores for a daylight landing. To avoid the possibility of colliding in the dark, each of the three planes flew separately from the others.

The flights went well until morning, when they were each approaching the Azores. A heavy fog rolled in, which was at times so thick that the pilots couldn't see their own wingtips. In the NC-1, pilot Bellinger couldn't find the string of destroyers in the fog and, running low on fuel, decided to put down on the sea and wait for the fog to lift so he could get some navigational bearings. But although he was able to land safely, the NC-1 was buffeted by 12-foot waves that prevented her from taking off again. Luckily, a Greek freighter happened to be nearby and picked up Lt Commander Bellinger and his crew. The Navy sent some ships to try and tow the NC-1 to safety, but this was prevented by the high waves, and after three days of pounding, the NC-1 broke apart and sank.

The NC-3, meanwhile, had also gotten lost. In the fog, Commander Towers had mistaken a British Navy cruiser for one of the American destroyers, and was drawn far off-course. When his fuel ran low, Towers also touched down onto the Atlantic, but the rough seas broke several of the plane's engine struts. The NC-3 could no longer take off, and was now a boat. It took two days for the NC-3 to sail the 200 miles to port.

The NC-4, meanwhile, had been able to follow the line of destroyers and reach the Azores, but was also low on fuel and fighting a thick fog when pilot Read set her down at the port in Horta. Of the three seaplanes, his was the only one still flying.

The NC-4 remained stuck in Horta for three more days until the weather cleared, then flew for Portugal, but suffered engine trouble and had to land after just 150 miles at Ponta Delgada. From there, another line of US Navy destroyers would guide her to the end of the trans-Atlantic flight in Lisbon. Once again, the weather caused delays, and it wasn't until May 27 that Read was able to once again take off. Twelve hours later, the NC-4 settled into Lisbon's harbor on the Tagus Estuary. The trans-Atlantic flight had taken almost three weeks, due mostly to weather delays. She had been actually in the air for 26 hours and 46 minutes.

The Navy, despite the difficulties during the flight, was happy with the long-range performance of the seaplanes, and built six more NC's, using them for anti-submarine and coastal patrols until 1922.

After her landing in Portugal, the NC-4 flew to England (first spending a night in Spain to fix a malfunctioning engine) and returned to the US by ship. After making a flying tour of the US ending at St Louis, the Navy put the seaplane on display at several places, including New York City's Central Park, before donating her to the Smithsonian, where she lay in storage until she was exhibited for the 1969 50th anniversary of her flight. In 1974 the NC-4 was loaned to the US Navy's National Museum of Naval Aviation in Pensacola FL, where she remains on display.

Boeing 40B Airmail Carrier

The development of air mail in the 1920s was intended as a practical service by the Post Office, but it also served as a way for the US Government to encourage and subsidize research into long-range air transportation.

In September 1911, there was a gathering of aviation enthusiasts on Long Island. As a stunt, one of the pilots, Earle Ovington, offered to fly sacks of mail back and forth between the meeting field and the post office in the nearby town of Mineola NY. Over the course of his daily trips, Ovington delivered about 38,000 pieces of mail.

At this time, most long-distance mail traveled by train. But watching Ovington's flights, the Post Office was impressed and saw in the "aeroplane" a potential new method for rapid delivery. When the Postmaster General asked Congress for an appropriation of $50,000 to obtain an aeroplane and begin some experiments, however, he ran into the same sort of benign ignorance that was hampering the US Army Signal Corps in its efforts to obtain more aircraft, and his request was rejected.

The Great War had, however, demonstrated that the airplane was rapidly becoming a mature technology. It also demonstrated that the United States was far behind other nations and needed to catch up. So the US turned to "air mail" as a way to encourage aeronautical research, promote new technologies, and subsidize the development of long-range aviation. This effort was endorsed by the military, who realized that the technical and logistical problems to be solved by the long-distance delivery of air mail were essentially the same as those faced by long-range deployment of bombers and fighters.

In 1917 Congress appropriated $100,000 for the Post Office to establish an experimental airmail route. This was set up the following year, with daily regularly-scheduled mail deliveries between New York City and Washington DC. At first the Army Air Corps provided the Jenny aircraft and pilots, but in 1918 the Post Office assumed control of the entire operation. This was further expanded into airmail service between New York and San Francisco. At first, the airmail service delivered mail from New York to Cleveland, where it met up with a westbound train to continue its journey. But as the planes got better, more airfields were built, and the Post Office gained more operational experience, more and more legs of the trip were flown by air. By 1920 it was possible for mail to fly, in a series of sections, straight from New York to California.

Initially, these services used Army-surplus Curtiss Jennies or DH-4s, left over from the war. By 1920, however, the Post Office was procuring specialized airmail planes, which served as test beds for a number of different techniques and technologies, from night flying to cross-country navigation.

In 1925, the Post Office issued a request for a standardized airmail plane, which would use the 12-cylinder Liberty engine that was still available in large numbers as war surplus. The design it adopted was the Boeing Model 40. The fuselage was made from steel tube and plywood, with fabric-covered wings. The Model 40 was somewhat limited in its performance by the now-antiquated Liberty engine that the Post Office required it to use, but by 1927 the Federal Government dropped that requirement, and Boeing mated the new 425-horsepower Pratt and Whitney Wasp engine to its airframe to produce the Model 40B.

It was a much better aircraft. Not only was the P&W engine 200 pounds lighter than the old Liberty engine, but the airframe, made of steel tube and aluminum skin, was also stronger and lighter. The 40B could carry up to 1200 pounds of mail. And, in an innovation that would soon turn the Boeing Company into one of the largest in the world, the plane had a special compartment, sealed from the weather, that could carry up to four long-distance passengers.

The Boeing 40B became the standard US Postal Service airmail plane from 1927 till 1932. Boeing continued to make improvements, and later models could carry up to four passengers.

Today, there is a 1927 Boeing 40B-2 on exhibit at the Henry Ford Museum in Dearborn MI. The Chicago Museum of Science and Industry has a Model 40B on display, built in 1928.

Ryan M-2 "Spirit of St Louis"

In 1927, Charles Lindbergh made what may still be the most famous flight in history, in a one-of-a-kind airplane called the "Spirit of St Louis".

After the war ended, the attention of the world was focused on civilian aviation. In May 1919, the US Navy seaplane NC-4 became the first plane to fly across the Atlantic, from Long Island to Lisbon with refueling stops at Newfoundland and the Azore Islands. Two weeks later, British pilots John Alcock and Arthur Whitten Brown, in a World War One Vickers Vimy bomber, flew nonstop from Newfoundland to Ireland.

That same month, a New York hotel owner named Raymond Orteig offered a $25,000 reward (about $350,000 today) for the first airplane that flew nonstop across the Atlantic between New York and Paris. For the next five years, nobody made an attempt to claim the Orteig Prize, and in 1924 Orteig renewed his offer. By then, technological advances had placed it within reach, and a number of aviation luminaries attempted to claim the prize. In September 1926, the highest-scoring surviving ace from the First World War, Frenchman Rene Fonck, attempted a flight from Paris to New York, but crashed on takeoff. In April 1927, American pilot Richard Byrd, famous for his flight over the North Pole, also crashed on takeoff during his attempt to fly from New York to Paris. By May 1927, four other pilots had been killed while attempting the flight.

On May 8, 1927, French WW1 ace Charles Nungesser made his attempt. Accompanied by navigator Francois Coli, Nungesser took off from Le Bourget airfield outside of Paris in a modified Levasseur PL.8 biplane that they had christened *l'Oiseau Blanc* ("White Bird"). Their planned route would take them across the English Channel, over southern England and Ireland, then across the North Atlantic to Newfoundland, south to Boston and then to a landing in New York. They never arrived.

That left two pilots as the only remaining teams who were ready to fly. One of these was Richard Byrd, who was ready to make another attempt after his crash. The other was a then-unknown airmail pilot from St Louis named Charles Lindbergh.

Lindbergh was being sponsored by the St Louis Chamber of Commerce and had a budget of just $15,000. By January 1927, however, he still didn't even have an airplane. Partly for economic reasons, but also for logistical advantage, he had made a couple of unconventional decisions. Unlike the other teams, who were using multi-engine aircraft, Lindbergh had opted for a single-engine plane. And while the others were flying with multiple crew members, Lindbergh decided that he could get better fuel mileage by reducing the weight as much as possible—which meant he would be flying alone. After much consultation the Ryan Company in San Diego agreed to special-build a high-wing monoplane, a modified and lengthened version of the company's Model M-2 crammed with extra fuel tanks for the attempt. One of the extra tanks was placed directly in front of the cockpit, meaning there was no forward windscreen and the pilot could not even see at all directly ahead (though a small periscope was placed in the cockpit). The entire plane weighed just over a ton, and could carry a ton and a half of fuel. With the Chamber of Commerce's blessing, Lindbergh christened the aircraft "The Spirit of St Louis". It was designed with just one purpose in mind — to make it across the Atlantic without landing.

The "Spirit" wasn't completed until the end of April 1927, and the St Louis team was in constant fear that someone would make the trans-Atlantic flight before they were ready. But after Byrd crashed and Nungesser disappeared, Lindbergh flew his plane from San Diego to St Louis and then on to Long Island, New York, (breaking the existing trans-continental speed record in the process), and over to the starting point at Roosevelt Field.

Byrd was already prepped for his flight, but decided to wait until a period of bad weather had cleared up. Lindbergh saw his chance, however, and decided to take the risk, and on May 20, 1927, after staying awake all night so he could leave early in the morning, he took off into a freezing rainstorm.

The flight took 33½ hours. To help stay awake, Lindbergh had intentionally installed an uncomfortable wicker chair in the cockpit, and he would also periodically open the small side windows to let rain and cold air in. At one point, he reports, while just barely skimming the waves at low altitude, he saw a fishing boat on the horizon and, as he passed it, yelled out the window "Which way to Ireland?" When he landed at the Le Bourget Airfield in Paris, radio reports of the flight had already reached France and an immense crowd was there to greet him.

The era of radio news had just begun, and "Lucky Lindy" was the first "media star". He instantly became the most famous person in the world. Ironically, though, Lindbergh is celebrated today mostly for the wrong reason — he was not the first person to fly nonstop across the Atlantic (Alcock and Brown had already done that, and a dozen others had followed them). But he was the first to fly nonstop from New York to Paris (and he did it alone, which was not even a requirement for the Orteig Prize — Lindbergh did it just to save weight).

In June, the "Spirit of St Louis" was returned to the US aboard the Navy cruiser *Memphis* and, along with Lindbergh, made a tour of the US and South America. Lindbergh then donated the plane to the Smithsonian, where it remains on display.

Winnie Mae

The Lockheed Vega was one of the premiere aircraft of the 1930's. Designed in 1927 as a long-distance passenger plane capable of carrying six passengers and a crew of two, the reliable and rugged Vega soon became a favorite with air explorers. Amelia Earhart used the Lockheed Vega in many of her flights. And Wiley Post, flying a Vega named "Winnie Mae", set two around-the-world speed records.

In 1929, the speed record for a round-the-world air flight was set—but not by an airplane. Captain Hugo Eckener had flown the German dirigible airship *Graf Zeppelin* around the world in 21 days. In 1931, aircraft pilot Wiley Post decided to beat this, and win the speed record for a fixed-wing airplane. Post had entered aviation as a barnstormer in the 1920's, then became the private pilot for Oklahoma oil millionaire FC Hall—all this despite losing an eye in an oilfield accident. In 1930, Hall and Post began to plan the speed record attempt. Hall purchased a Lockheed Vega 5C which he named after his daughter, "Winnie Mae". Post installed a modified Wasp engine to increase the speed and range. After flying the Winnie Mae in the 1930 Men's Air Derby from Los Angeles to Chicago (and winning the race), Post was ready to circumnavigate the globe. He picked Harold Gatty as his navigator and, on June 23, 1931, the Winnie Mae took off from Roosevelt Field in New York.

The first stop was at Harbor Grace, Newfoundland. From there, Post and Gatty crossed the Atlantic to the RAF airfield in Flintshire, England, and then to Hanover, Germany. After taking off from Hanover for Berlin, they decided to return for more fuel, and thus ended up taking off from Hanover twice. From Templehof Airdrome in Berlin, they went on to Moscow's October Airport, then flew all the way to Siberia, making stops in Novosibirsk, Irkutsk, Blagovyeschensk, and Khabarovsk. At Blagovyeschensk they were delayed several hours when the Winnie Mae got stuck in the muddy landing strip and had to be pulled out with a tractor, then were delayed again in Khabarovsk while mechanics checked the plane for damage.

From Siberia, Post and Gatty made the 17-hour flight to Nome, Alaska, landing at Solomon Beach. When they tried to take off from Nome on June 30, loaded with extra fuel, the Winnie Mae sunk into the soft sand and struck the propeller on the ground, bending the tips. Post and Gatty hammered the prop back into shape with a rock. While starting up the engine to check the propeller, Gatty was accidentally whacked by a propeller blade, fortunately without serious injury. They then took off, landing at Fairbanks, where they obtained another propeller from Alaska Airways and repaired the Winnie Mae.

With her new propeller, the Winnie Mae took off again, and flew from Fairbanks over the Rocky Mountains to Edmonton, Canada. When they got there, they found that the airstrip, Blatchford Field, had become a muddy swamp after a storm, and they would not be able to take off from it. So with the help of a few dozen locals, they pulled the Winnie Mae to the center of town, and took off from one of the city streets with just inches to spare on either side. From Canada, Post and Gatty went to Cleveland, and finally returned back to Roosevelt Field at Long Island on July 1. They had gone around the world in 8 days, 15 hours, and 51 minutes.

After the flight, Post and Gatty were fêted as celebrities—they were guests at the White House, and were honored with a ticker-tape parade in New York. For Post, the best honor came from FC Hall, who gave the Winnie Mae to him as a gift. The two pilots wrote an account of their trip titled *Around the World in Eight Days*. The Foreword to the book was written by humorist Will Rogers, who was a friend of Post's and who often flew as a passenger with him.

Almost immediately, Post began making plans for a second around-the-world flight—this time solo. The Winnie Mae's engine was overhauled, and she was fitted with a new automatic pilot system that had just been developed by the Sperry Gyroscope Company. Also added was a new radio-homing system developed by the US Army. On July 15, 1933, Post took off in the Winnie Mae from Brooklyn, following much the same route as his 1931 flight. The automatic pilot system did not work as expected, and Post ended up sleeping only 24 hours total during the flight. His sole major mishap occurred when he got lost in Alaska and had to land in the tiny mining town of Flat, nosing over in the mud and wrecking his propeller during the landing. A new propeller had to be flown in for him. Post landed back at New York on July 27, with a new circumglobal speed record of 7 days, 18 hours, and 49 minutes.

After his record-breaking solo flight around the world, Post laid plans to fly in the 1934 MacRobertson Race from England to Australia. Concluding that he could fly faster if he flew high enough to ride the jet stream air current, Post modified the Winnie Mae for extreme high-altitude flight (up to 30,000 feet). Because the Lockheed Vega's cockpit could not be pressurized, Post had to work with the BF Goodrich Company to design and test a special pressure suit. After deciding not to enter the now-aging Winnie Mae in the MacRobertson Race, Post continued to work on his pressure suit, which he flight-tested in March 1935, riding the gulf stream from California to Ohio in seven hours. The Wiley pressure suit would later become the basis for the Air Force's high-altitude flight suits.

In August 1935, Post and his friend Will Rogers decided to fly on a fishing trip to Alaska, using a prototype airplane that Post was working on using parts from two different airplanes, the "Orion-Explorer". Post asked the engineers at Lockheed to replace the plane's landing gear with water-landing pontoons for the Alaska trip, but they refused, concluding that it would alter the aerodynamics and make the plane too nose-heavy. Post, on his own, added pontoons anyway. With Rogers, he flew to Alaska and made several stops. On August 15, 1935, as they took off from a lake near

Point Barrow, Alaska, the plane nosed over into the water and crashed. Both Post and Rogers were killed instantly.

In 1936, Wiley Post's widow sold the Winnie Mae to the Smithsonian. The plane is now exhibited in the Air and Space Museum.

Ford Tri-Motor

Although Henry Ford is best-known for introducing the mass-produced automobile to the world, he also played a significant role in helping to establish the passenger airline.

By 1908, Henry Ford had changed the face of America by introducing the Model T automobile. Simple, reliable and so cheap that virtually anyone could afford it, the "Tin Lizzy" made the horse-drawn carriage obsolete virtually overnight. In just 20 years, over 15 million Model T's had been sold, and America became a nation of car owners. In the post-war years, though, and especially after Lindbergh's flight, Ford became interested in aviation, and saw the potential for long-distance passenger and freight air travel.

After the war, a number of American industrialists received a mimeographed copy of a form letter from someone named William Stout, who wanted to start an aircraft company. Stout was an engineer who had worked for Packard during the war, producing Liberty engines. In the 1920's, he formed his own aircraft company and designed the Stout 2-AT, the first all-metal airplane certified in the US. Designed to carry both mail and passengers, the 2-AT was a high-wing monoplane with a single Liberty engine. With its thick wings and corrugated-aluminum skin, the "Pullman", as it was called, was based on the Junkers and Fokker designs then being produced in Germany. (Indeed they were so similar that the Germans later sued for patent infringement.) In his form letter, Stout offered shares in his company for an investment of $1,000, boldly declaring, "For your one thousand dollars you will get one definite promise: You will never get your money back."

Henry Ford and his son Edsel, perhaps impressed by Stout's sheer pluck, each ponied up $1,000, then in 1925 purchased the entire Stout Metal Aircraft Company. By this time, Stout was already working on a new design, the 3-AT, which replaced the 2-AT's single Liberty engine with three lighter Wright Whirlwind radial engines, one on the nose and one on each wing. But on its first flight, the 3-AT proved to be seriously underpowered: its test pilot could barely maintain altitude and refused to fly the plane again. Ford in turn angrily declared, "This plane is a mechanical monstrosity and an aerodynamic absurdity. From now on keep Stout out of the design room." Ford's own design team went to work to modify the 3-AT, replacing the engines with more powerful J-5 versions of the Whirlwind. Given the model number 4-AT, it became known as the Ford Tri-Motor.

From the beginning, the Tri-Motor was designed with safety in mind: Ford knew that his company name had been associated with safe and reliable automobiles, and he wanted that to carry over into the air passenger market as well. The Tri-Motor could fly safely on just two engines, and could even maintain altitude with just one, making it safe for long-distance flights even over water. Its rugged all-metal construction and sturdy landing gear meant that the plane could take off and land even from rough grass airstrips, and the wheels could also be replaced with skis or floats. Over the years newer versions, the 5-AT and 6-AT, appeared, which had even more powerful engines. They were capable of carrying up to 15 passengers along with two flight crew and one flight attendant for the passengers.

Ford's Tri-Motor became the air equivalent of the Model T—the first mass-produced aircraft for the civilian market (it even earned the nickname "Tin Goose"). Nearly all of the major airlines in the US, including American, Eastern, Pan Am, Transcontinental, and United, began their life by flying passengers in Ford Tri-Motors. When bigger and better passenger planes began to appear, Ford halted production in 1933, but the rugged little aircraft continued, serving as freight carriers or crop dusters, and still carrying passengers at rough airstrips in remote areas. A few of these are still flying today, carrying fans at aviation shows for joyrides around the field.

Ford produced 199 Tri-Motors between 1926 and 1933. Today one of these is on display at the Smithsonian Air and Space Museum. Registration number NC9683, a 5-AT-B model, was built in 1929 and sold to Southwest Air Fast Service (SAFE), which was then bought out by American Airlines in 1930. American flew the Tri-Motor on a number of passenger routes, including the transcontinental Cleveland to Los Angeles route, until 1935, when it was sold to the regional TACA airline in Nicaragua. Over the years the plane was sold to operators in Mexico, Montana, Alaska, and finally back to Mexico.

Here the Tri-Motor somehow ended up grounded and transformed into someone's house, with a stove and chimney installed through the roof. American Airlines found it, purchased and restored it, and began flying it on goodwill tours in the early 1960s. The plane was then donated to the Smithsonian, where it remains on display.

Martin B-10 Bomber

The Martin B-10 is considered to be the first "modern" military bomber. At the time it was introduced, the design, featuring retractable landing gear, turreted defensive machine guns, and an internal bomb bay, was considered revolutionary.   On the eve of the Second World War, the B-10 changed the entire face of air combat.

In 1931, the US Army Air Force was looking for a new heavy bomber, to fight a new kind of war.

At the beginning of the First World War in 1914, "aerial bombing" consisted of slow ponderous biplanes, in which an observer could manually toss grenades or small finned bombs out over the side of the plane onto enemy trenches. But the technology advanced rapidly, and four years later when the war ended, German Gotha and British Vickers long-range bombers were carrying out strategic attacks on each other's cities.

This new capability inspired a completely new way of looking at war. With strategic bombing, some military theorists concluded, it was now possible to avoid the long drawn-out bloody trench battles of the Western Front and defeat an enemy solely through air power, using heavy long-range bombing raids to destroy his industry, terrorize and demoralize his population, and make it incapable for the enemy to continue to fight.

But this could not be done with the slow vulnerable canvas-covered biplanes from the First World War. It required new technology — which came in 1931.

The Martin bomber didn't start out as a revolution. The original design for the B-10 was fairly conventional: its major innovation was that it was a newer monoplane instead of the traditional biplane, and was built entirely of metal skin instead of a canvas-covered frame. The bomb load was carried on standard racks located under the wings. But this design produced too much drag, leading to slow speed and poor performance. To decrease the drag, engineers decided to remove the bomb racks from the wings and place them inside the fuselage instead. That made all the difference.

That change in turn led to a cascade of other improvements. An internal bomb rack required a larger and roomier fuselage. This allowed enough internal space for retractable landing gear in which the wheels folded up inside the plane after takeoff, greatly increasing the speed. The bigger fuselage required a larger wing for more lift, which in turn allowed for more powerful engines. So not only could the plane now carry a bigger and heavier bomb load — 2,000 pounds of bombs — but it could carry the extra weight of three defensive .30-caliber machine guns including a rotating turret, giving it unmatched defensive firepower. And, with its powerful engines, the streamlined bomber could fly at over 200mph, faster than nearly any existing fighter plane.

In one stroke, the Martin B-10 made every other bomber in the world — and most fighter planes — obsolete. Though given the unglamorous nickname of "The Whale" (because of its bloated belly), it was the dream plane that every strategic air war theorist had wanted. Vast formations of such bombers could, the reasoning now went, fly long distances to pummel any opponent's industrial cities into ruins, outrunning enemy fighters and using its bristling machine guns to fight off any interceptors that were able to catch them. It led to a slogan that summed up the new military outlook: "The bomber will always get through."

In 1934, the United States undertook a project which showed off the full potential of its premiere new bomber. Led by Lt Col Henry "Hap" Arnold, a group of 10 B-10s took off from Washington DC. Over the next week, the aircraft flew all the way to Alaska, then made a series of long-range flights over the Arctic. Officially, the purpose of the mission was to photograph the northern regions and to map new flight paths to Asia and Europe. Unofficially, it was a show of power directed at what were already potential US enemies in Japan and Germany.

In 1935, the capabilities of the B-10 were improved when it was used to test the new Norden bombsight, which was intended to allow pinpoint-accurate bombing of enemy industrial and war-production targets.

By the time the Second World War broke out, however, the B-10 was the victim of its own success. Shaken by the revolutionary new design, other nations were forced to quickly find a way to meet the threat. By 1939, a new generation of fighter planes was in the works—fast heavily-armed all-metal mono-wings like the German Messerschmitt, the Japanese Zero, and the British Spitfire—all designed to take on bombers like the B-10. In the strategic bombing role, meanwhile, the B-10 was surpassed by larger, faster, more heavily-armed planes like the Lancaster and the B-17.

The B-10 did play a peripheral role during the early part of World War II. Export versions had been sold to China, where they served during the war against Japan. The first air raid on Tokyo was carried out by two Chinese B-10s—though they dropped propaganda leaflets instead of bombs. A number of B-10s were also sold to the Netherlands, where they fought against the Japanese in the East Indies from 1941 to 1942.

In all, the US produced 348 B-10 bombers, selling 182 of these overseas. Today, only one still remains. Originally part of a group of 40 sold to Argentina in 1938 and used for coastal patrol, this sole survivor was still being used as a training aircraft for ground crews in the 1960's. In 1970, it was donated by the Argentine Government to the US Air Force Museum, which restored it in the markings used by the 1934 Alaska Expedition. It is now on display at the Museum.

Texaco Model R Racer

In addition to helping to promote aviation to the public, air races in the 1920s and 1930s helped spur technological innovations.

The first "air competition" was held in France in 1909, billed as "Champagne's Grand Week of Aviation". It introduced the Gordon Bennett Trophy for aviation and attracted aircraft designers and pilots from all over the world, as well as a huge audience including European royalty. The event was won by the American Glenn Curtiss.

In 1913, the first Schneider Trophy race for seaplanes was held. It was then suspended during the First World War, resuming in 1919. Perhaps the most notable of the Schneider races was in 1931 when the British Supermarine Company's winning seaplane set a record of over 400mph: features from this design were incorporated into the Spitfire fighter.

In the US, the newspaper publisher Ralph Pulitzer sponsored an air race in 1920, which was then continued on an annual basis, dubbed the "National Air Races" and featuring both pylon-courses and cross-country races. In 1964, the National Air Races moved from Cleveland to Reno NV, where they are still held each year.

In 1927, the Texaco Oil Company bought a Ford Tri-Motor which it flew across the country to promote and advertise its product, and when the Tri-Motor crashed in December 1928 it was replaced with a Lockheed Vega.

By 1930, Texaco decided to sponsor its own entries into the National Air Races. It turned to the Travel Air Manufacturing Company in Wichita, which had been founded by three men who went on to become aviation legends: Walter Beech, Clyde Cessna, and Lloyd Stearman. The company had been producing a specialized air racer which it called the Model R, but which had been dubbed "Mystery Ships" by the press because Travel Air released no details about the aircraft and kept their manufacture a secret, going so far as to drape the planes with a tarp and post an armed guard in front of the locked hangar. The Model R that went to Texaco was the fourth Mystery Ship to be produced (Travel Air made only five in total), and bore the civilian registration number NR1313. Texaco dubbed it "Number 13".

It turned out to be a lucky number for Texaco. Powered by a nine-cylinder Wright Whirlwind R-975 engine and a thin low mono-wing, Number 13 quickly set two transcontinental speed records. It won the pylon race at the 1929 meet in Cleveland with an average speed of 194.9mph, even though it had missed one of the pylons and had to circle back. The Model R was also a champion cross-country racer and set over 200 speed records. And the aircraft gave a shocking surprise to the US Army Air Force: two of the entrants in these races were a Curtiss P-3-A and a Curtiss F6C-C, both biplane pursuit fighters that were then in active military service. It provoked embarrassing questions from Congress about how America's frontline fighters had been beaten by an off-the-shelf civilian airplane, and was one of the factors that led the military to phase out canvas-covered biplanes and move to all-metal monoplanes like the P-26. The Fascists in Italy, meanwhile, were so impressed with the Model 13 design that they purchased one of the aircraft, pieced together from spare parts, to study it, hoping to adapt some of its features for their own military fighters, resulting in the Breda Ba27.

Today, the Texaco Model R N1313 is on display at the Museum of Science and Industry in Chicago.

Douglas DC-3

The DC-3 airliner changed the face of commercial aviation, made long-distance passenger flying a routine, and is still flying today.

In 1935, American Airlines was looking for a new airplane. Boeing had introduced its Model 247, and Douglas had responded with the DC-1 and then the improved DC-2, but American Airlines, which was still flying Ford Trimotors, was not satisfied with either of those. They wanted something bigger, more economical to fly, and more roomy and comfortable for passengers—especially on overnight flights. In short, they wanted a better version of the DC-2.

Douglas Aircraft, on the other hand, was not enthusiastic. They were still manufacturing DC-2s and did not want to have to retool a factory to produce a new design, especially when they were not sure that other airlines would chip in with enough orders to make it practical. But American was insistent, and, taking advantage of one of FDR's New Deal programs, borrowed enough money from the US Government to place a pre-order for twenty of the new airliners, sight unseen—enough to fund the entire development program.

The new DC-3 was essentially a modified and improved DC-2. It would begin by widening the fuselage by one-third and rounding it to make more passenger space. It would be driven by two Wright R-1820 Cyclone radial engines, each with 1,100 horsepower (this was upgraded in later versions to use Pratt and Whitney R-1830 Twin Wasp engines). The DC-3 was capable of speeds up to 230mph, and its added fuel capacity meant it could fly nonstop from New York to Chicago, something no other passenger plane could do—and it could do it in about four hours. Douglas would make two versions of the plane: the standard "day plane" could carry 21 passengers, and the DST ("Douglas Sleeper Transport", usually advertised as the "Skyliner") version was intended for overnight routes and provided private sleeping berths, similar to those in railroad cars, for 16 passengers. DST versions could travel, in segments with fuel stops, from coast to coast in about 19 hours.

The plane began entering service in June 1936—and was an instant hit. Passengers loved the room and comfort, and airlines loved the range and fuel economy which made it quite profitable to operate. As orders poured in, the DC-3 quickly eclipsed the DC-2 and Boeing's Model 247, and came to dominate long-distance commercial air travel. By 1939, some 90% of all long-distance commercial passenger travel was being carried by DC-2s and DC-3s.

Another important customer was the US military, which made some changes, added a few doors, and converted the airliner into a transport and cargo plane, the C-47 Skytrain. Dubbed the "Gooney Bird", it became the workhorse of the Army and Navy supply networks during the upcoming Second World War. It was also used for dropping paratroopers.

Douglas also gained considerable foreign sales from the DC-3. Holland wanted the DC-3 for European service and also to fly out of its colonies in the Pacific East Indies, but the Nazis invaded and conquered the Dutch before any could be produced. British airlines purchased the civilian versions, while the RAF obtained a large number of C-47 transports, dubbing them the "Dakota". The Russians negotiated to manufacture the transport version with Soviet engines as the Lisunov Li-2: they produced around 5,000 of them but never paid any of the license fees. Even the Japanese, faced with the problem of ferrying supplies between their far-flung outposts in the Pacific, saw the DC-3/C-47 as the solution. They purchased several of the planes through dummy companies to hide their destination, copied them with Mitsubishi engines, and manufactured them throughout the war as the Showa L2D "Tabby", making the transport unique as the only military aircraft to be flown in the Pacific war by both the Americans and the Japanese.

After 1945, Douglas was once again able to concentrate on the civilian market; although the DC-3 had stopped production in 1942, the postwar world was flooded with surplus C-47s, which Douglas converted back into new DC-3s. With America entering its postwar economic boom, "travel" became affordable for many, the airline business exploded rapidly, and the DC-3 dominated air travel throughout the 1960s, declining only after Boeing introduced its Model 707. In all, some 16,000 planes, in different versions, were built. Even today, 80 years after the last one rolled off the production line, there are still dozens of DC-3s in active commercial service, flying routes between small airfields in outlying areas where the bigger planes cannot go.

Stearman PT-17 Kaydet

The PT-17 was the most numerous of several different trainers that were introduced by the Stearman Company. Nearly every American pilot who flew fighters, bombers, or cargo planes during World War II got their first flying lessons in a PT-17.

By the mid-1930s, the US needed a new airplane for basic flight training. Warplane design had advanced rapidly, from cloth-covered biplanes to all-metal mono-wings, but the United States had not kept up—the US Army Air Force and Navy were still using versions of the PT-3 Trusty, introduced back in 1927, as their primary trainer for new pilots. At this time, the training for American military pilots happened in three stages with three different airplanes: the "primary trainer" was used for teaching new students how to fly, the "basic trainer" was used for instruction in subjects such as formation flying and aerial gunnery, and an "advanced trainer" was a more powerful aircraft intended to prepare students in air tactics before they began specific training in the type of airplane they would be using in their combat assignment. The rate of student failure, known as "washing out", usually got higher with each step.

In the inter-war years, though, America was stuck in a wave of isolationism, and nobody in Congress wanted to spend money to modernize the military. It wasn't until 1935, with war clouds looming in both Europe and the Pacific, that enough funding was finally provided for a new training aircraft.

The Stearman Company, however, anticipating that the military would be looking for a new trainer soon, had already begun design work on its Model 75 airplane in 1934. It was, at the time it was introduced, already an obsolete design: a fabric-covered biplane in an era when all-metal mono-wings were supreme. But the Stearman was very stable at low speeds and was easy to control, making it very good for training rookie pilots. It also used a radial engine, which was reliable, durable, and easy to repair. Both the Army Air Corps and the Navy began ordering two-seat versions of the biplane for use as basic trainers.

There were a bewildering variety of Stearman trainers, differing mostly in which engine had been fitted to them. The first production models obtained in 1935 used a Lycoming R-680 engine, and they received the Army designation PT-13. After the Boeing Company purchased Stearman in 1936, they continued to produce PT-13s. But as war came closer, the military began ordering them in increasing numbers—3500 in 1940 alone—and the manufacturers were unable to keep up. When bottlenecks began to appear in the fabrication of Lycoming engines, the Army Air Corps, anxious to maintain production, ordered that the more readily-available Continental R-670 engine be fitted to the same airframe, designating the resulting plane as the PT-17. With a 220-horsepower radial engine and a top speed of around 125mph, this would be the most widely-produced variant, but others followed. In 1942, in turn, now faced with a shortage of Continental engines, Stearman began using the Jacobs R-755-7 instead, and this variant was listed as the PT-18.

The Navy, meanwhile, was using the same airframe for its own primary trainer, but with a different variety of radial engines, and they used the designation N2S instead of PT. At one point in 1942, both the Army and Navy found themselves using the same Lycoming R-680-17 engine, and the Army PT-13D and Navy N2S-5 were identical—the only time this ever happened. A number of the Army versions were also sent to Canada under Lend-Lease. At first these were equipped with the standard open cockpits, but during winter training the Canadians decided that they didn't like this very much and installed enclosed cockpits.

The Stearman was a superb training platform. As with all trainers, the plane had dual cockpits, with the student sitting in front and the instructor in back. The instructor had a duplicate set of flight controls and could take over immediately if the student got himself into trouble. The big engine was powerful but the airframe had handling characteristics that were forgiving, especially for takeoffs and landings, making it easier for student pilots to learn the basics. Somewhat inconsistently, it soon earned the nickname "The Yellow Peril"; this was perhaps because of its bright yellow and blue paint scheme, perhaps because the high washout rate was hazardous to a young pilot's career, or perhaps because whenever a student pilot was flying it near you never knew *what* he was going to do next. But it was the Canadians who gave the plane the nickname by which it is still most widely known: the Kaydet.

In all, over 10,000 Kaydets of various models (mostly PT-17s) were produced during the war, with the last one rolling off the Boeing assembly line in Wichita KS in February 1945. Although the Air Force continued to use the Stearman as a basic trainer well into the jet age, after the war several thousand of the planes were declared surplus and sold. Through the 1950's, many found use as agricultural crop dusters; large numbers of these were fitted with newer Pratt and Whitney R-985 engines with 450 horsepower. By the 1960s, restored to their original military specs, they were appearing at air shows. Today, 75 years after production stopped, there are at least 1,000 Kaydets still flying.

The PT-13D obtained by the Smithsonian Air and Space Museum was manufactured in 1944 and used at the Moton Field training base in Tuskagee, Alabama, to train members of the famous "Tuskagee Airmen", the first African-American fighter squadron. Originally exhibited at the Museum's Udvar-Hazy Center, it is now housed in the National Museum of African American History and Culture.

Polikarpov I-16

Designed inside a prison labor camp, the Soviet I-16 was the first "modern" fighter, with mono-wings, enclosed cockpit, and retractable landing gear.

Nikolai Polikarpov had already became a successful aircraft designer in the 1920s. After Igor Sikorsky defected to the West, Polikarpov had taken over management of the Russo-Baltic Railcar Factory, which produced the Ilya Muromets bomber. He then designed the R-5 reconnaissance plane, followed by the Polikarpov Po-2 trainer, and the success of these biplanes led to his appointment, along with Dmitri Grigorovich (who had designed a series of seaplanes during the First World War), to produce a new generation of modern Soviet fighter planes that would allow the USSR to catch up with the West. When Polikarpov and Grigorovich came up with a number of designs which, however, proved to be unsuitable or unworkable, Stalin was displeased with their apparent lack of progress, and in 1929, during one of his periodic purges, he had them both arrested and exiled to a prison camp—charged with "sabotaging" the Russian military.

But not just any prison camp. Still recognizing their talent and their potential value, Stalin had them sent to State Aircraft Factory No. 39, near Moscow, which was in fact an "Internal Prison" manned by political inmates, including a number of aeronautical engineers, under the watchful eye of the Central Aero and Hydrodynamic Institute (known by its Russian initials TsAGI). Here, Polikarpov and Grigorovich were again put to work designing fighter planes.

During this time, Andrei Tupolev needed engineers to work on a new biplane fighter, and in August 1932 Polikarpov and Grigorovich were released from prison to work on the "I-14A". Their work would result in the I-15, a fast snub-nosed maneuverable biplane fighter with a huge radial engine. It entered service in 1933.

The now-freed Polikarpov already had ideas for a revolutionary new aircraft, however, one that would push the USSR to the forefront of military aviation. Essentially, the I-16 was to be a monoplane version of the I-15. But it was far more advanced, yet was intentionally designed to be simple enough to be produced by unskilled factory workers. The body, unlike the fabric-covered biplane, would be a monocoque plywood/fiberglass shell. The monoplane wing gave it superb maneuverability, while the retractable landing gear, operated by a hand crank inside the cockpit, would be the first on a military airplane. Early versions had an enclosed cockpit, but the canopy often became stuck, so it was later replaced by a simple windscreen in front of an open cockpit.

The I-16 was originally designed for a Soviet-built licensed copy of the Wright Cyclone R-1820 engine, but when negotiations for that fell through, Polikarpov substituted the Russian 1,000-hp Shvetsov M-62 supercharged 9-cylinder radial engine instead, turning a two-blade variable-pitch propeller. The plane was armed with two .30-

caliber ShKAS machine guns in the wings, and could carry 200kg of bombs.

The first prototype flew in December 1933, and production models entered service in 1935. The stubby little plane, just twenty feet long, reached a top speed of 283mph, making it the fastest fighter in the world at the time. Pilots called it *Ishak*, or "Little Donkey". Polikarpov, once a prisoner in one of Stalin's gulags, was now presented with the Order of Lenin.

When the Spanish Civil War broke out in July 1936, Hitler threw his support behind the Nationalist forces of Francisco Franco, while Stalin began sending military equipment to the leftist Republicans. Among the guns, ammunition and airplanes sent by the USSR were 475 I-16s. The Spanish Republicans dubbed the little fighter *Moska*, "the fly", while the Nationalists referred to it disparagingly as *Rata*, "the rat". The stubby little I-16 did well against the German-built Heinkel He-51 and Arado Ar-68 biplane fighters that were being flown by Franco's pilots.

But in 1937 the Nazis began introducing their new Messerschmitt Bf-109B fighter into Spain, and the *Moska* found itself outclassed. Compared to the 109, the I-16 was underpowered and outgunned. Soon, the Russian plane was being produced with a larger twin-row M-88 radial engine, pushing the I-16 to 342mph. The armament was also increased by adding two more machine guns to the nose, and some versions were fitted with two 20mm cannons replacing the wing guns and with unguided RS-82 air-to-ground rockets under the wings.

By the time the Spanish Civil War ended in 1939, however, the Russians had already withdrawn all of their I-16s, which were being pressed into service in other places. Russia invaded Finland in what became known as the "Winter War", and the Finns did surprisingly well against Soviet ground forces and Polikarpov fighters. Some 250 *Ishaks* were also sold to China, where they performed well against Japanese A5M Claude fighters. When a border dispute broke out in Mongolia between Japan and the USSR, the Soviet fighters won air superiority against the Japanese Ki-27 Nates, forcing the Imperial Army to withdraw.

Over the next year, however, with the appearance of the American P-40, British Spitfire, Japanese Zero, and newer models of the German Bf-109, it was clear that the I-16 had reached the end of its useful life. But the Soviets had no good fighter design yet to replace it, and so when the Nazis invaded Russia in June 1941, the Polikarpov was still the frontline fighter for Stalin's forces. The German Luftwaffe caught the Soviet Air Force by surprise and destroyed most of it on the ground. In the air, the I-16 was no match for the Nazi Me-109Es, and desperate Russian pilots of the "Great

Patriotic War" took to ramming German airplanes to knock them out of the sky—a tactic known as *taran*. It wasn't until 1942 that newer and better Soviet fighters began to appear, and the little *Ishak* was withdrawn from service. In all, between 8,000 and 10,000 I-16s, of various models, had been produced.

In 1992, six Polikarpov I-16s and three I-15s, all of them manufactured in 1939, were found on a former battlefield north of St Petersburg, where they had crashed during the siege of what was then known as Leningrad. They were taken to Siberia, where they were restored to flying condition in the same factory in Novosibirsk where they had been originally built, using parts made from original design drawings. The restored fighters were then crated and shipped to New Zealand, where their first flights were made in 1995 by Sir Tim Wallis' Alpine Fighter Collection.

One of these restored Polikarpov I-16s is now on display at the Military Aviation Museum in Virginia Beach. Another is in the exhibit of the Flying Heritage Collection in Everett WA. There are other *Ishaks* at museums in Russia, Finland, and Spain.

Boeing P-26 Peashooter

When it was first introduced, the Peashooter was one of the fastest fighters in the world, but it was quickly outclassed by better designs. Nevertheless, even though obsolete, it managed to hold on until the beginning of World War Two, when it scored some of the first air victories against the Japanese.

In 1931, designers at Boeing began work on a new fighter concept. At the time, the US Army Air Corps was flying the Boeing P-12, a rugged biplane fighter. But Boeing, like most warbird manufacturers, already realized that the days of the biplane were over, and the future lay with low-wing all-metal monoplanes. And so they drew up plans for a sleek futuristic-looking fighter that they designated the Model 248. It would be the US's first metal mono-wing fighter. The prototype flew in March 1932.

At first glance, Boeing's new fighter looked a lot like the Russian I-16 then being worked on in the USSR (though of course Boeing didn't know anything about the Soviet design). But in many ways, the American design fell short—mostly due to the inherent conservatism of the US military. The Army, for instance, knew that retractable landing gear would reduce drag and increase the speed, but they feared that the complicated cranking mechanism would be prone to failure and that its added weight would impact the plane's performance. So the Model 248 had fixed landing gear. Military experts were also unsure if a single cantilevered mono-wing would really be able to withstand the stresses of high-speed maneuvering in combat, so Boeing placed a series of external bracing wires to strengthen it, though this produced drag. Conversely, Boeing also knew that an enclosed cockpit would decrease drag and help performance, but American military pilots wanted an open cockpit, both to help with visibility in searching for enemy aircraft and to make it easier to see hand signals from flight leaders and fellow pilots in these pre-radio days.

Despite all of these built-in limitations, however, the P-26 fighter, upon its introduction, still managed a speed of 235mph, faster than anything else in the sky (though it was soon to be eclipsed by the Soviet I-16). This was despite the fact that the P-26 used the very same engine as the P-12. The P-12 with its biplane wing, nevertheless, had a faster climb rate and a higher ceiling than the new monoplane. The Army also did not like the rather high landing speed of the P-26, and ordered wing flaps to be retrofitted to all of them to reduce it. This in turn made the plane difficult to handle on landing, which ruled out any possible use as a Navy carrier-based fighter.

Most Army pilots simply didn't like the stubby little fighter. It was fast and maneuverable, but it handled differently than the biplanes they were accustomed to. If the plane crashed upon landing and flipped over, the cockpit exposed the pilot to being crushed in the wreck: Boeing responded to this by adding a bigger protective "hump" to the fuselage just behind the pilot's seat. Most of all, though, the pilots didn't like the weak armament of two .30-caliber machine guns that were set underneath the floor of the cockpit and synchronized to fire through the propeller. And the gunsight worked by using a long blast tube mounted in front of the window, which looked like a schoolboy's peashooter—thereby giving the little fighter its nickname. It was not meant as a compliment.

Ultimately, the design decisions that the military had itself insisted upon had doomed the Peashooter to an early grave. Within three years it was already being replaced by newer and better mono-wing designs like the P-35, P-36 and P-39. The Peashooters were demoted to the role of "advanced trainer".

But a number of P-26s still remained operational in remote areas that were considered of lesser importance; at this time, the Army Air Corps considered the defense of the American mainland to be its primary role, and outlying areas like Hawaii, the Philippines, and Panama were neglected. By 1940, the American fighter force in the Philippines consisted solely of obsolete Peashooters.

When the Japanese invaded China, the United States shipped a number of P-26 fighters to help them. In one action, a flight of Peashooters intercepted a group of Japanese medium bombers that were flying without escort and shot most of them down. But when faced by Japanese Nate and Claude fighters, the P-26s were entirely outclassed. By the end of 1937, all of the Chinese Peashooters had either crashed, failed mechanically, or been shot down, and they were replaced with British Gloster Gladiator biplanes, which were even more obsolete.

During the summer of 1941, the US finally began to replace the P-26s in the Philippines with P-35s and P-36s. Most of the Peashooters were moved back to Hawaii, but on December 7, 1941, nearly all of those were destroyed on the ground during the Japanese attack. In the Philippines, the Japanese also caught most of the American planes on the ground. But during the ensuing weeks of air raids, a squadron of pilots flying P-26s managed to take off from Batangas Field and engage the Japanese. Despite the fact that they were flying an outdated relic, the Filipino pilots were able to score two victories, with one pilot shooting down a Betty medium bomber and another managing to score against a Japanese Zero. They were two of the earliest Japanese planes shot down during the war.

Meanwhile, a squadron of American pilots was still flying P-26s as patrol aircraft in the Panama Canal Zone. In 1943, the last 11 of these were sold to the Panamanian Air Force, which in turn sold them to Guatemala later that year. The Guatemalans flew them until 1950, when the US replaced them with surplus P-51 Mustangs. The remaining Peashooters were returned to the US and refurbished. One of them was then donated to the Smithsonian Air and Space Museum's Udvar-Hazy Center in Washington, and the other went to the Planes of Fame Museum in Chino CA.

Curtiss P-36 Hawk

The American-designed P-36 saw most of its action in early World War Two while flying for the French.

With the failure of the P-26 Peashooter, by 1935 the US Army Air Corps was already looking for a new fighter plane. Three companies submitted proposals: learning their lessons from the P-26, all of the proposals were for an all-metal low-wing mono-plane with retractable landing gear. In 1936 the Army awarded a contract to the Seversky company, whose prototype was adopted as the P-35. The US deployed P-35s to the Philippines and also based several squadrons in Michigan. Sweden tried to buy a number of them, but these were diverted to the Philippines instead. Ironically, the Japanese Navy bought 20 two-seat versions of the P-35 to use as trainers.

But the Army also liked Curtiss's P-36 design, and ordered three prototypes for further evaluation before in 1938 placing a request for 210 of the fighters. In accordance with American military doctrine, which placed first priority upon defense of the American homeland, most of these were based in the United States, but several squadrons were also deployed in Hawaii, the Panama Canal Zone, and the Philippines.

In 1939, France was facing the Nazis and their new Messerschmitt fighters, and, facing production issues with their own Bloch and Morane-Saulnier fighters, needed to supplement their squadrons quickly. They turned to the US and asked for 300 Curtiss Model 75 Hawks, the export version of the P-36. The American military, anxious over its own need to re-equip its fighter squadrons, opposed the deal and delayed it, and the first Hawks did not reach French units until March 1939. In all, France received 316 Curtiss Hawk 75s before her capitulation in 1940. Those that had not yet been delivered to France were sent instead to Britain, where they were designated as "Mohawks". Smaller numbers of Hawks were also delivered to Holland, Norway, and some South American countries, and a handful were built in China under license. Some of the Model 75s captured by Germany from France were later given to Finland for use against the Soviets.

The experience in France, however, demonstrated that the P-36 was not up to the level of the Messerschmitt or Spitfire; at 250mph it was too slow, and, with just two machine guns, it was underarmed. The US first upgraded the P-36 by adding two more guns to the wings, but it was not enough, and the Army Air Corps began making efforts to replace its frontline Hawks with newer P-40 Warhawks, the best American fighter available. (The P-40 was itself a P-36 airframe with its radial engine replaced by a slimmer liquid-cooled inline.)

By December 1941 only two American fighter groups were still flying P-36s: one in Alaska and one in Hawaii. During the Japanese attack on Pearl Harbor six of those P-36s were able to get into the air, where they managed to shoot down two Japanese aircraft while having one of their own shot down. But by June 1942 nearly all of the surviving Hawks had been withdrawn from combat.

Of the 1200 Hawks produced during the war, 900 were sent overseas. Today only two examples of the P-36 and three Hawk 75s still survive, three of them airworthy. One is in Thailand, one in New Zealand, and two in the UK. The US Air Force Museum in Dayton displays the first P-36 that was provided to the Army, delivered to Louisiana's Barksdale Field in April 1938. It is presented in the markings carried by one of the Hawks that flew against the Japanese during the Pearl Harbor attack.

Bell P-39 Airacobra

Originally designed to intercept high-altitude heavy bombers, the P-39 ended up performing low-altitude fighter-sweep duties for the Soviets.

Throughout the 1920s and 1930s, the US military had been preparing exclusively for a defense against seaborne invasion. Since no nation had aircraft capable of crossing the vast oceans to reach the United States, not much thought was given to any capability to counter high-altitude bombers. But by the late 30s it was becoming clear from events in Europe that strategic bombers could indeed pose a serious threat to the US mainland in the near future.

In 1937, the US Army Air Corps finally released a "request for proposals" for an interceptor that would be capable of shooting down heavy bombers approaching at high attitude. The design would have to use the liquid-cooled inline Allison engine, it would need to reach a speed of at least 360mph, and it had to be capable of reaching an altitude of 20,000 feet in just six minutes.

In response, the Bell Aircraft Company proposed a revolutionary airplane that was different from anything else that had ever been built. The key to the P-39 Airacobra design was its gun. Since the time of World War One, fighter planes and interceptors had been armed with machine guns, sometimes of .30-caliber or, in more modern designs, .50-caliber. But in the eyes of Bell's design team, this armament was reaching its limits and was already proving to be insufficient to bring down the kinds of big four-engined high-altitude bombers that the United States could expect to face soon. And so, they decided, they needed to upgrade the fighter's armament to a cannon. This had already been done in some places: the Japanese Zero was armed with 20mm cannons, and so was the Messerschmitt. But Bell concluded that their new interceptor would carry a single M4 37mm cannon—twice as big—with exploding shells that were capable of destroying a bomber with just one hit. And for maximum accuracy, this would be mounted in the nose and fire through the propeller hub.

That decision dictated the rest of the P-39's design. With the huge cannon and its ammo filling up much of the nose of the airplane, there was no room for an engine there, so the liquid cooled Allison and its radiator would have to be mounted further back, behind the cockpit. That in turn left just enough remaining space inside the nose for two .50-caliber machine guns above the cannon, and in some later models, additional .30-caliber machine guns were mounted in the wings. The Airacobra would have devastating firepower.

The propeller shaft, meanwhile, would need to stretch all the way through the front of the plane to the propeller, passing through the cockpit underneath the pilot's seat. This necessitated placing the cockpit higher in the fuselage, covered by a bubble canopy—which gave increased visibility for the pilot. Finally, the shifting center of gravity produced by having the heavy engine at the middle of the fuselage meant that a tail wheel would be ineffective, so the P-39 was fitted with "tricycle" landing gear at the nose and each wing. And finally, to give sufficient performance at high altitude, the Allison V-1710-17 engine would be fitted with a turbo-supercharger to suck in extra oxygen for additional power.

It was a radical design that all looked great on paper. And then it all fell apart.

When the prototype took to the air in April 1939, it hit speeds of 390mph at 20,000 feet, but the plane's speed at lower altitude was not as great as expected, and although the P-39 had been designed for high altitudes, now the Army decided that it also wanted better performance at low altitude as well. When experts from the National Advisory Committee for Aeronautics studied the problem, they decided that the issue was with the air intake that fed oxygen into the turbo-supercharger—it was creating enough drag to affect the airplane's performance, and if it were moved to somewhere inside the fuselage it would increase the speed by as much as 16%. This was not something that Bell wanted to hear: moving the turbo-supercharger somewhere else would require a slew of other design changes, costing time. And so, in a decision that would prove to be disastrous, Bell agreed to drop the supercharger altogether. While this gave the preferred increase in speed at low altitudes, it meant that the plane's ability to fly well at high altitude was severely crippled—a fatal flaw in a design that had been intended to attack enemy bombers.

Nevertheless, the Army ordered eighty P-39s in August 1939. A month later, Germany invaded Poland.

The initial design for the Airacobra, like most other fighters of the period, had no provisions for self-sealing gas tanks or for armor in the cockpit to protect the pilot. But after the war began, the Army decided that these things were necessary, and although it was a simple matter to add them, the unplanned-for weight also reduced the plane's performance.

By 1940, France and England were facing the Nazi onslaught and were frantically looking for fighters—any that were available. Under Lend-Lease, the US offered them P-39 Airacobras. France surrendered before any could reach her in significant numbers, but England asked for 675 of the fighters to be shipped. When they reached the RAF 601 Squadron, the British flew four missions with them against the Luftwaffe bombers, discovered that the Airacobra's performance at high altitudes was terrible, and refused to fly them again. Some 200 of the planes were passed on to Russia, who was also desperate for fighter planes. A handful were sent to North Africa to serve as ground-attack aircraft with the RAF. The rest were sent back to the US.

After December 1941, the United States was also desperate for fighters, and it quickly took all of the P-39s intended for England and sent them to the Pacific. Many of these were armed with 20mm nose cannon instead of 37mm, a variant known as the P-400. As it happened, most of the fighting against the Japanese took place at low altitudes, where the Airacobra's lack of a turbocharger did not hamper it, and although it was outclassed by the Zero it still held up reasonably well, and by some accounts even managed a 1:1 kill ratio with the Japanese fighters. The P-39 stayed on the Pacific frontlines until it could be replaced by P-38s and P-47s.

But it was in Russia that the Airacobra came into its own. As the US replaced its P-39s with Thunderbolts and Mustangs, it began sending Airacobras to the USSR under Lend-Lease. The Soviets quickly realized that the P-39 was not a high-altitude interceptor, but if utilized at low altitude, where most of the combat on the Eastern Front tended to be anyway, it was a very capable and heavily-armed platform for shooting down German fighter-bomberss and dive bombers. (Note that the Soviets did *not* utilize the Airacobra in the ground-attack role, despite many postwar histories that say otherwise—they already had the Shturmovik for that, and this was part of an intentional Russian campaign to mislead the Americans about how they were using the planes.) In total, around half of all the P-39s produced during the war went to Russia, along with about three-fourths of the later larger variant called the P-63 Kingcobra.

In Soviet hands, the *Kobrushka* ("Little Cobra") was devastating against the Nazis. Of the top ten Soviet aces of the war, five scored most of their victories in P-39 Airacobras, including Aleksandr Pokryshkin with 48 victories and Grigori Rechkalov with 44. At least 28 Russian Airacobra pilots scored 15 or more.

Around 20 wartime P-39s still exist, with around a dozen of these being flight-capable. In the US, the Pima Air and Space Museum has a P-39N model on display, while the Air Force Museum in Dayton exhibits a reconnaissance version of the P-39Q.

Curtiss P-40 Warhawk

The P-40 is best known as the shark-mouthed Flying Tiger. But it was a versatile aircraft that was used in virtually every theater of the war by several different nations.

As war was looming in Europe in 1938, the US Air Force was desperate to replace its P-36 Hawk fighter with a faster and better-armed model. In response, the Army Air Corps received proposals from Lockheed (which became the P-38), and Bell (which became the P-39). Curtiss-Wright, the manufacturer of the P-36 Hawk, also submitted a design for a much-improved version, which was known as the P-40. The US would go on to develop all three.

Essentially, the P-40 prototype, which flew in October 1938, was a modified P-36 airframe with its Pratt and Whitney radial engine replaced by a new Allison liquid-cooled inline V-12. Although the twin-engined P-38 was a better aircraft, the Army needed something that could be produced quickly, both for itself and for American allies in France, England and China. Since the P-40 used much of the same machine tools as the already-existing P-36, it could be put into production almost immediately, and because it was cheaper to make, the Army could afford to buy a lot of them. So Curtiss got an initial contract for 540 of the new fighters, to be delivered as soon as possible. It became known as the "Warhawk".

From the landing gear and cockpit back, the P-40 was essentially the same aircraft as the P-36. The major differences were in the engine and the armament. The big radial engine used by the P-36 was replaced by the inline Allison V-1710. This was not a great improvement in horsepower, but even with the necessary added radiator and cooling systems, the slimmer streamlined nose on the P-40 greatly decreased drag and boosted the speed. The Warhawk was the first American warplane to exceed 300mph in level flight, and was for a time the fastest fighter in the world. However, the original production Allison engine did not have a turbocharger, which greatly decreased its performance above 12,000 feet. Since the Army Air Force was most interested in a ground-attack fighter, for use against German armored Panzer columns, this was not considered to be much of a disadvantage.

The other major improvement in the Warhawk was the armament. The original prototype carried two .30-caliber guns on the engine cowling, but this was quickly upgraded by adding four .50 caliber guns on the wings, then modifying the P-40E model to carry six wing-mounted .50-calibers, making the Warhawk one of the most heavily-armed fighters of its time, outgunning the German Messerschmitt and the newest British fighters. The prototype plane could also carry a load of 700 pounds of bombs for attacking ground targets—later upgraded to three 500-pound bombs.

The first Warhawks rolled off the assembly line in May 1940. By the end of the year, 185 P-40s were delivered to England, which called them the "Tomahawk". During the war the UK would receive some 930 P-40s. Many of these were later models which were sent to

Australia and New Zealand, where they were known as the "Kittyhawk". France placed an order for 140 P-40s, but surrendered to German invasion before any of them could be delivered. Many of those went to England and Russia instead, and the Soviets received around 2,000 Warhawks up to 1944 through the Lend-Lease program. Another 100 P-40B models were sent to China in early 1941 along with American volunteer pilots, where they formed the American Volunteer Group, which famously became known as "The Flying Tigers" with their iconic and much-copied shark's mouth paintjob.

By the time of the Japanese attacks in December 1941, 100 P-40s had been delivered to American bases in Hawaii. Some were deployed around Pearl Harbor, a handful managed to take off during the raid, and two pilots, George Welch and Kenneth Taylor, shot down a number of Japanese planes. In the Philippines, there were a little over 100 P-40s, but most of them were destroyed on the ground.

For most of 1942 and 1943, the Warhawk was America's frontline fighter. In combat against German and Japanese planes, the P-40 was already outclassed, but it was the only American fighter that was available in any significant numbers. By late 1942, newer models were being made with supercharged engines and better performance. The P-40F model was fitted with the British Merlin engine, built in the US by the Packard Auto Company under license. The final (and most numerous) version was the P-40N, introduced in late 1943—it could make 380mph.

But the Warhawk was still outperformed by its opponents. In Europe, as the British Spitfire appeared, the Warhawk was relegated to combat against less-capable Italian aircraft and to ground-attack and close-combat support duty in the North African desert, where it proved effective and was used by the Americans, the British, and the South Africans.

In the Pacific, the Warhawks struggled but held their own against Japanese Zero and Oscar fighters until they could finally be replaced with newer Army Air Force P-38s in 1943. Warhawk pilots learned to take advantage of their superior diving speed to climb above the Zeros, make a diving attack, then zoom down and away to climb for another pass, but some Japanese fighter pilots held the Warhawks in contempt, and were able to score as many as 80 air victories against the American P-39s and P-40s.

Nevertheless, by the time the Second World War ended in 1945, there were still a number of P-40N model Warhawks in service in the China-Burma-India theater. In all, some 14,000 P-40s had been built, and they had served in the armed forces of 28 different nations. Although the US halted production of the Warhawk in November

1944, it continued in service with some smaller nations throughout the 1950s. The last frontline P-40s were retired by Brazil in 1958.

Today, there are around 50 surviving P-40 Warhawks, with around half in flyable condition. The Naval Aviation Museum in Pensacola FL displays a P-40 that was originally ordered for France as a Hawk 81-A export variant but was transferred to England and adopted as a Tomahawk II. It is displayed in the markings of the Chinese Flying Tigers. The P-40E Warhawk at the Smithsonian Udvar-Hazy center was originally sent to Canada in 1941 as a Kittyhawk I, was assigned to the Aleutians and was declared "surplus" in 1946 and passed through several American owners. It was obtained by the Smithsonian in 1964. The US Air Force Museum in Dayton OH also has a Kittyhawk that served in England during the war. The Duxford RAF Museum in England has the only surviving flyable P-40B model, which was present at Pearl Harbor during the Japanese attack.

North American AT-6 Texan

Often overlooked in the history of the Second World War, the AT-6 trainer was where most of the American pilots who fought in the conflict learned to fly.

In 1934, the US adopted a design from the North American Aircraft Company as its new "basic trainer". The BT-9 had dual cockpits with duplicate controls, and could be used to teach the essentials of military flying to students who had already received beginner's flight training in a "primary trainer". The BT-9 could also serve as a transport plane for officers and VIPs.

As the world's political situation heated up, the armed forces began to beef themselves up in response. The BT-9 had some improvements made to it—retractable landing gear and a bigger engine—and was redesignated the BC-1 (for "basic combat"). The Army began obtaining the BC-1 by the hundreds, in preparation for handling the new pilot trainees it would soon be receiving, and the Navy, undergoing a similar expansion, also adopted the new trainer, designating it the SNJ-1.

Modifications continued to be made to the design, particularly by adding more powerful engines. By the time the Second World War broke out in September 1939, the "basic combat trainer" was almost as powerful as some of the US's frontline fighters, and was intended to teach advanced students the fundamentals of air warfare (such as aerobatics, formation flying, gunnery, dogfighting tactics, strafing and bombing, or instrument flying) before they began specialized instruction with the particular type of fighter or bomber that they had been assigned to fly in combat. To reflect this, the trainer's designation was changed again, from BC-1 to AT-6 (for "advanced trainer").

By this time, air forces from other nations had also adopted the American trainer. The Canadians and British used it under the name "Harvard". With so many Allied nations also hard-pressed for fighters, it was decided that the AT-6 might, if fitted with machine guns and bomb racks, be useful in actual combat, and a number of these were sent to France, England and Australia.

In the United States, meanwhile, the demand for trainers was so great that North American opened a new factory in Dallas just to make AT-6s, and this led to the nickname that the plane still carries—the "Texan". For the rest of the war, a variety of different models appeared, and some 16,000 Texans were eventually produced, making it one of the most widely-made aircraft of the era.

When the Korean War broke out in 1950, AT-6s were rushed into service as unarmed spotters who could loiter over the battlefield and call in artillery or air strikes on ground targets, a task they also performed later in Vietnam. The Texans continued to serve as trainers until 1958, when they were finally phased out. In all, the plane was flown by 34 countries, and some small nations kept the AT-6 in service, both armed and unarmed, until the 1970s: the South African Air Force was still using Texans as trainers in the 1990s. Well over a thousand AT-6s of various models are today in private hands, and they are regular visitors to air shows and warbird displays. The National Air Races in Reno have a special race category just for AT-6 Texans.

When the movie *Tora, Tora, Tora* was being made in 1970, the producers could not find any flyable Japanese Zeros still in existence, and so they painted a flight of AT-6 Texans in Japanese markings and used them as stand-ins for the film's air combat scenes. Years later, some of these "Zeros" also found their way into the television show "Black Sheep Squadron".

Macchi C.200 Saetta

One of Italy's first all-metal mono-planes, the Saetta was outmatched by Allied fighters.

When Benito Mussolini took power in Italy in 1922, he spoke grandly of re-establishing the splendor and power of Rome, and envisioned a new Italian Empire that dominated the Mediterranean. He rapidly militarized Italian society, enrolling youth in a "New Empires" paramilitary, taking steps to increase the population of Italy by encouraging women to have more children, and began massive re-armament programs.

But the Italian military campaigns in Northern Africa in the 1930s demonstrated that the Fascists still did not have the military strength to confront France or England. In particular, the Fiat CR.32 biplane fighter was obsolete.

As a result, in February 1936 the Regio Aeronautica issued a call for a new design that would be capable of taking on the most modern British and French fighters, with a speed of at least 300mph. Because the Italians were having trouble producing reliable inline aircraft engines, it was specified that the new fighter use an air-cooled radial engine.

At the Macchi company, Mario Castoldi, who had already produced a number of racing planes, submitted a design for an all-metal mono-wing with retractable landing gear and an enclosed cockpit. Dubbed the C.200 Saetta ("Lightning Bolt"), the prototype first flew in December 1937. It was driven by a 14-cylinder Fiat A.74 RC-38 radial engine with 870 hp (a redesigned copy of the Pratt & Whitney R-1830 SC-4 Twin Wasp from the United States), capable of 315mph. To give the pilot better visibility forward over the engine, the cockpit canopy was mounted on a distinctive "hump" in the fuselage. The new fighter was armed with two .50-caliber machine guns mounted on the engine cowling, which was the standard for most other fighters of the time. Production began in June 1939, with Macchi, Breda and SAI Ambrosini all manufacturing the design. By the time the Second World War broke out in September, about 150 Saettas had been deployed as part of the Italian air force's frontline fighter force, along with a competing design from Fiat known as the G.50 Freccia "Arrow", which was placed into production because it could be manufactured more quickly. In all, around 1,100 C.200 Saettas were produced during the war.

The Saetta saw combat in Malta, Greece, Yugoslavia, and North Africa, and was later deployed with an Italian squadron to Russia. But immediately the plane ran into difficulties. The engine proved to be both underpowered and unreliable, and the twin machine gun armament was woefully inadequate. The plane also had a tendency to go into a flat spin, making it dangerous for inexperienced pilots, and Castoldi made several attempts to change the wing profile to correct this problem. Early models did not have any armor plating, and when this was added later it interfered with the airplane's center of gravity. More important, the slower C.200 was unable to stand in a dogfight with newer Allied fighters like the Spitfire. By 1942, the Saetta was being replaced by the newer Macchi C.202 Folgore, and was relegated to the role of fighter-bomber. Although it worked well as a ground-attack plane, by the time Fascist Italy surrendered in 1943 the C.200 was no longer being produced and less than 50 flyable planes still remained. They were used as trainers by the remaining Fascist forces.

In November 1942, during the battle of El Alamein, British troops captured an Italian airfield at Benghazi, in what was then known as Cyrenaica. An abandoned C.200 Saetta was found sitting at the airfield, and it was sent to the United States where it was taken on tour as part of a war-bond drive. After the war the aircraft was obtained by the New England Air Museum, where it went on display before being purchased by a private buyer in 1989, and restored in Italy by the Macchi company. It was then obtained by the US Air Force Museum in Dayton OH, where it is on display.

Junkers Ju-87 Stuka

One of the most famous aircraft of the war, the Stuka dive bomber is a familiar icon of the Nazi Luftwaffe. But its actual lifetime as an effective combat airplane was limited because of its deficiencies in design.

Within months of taking power in Germany in 1933, Adolf Hitler and the Nazi Party were already planning on a war with France and England. To rebuild the German Air Force, World War One fighter ace Ernst Udet was placed in charge of developing new combat aircraft for the Luftwaffe. The Nazi military was developing the new concept of *Blitzkrieg* or "Lightning War", which would avoid the long drawn-out trench warfare of 1914-1918 with rapid thrusts deep into the enemy's rear area, spearheaded by columns of tanks and armored vehicles and supported by tactical air strikes. Other nations had already carried out some experiments with dive-bombing—in which a bomber delivered its bombs by dropping them almost straight down onto a target before pulling up and away—but it was Udet who became the most enthusiastic advocate of the concept.

In 1933, Udet approved a design submitted by the Junkers company for a two-seat dive bomber which would function almost as aerial artillery, sweeping down onto the battlefield to strike at tactical targets with pinpoint accuracy. The project was designated the Ju-87 *Sturzkampfflugzeug*, or "Stuka" for short. Intended as a short-range ground-support bomber, the Stuka would carry an 1,100-pound bomb under the fuselage and two 110-pound bombs under the wings. To withstand the stress of a high-G dive, the wings were double-sparred and configured in an upward-curving "inverted gull wing" pattern, and were fitted with dive brakes for bombing accuracy and an automatic system to pull the plane out of its dive and into level flight, in case the pilot passed out from the G-forces. The landing gear was extra-strong to allow the plane to operate from crude grass fields close to the front, and for extra effect Hitler ordered a siren, called the "Jericho Trumpet", installed into the landing gear, which produced a shrieking scream during its dive intended to provoke terror in the target. The Stuka had forward-firing machine guns in the wings for suppressing enemy anti-aircraft gunners, and the rear gunner had his own machine gun to defend against fighters. In the original version, the tail rudder was double-finned, but after this proved too weak (and caused a crash in one of the prototypes) this was replaced with a single strengthened tail fin.

From the beginning, however, the project was delayed, partly because of difficulties in obtaining a suitable engine and partly because of opposition from other Luftwaffe officers, including Wolfram von Richthofen, who considered the Stuka to be too slow and too vulnerable. Richthofen championed a rival design, the Heinkel He-118, and the arguments continued for years until the Heinkel prototype crashed during a test flight in 1936. The Stuka began production later that year. Early models saw their first combat during the Spanish Civil War, where they were used to bomb civilians as well as military targets. When the Second World War broke out in 1939, the Stukas decimated enemy positions in Poland and France, clearing the advance for columns of Panzer tanks, and their screeching sirens became an iconic image of the Nazi *Blitzkrieg*.

In these campaigns, however, the Luftwaffe had enjoyed virtually uncontested air superiority. When the Battle of Britain began in the summer of 1940, the Nazis had no such advantage, and the Stuka paid the price. In the early stages of the air campaign, Stukas were sent to bomb ships in the English Channel and then to attack point targets in England, including the all-important radar sites. But now, facing modern British Hurricane and Spitfire fighters, the limitations of the Stuka design became apparent. Without effective fighter protection the dive bombers were painfully slow—barely 200mph—and their lack of armor made them extremely vulnerable. Unlike their American and Japanese counterparts, which were relatively maneuverable once they had dropped their bomb load, the Stuka was ponderous and clumsy, easy prey for fighters. In just a few weeks of combat, so many Stukas were shot down over England that they were withdrawn, and never operated in large numbers in the European Theater again.

Many Stukas were now retrofitted with sand filters for desert conditions, and these "tropicalized" versions, designated Ju-87B-2 Trops, were sent to North Africa. Here, facing less capable Allied fighters like the P-40, they proved useful against enemy tanks.

One little-known variant of the Stuka was the Ju-87C, a "navalized" version, capable of delivering either bombs or a torpedo, that was intended to be carried by the German aircraft carrier *Graf Zeppelin*. But the Nazis never finished the ship and no naval Stukas were ever produced.

When Germany invaded the Soviet Union in June 1941, another version of the Stuka, fitted with two 37mm cannons under the wings for tank-busting, was designated the Ju-87G. These were not capable of penetrating the front armor of a T-34 tank, but were lethal against the thinner sides and top. In the initial stages of the campaign, when the Soviet Air Defense Force was crippled and was flying inferior older models, the Stukas enjoyed success against formations of Russian tanks. The most highly-decorated German pilot of the war, Hans Ulrich Rudel, was a Stuka pilot who was credited with destroying 519 Soviet tanks while flying over 2500 combat missions. But as the war went on and the Soviets were able to produce large numbers of newer and better fighters, the Ju-87G's proved once again to be too vulnerable, and losses were heavy. After the Battle of Stalingrad, the Nazis began replacing their Stukas with ground-attack versions of the Focke-Wulf Fw-190. By the time Berlin fell in 1945, the once-iconic Stuka had all but disappeared.

Today, only two Stuka dive bombers remain in existence from the 5700 that were produced during the war. In 1941, British troops in North Africa overran a Nazi airbase and captured a damaged Stuka Trop that had been awaiting repair. The airplane was sent back to England where it underwent technical evaluation and then was given to the US Army Air Force and sent to America. In 1974 this aircraft was restored as a static display by the Experimental Aircraft Association in Wisconsin, and was obtained by the Museum of Science and Industry in Chicago, where it is on exhibit. The bullet holes can still be seen on the wings and fuselage.

In 1945, a Ju-87 was captured by British troops in Germany. Originally built as a dive bomber, it had been remodeled during the war as a G-model ground attack plane. This aircraft was given to the Air Historical Branch to be preserved, and is now on display in the RAF Museum.

Hawker Hurricane

Although outshined by the more famous Spitfire, the Hurricane bore the brunt of the fighting during the Battle of Britain.

In the early 1930s, the United Kingdom was flying the Hawker Fury biplane as its frontline fighter. For its time it was fast and maneuverable, but as war clouds appeared in Europe and the Nazis began rearming their Luftwaffe, it became apparent that the Fury would be no match for the new German fighters.

So in 1933 Hawker began designing a replacement: a mono-wing version that would use the same Goshawk engine, but which would be much faster and better-armed. Dubbed the "Hurricane", it would have retractable landing gear, house the engine compartment inside an aluminum skin, and use fabric to cover the wings and the rest of the fuselage. And when the Rolls-Royce Merlin engine was introduced, it was decided to drop the old Goshawk and use this instead.

When the prototype first flew in November 1935, it reached speeds of almost 400mph. The Air Ministry immediately placed an order for 600 fighters. This proved to be too much for Rolls-Royce to handle, though, so the engine was switched over to the Merlin II instead. When the first production Hurricane Mark Is began reaching British squadrons in 1937, they had also been fitted with self-sealing gas tanks and armor plating in the cockpit, and shortly later the wings were covered with sheet aluminum instead of canvas, and all of this extra weight dropped the speed to around 340mph. But the Hurricane, with its eight .303-caliber machine guns, was still a lethal machine. To speed deployment, the Gloster Aircraft Company also began turning out Hurricanes.

By the time Hitler invaded Poland in 1939, nineteen RAF fighter squadrons had been equipped with Hurricanes. Four of these were sent to France, which expected invasion at any time. When it came, the Hurricanes suffered 25% losses from German Messerschmitts and bombing raids, and were forced to withdraw when France surrendered.

Hitler next turned his sites onto England. Britain's Fighter Command now had 32 squadrons of Hurricanes, both Mark I and Mark II, and 19 squadrons of the newer Spitfire at its disposal. While outnumbered three to one, the RAF had the advantage of radar, which could direct the fighters to the area where they were most needed. It was decided that the Hurricanes would be sent against the German bombers, while the more capable Spitfires would attack the German Me-109 fighters that were escorting them.

English losses were heavy, but the Luftwaffe proved unable to overpower the RAF, and the Battle of Britain drew to a close in September 1940. About two-thirds of the German losses were attributed to Hurricanes.

In 1941, the Hurricanes were updated with a more powerful engine and a plant was opened in Canada to produce them, using

American-built copies of the Merlin III engine. Many of these were sent to North Africa where, armed with four 20mm cannons, they served as ground-attack fighters. As new models of the Spitfire appeared, however, the Hurricane fell more and more behind. By 1942 it had been relegated to minor theaters, where it was fitted with air-to-ground rockets and continued as a close-support platform until the end of the war. They were dubbed "Hurribombers". About 3,000 Hurricanes were also sent to the Soviet Union under Lend-Lease, but the Russians didn't really like the plane, considering it to be inferior to the German fighters. And a navalized carrier-based version known as the Sea Hurricane was used in the Pacific against the Japanese. In various models, the Hurricane was not officially withdrawn from RAF service until 1947.

In all, around 14,000 Hurricanes were produced during the war. One of these was serial number LF686, a Mark IIc manufactured in February 1944 and used to train ground mechanics. In 1969, this Hurricane was sent to the United States in exchange for a Hawker Typhoon and given to the Smithsonian. Hurricane LF686 was refurbished and placed on display in 2001. Today it is in the Udvar-Hazy Center.

Supermarine Spitfire

Perhaps the most famous fighter plane of the Second World War, the Spitfire was produced in numerous versions throughout the entire conflict and saw service in every theater.

In 1931, the Supermarine S6-B racing seaplane was able to reach the then unheard-of speed of 407mph, faster than any other aircraft had ever gone, and twice as fast as most of the biplane military fighters then in service. It had been designed by Reginald Mitchell.

Later, as another world war seemed to be looming, the Royal Air Force needed a new fighter that could outclass the designs that were appearing in Germany. Mitchell in turn designed a low-wing all-metal mono-plane that was based on aspects of the S6-B seaplane and used the new Rolls-Royce Merlin engine. It became the Spitfire. Work began on a prototype in 1935 and it first flew a year later.

Mitchell himself died of cancer in 1937. But the plane he had birthed was revolutionary. Rather than bracing wires, the internal frame was made from laminated pieces of aluminum and covered with stressed skin. The distinctive elliptical wings carried eight .303 machine guns, and the plane had thin airfoils and a supercharged engine for superb high-altitude performance. With its heavy military equipment, the Spitfire could only manage 360mph, not the 400 of its record-breaking seaplane progenitor, but it was still one of the fastest fighters in the sky.

The British, however, decided that the Hurricane, though less advanced than the Supermarine design, could be produced more rapidly and less expensively, and placed an order to procure 600 Hurricanes. But they also saw the promise in the Spitfire, and ordered 310, then 200 more a year later despite technical delays in the program. In 1938, deliveries of frontline fighters finally began, and, with war clouds gathering, the RAF asked for 1,000 Spitfires, then a thousand more. By the time Germany invaded Poland in September 1939, the British had provided nine fighter squadrons with Spits and were in the process of re-equipping two more. Although it was not a difficult airplane to fly, the Spitfire handled differently than the older biplanes, and about ten percent of prewar Spits were destroyed in training accidents.

After overrunning Poland, Germany turned to France, knocking her out of the war in the summer of 1940. And then Hitler faced England. For several months, the RAF and the Luftwaffe fought daily air duels as the Germans sought the air superiority which would allow them to launch a cross-Channel invasion.

In many ways, the Spitfire and the Me-109 were evenly matched, with each having advantages over the other, but the English were outnumbered two to one, and the RAF's losses were heavy. The Germans, however, were hampered by their short range, which allowed them to engage in combat for only a short period before they had to turn back to their bases in France. The British also had the huge advantage of a sophisticated early-warning radar system, which allowed them to deploy their scarce fighters where they could be most effective. In the end, it was enough to fend off the Nazis. Hitler turned towards Russia instead.

The Spitfire was constantly being upgraded and remodeled, as well as adapted for different tasks. Some versions were stripped of their guns and armor to lighten them as much as possible, turning them into high-speed photoreconnaissance craft. Others were fitted with underwing bomb racks and used as ground-attack fighter bombers. Late-war models were fitted with Rolls-Royce Griffon engines of 2,000 horsepower. In the Atlantic and Pacific, carrier versions were known as Seafires. A few Spits were sent to Russia on Lend-Lease, but the Soviets were engaged mostly in low-altitude air combat, and that was a role that the Spitfire was not very good at. Some Americans in the 4th Fighter Group, based in England, also flew Spitfires for a while, until they were replaced with P-47s.

After the war, the Spitfire continued in production until 1948. The following year, it was adopted by the newborn Israeli Air Force. It also continued in service with the RAF and was occasionally used as a trainer and a ground-attack fighter in the Korean War.

In total, the UK manufactured over 20,300 Spitfires of various models. It was the only Allied fighter to be in continuous production from the beginning of the war till its end. Today, about 100 remain in private hands or in various museums around the world, with about half being airworthy. The oldest of these is a Mark I on display at Royal Air Force Museum Cosford, manufactured in 1939. The only still-flying survivor that fought in the Battle of Britain is a Mark Ia owned by the Battle of Britain Memorial Flight in the UK.

In the US, the Military Aviation Museum in Virginia has a Mark IX that flew 95 missions in Italy, and the Commemorative Air Force flies a Mark XIV that was based in India during the war. The Museum of Science and Industry in Chicago exhibits a Mark Ia that flew in the Battle of Britain but is now a static display, and the US Air Force Museum in Dayton displays a Mark V that originally flew in Australia and is now in USAF markings. The Pima Air and Space Museum exhibits a Mark XIV.

Grumman F4F Wildcat

The first widely-deployed mono-wing American carrier fighter, the Wildcat was the US Navy's frontline fighter during the first years of the Pacific War.

In 1935, the US Navy adopted the Grumman F2F as its carrier-based fighter. A stubby-nosed biplane, the aircraft proved to have issues with directional stability, and Grumman fixed these problems with the F3F, another biplane. By this time, the Army Air Corps had been flying mono-wing fighters like the P-26 for years, but the Navy was reluctant to use mono-wings because of their high landing speeds and their wider wingspans, which caused difficulties in landing on carriers and storing them below the flight deck.

But by the late 1930s it was apparent that the biplanes had reached the edge of their performance, and that the drag induced by biplane wings and their supporting struts was now a severe limiting factor. So, in 1936, the Navy began seeking a new mono-wing carrier fighter. It settled on the Brewster F2A Buffalo, but that plane suffered from production problems and also proved to be inadequate for carrier landings. The Navy sought an alternative.

Grumman responded by taking the fuselage of the F3F, modifying it a bit, and fitting a mono-wing to it. This did not prove to be much of an advantage over the biplane, so the design was reworked further. In 1939, a suitable prototype was produced. It was dubbed the F4F Wildcat, and began production in August.

Superficially, the Wildcat still looked a lot like a monoplane version of the F3F. It had the same stubby nose and rotund fuselage, and the retractable landing gear that folded up into the side of the nose. But it featured a moveable wing that folded back along the sides to reduce the airplane's footprint, allowing more of them to be stowed on the flight deck and in the carrier's hangar. Unlike most of the newer fighters, which used inline engines for reduced drag and higher speed, Grumman decided to stay with a radial engine for the Wildcat, since it required less maintenance and was more rugged in combat. The 1,050hp Pratt & Whitney Twin Wasp pushed the Wildcat to 330mph. The fighter was armed with six .50-caliber machine guns, and could be fitted with two small bombs.

The Wildcat was also adopted by the British Royal Navy and the French, though the French versions were not delivered before the Nazis invaded and took France out of the war. The Royal Navy began flying F4Fs, designating them as the "Martlet". The initial shipments of Martlets lacked folding wings and were assigned to ground duty. Later versions with folding wings were assigned to British escort carriers for antisubmarine duty.

By 1940, the Wildcat had replaced the F2A Brewster Buffalo and the F3F as the frontline fighter for both the US Navy and the US Marines. It was already obsolete. Although the Wildcat was rugged and could take a lot of punishment, and could also readily outdive a Zero, the Japanese fighter was faster, more maneuverable and flown by superbly-trained pilots who viewed the F4F as an easy target.

During combat in the Pacific, the Americans quickly learned that getting into a turning dogfight with a Zero was suicidal. The tactic of choice became the "Thach Weave", in which two Wildcats would fly a criss-cross pattern to cover each other's tails. Although the Wildcat was constantly updated and improved, with some using the Wright Cyclone engine, it was never able to outclass the Zero. However, as the war went on, the lightly armored Zeros suffered heavy pilot losses, and by 1944 the Japanese were sending poorly-trained pilots into combat where they were shot down by the now-more-experienced Americans. In total, the Wildcat ended up with a 7 to 1 kill ratio against Japanese fighters.

By the middle of 1942, the Navy was concentrating on the new F6F Hellcat fighter and the larger *Essex*-class aircraft carriers. But the Wildcat still retained a useful role: a whole fleet of American escort carriers, also known as "jeep carriers", was being built to protect convoys from submarines, and their decks were too short for Hellcats. So production of Wildcats was maintained by transferring them to the General Motors company, which made them under license until the end of the war. Since these were intended mostly for antisubmarine duty rather than air superiority, two of the wing machine guns were removed to reduce the weight. Some models were fitted with unguided rockets under the wings for attacking ground targets or submarines.

In total, around 8,000 Wildcats were made during the war, with 6,000 of these being the General Motors version, known as the FM. Today, about 45 remain, with around 15 of these being in flyable condition.

The Wildcat on display at the Smithsonian Air and Space Museum is an FM-2 model produced by General Motors in 1943. It was assigned to a Navy base in Oklahoma, was deactivated and placed in storage and was finally transferred to the Smithsonian in 1960. The Naval Aviation Museum in Pensacola has both an F4F-3 model and an FM-2 model on exhibit.

Grumman TBF Avenger

Designed as a replacement for the TBD Devastator, the Avenger torpedo bomber began entering the Pacific War in June 1942 — just in time for the Battle of Midway.

When the first practical submarines began to appear in the years before the First World War, naval experts recognized that, apart from their underwater stealth ability, it was the torpedo weapons they carried that made the "U-boats" so deadly. Rather than an intense bombardment of heavy guns, ships at sea could now be sunk with just one or two torpedoes—and ship-borne aircraft offered another possible method of delivering those weapons.

The first tests with aerial torpedo-bombing, however, were all failures. Various navies, including the British, American and Japanese, were experimenting with deploying seaplanes from ships at sea, but these did not have the power to carry the heavy torpedoes of the day. It wasn't until August 1915 that a British Short 184 floatplane, based on the seaplane tender HMS *Ben-My-Chree*, was able to successfully deliver a torpedo attack, sinking a Turkish merchant ship. The Royal Navy quickly rigged up a sturdier method of carrying and releasing a torpedo slung under the Short's belly and ordered more, producing almost a thousand by the end of the war. The Japanese Navy also purchased a number of Model 184 floatplanes and began its own experiments.

By 1917, the British had developed the Sopwith Cuckoo, a large biplane bomber that was specifically designed to fly from the Royal Navy's experimental aircraft carriers. The Cuckoo had folding wings and could carry a 1,000-pound torpedo, but with carrier takeoff and landing procedures still in their infancy it proved able to take off from a carrier deck but was too heavy to land on it without better arresting gear. The Navy recognized the power of its new weapon, though, and was making ambitious plans to attack the German fleet in harbor with a force of as many as 120 torpedo-armed Cuckoos launched from five aircraft carriers, but the war ended before such an attack became possible.

Research continued, and by the time the Second World War could be seen approaching, each of the naval powers had developed lethal torpedo bombers. The British were still using biplane Fairey Swordfish, introduced in 1934, to deliver torpedoes, but the Americans had deployed the modern mono-wing TBD Devastator the year after that.

In 1936, however, the Japanese took the lead in torpedo-bombing capability when their carrier fleet began using the Nakajima B5N torpedo bomber, known to the Allies by the codename "Kate". The Kate was faster and had longer range, and it could also function either as a torpedo bomber (the Type 91 torpedo had a warhead of up to 1,000 pounds) or as a high-altitude level bomber (carrying 1800 pounds of armor-piercing bombs). Even before the Pearl Harbor attack, however, the Japanese recognized that the Kate was becoming outdated, and they were already working on a replacement; the B6N would be known by the Allied codename "Jill".

The Americans also knew that their Devastator was too slow and too lightly-armored to face Japanese fighters, and had begun work on a replacement. The much-larger Grumman TBF Avenger was planned to have a range of 1,000 miles, a speed of 300mph, and an internal weapons bay with a Mark 13 aerial torpedo or four 500-pound bombs. A powered ball turret helped protect it from fighters.

To produce the new bomber, Grumman built an additional factory in its complex at Bethpage NY. It opened on December 7, 1941: company officials received word during the opening ceremony that Japanese dive and torpedo bombers had attacked Hawaii. The plant immediately went on a war footing.

By June 1942, 145 Avengers had been delivered to the Navy. Of these, only six had reached the frontlines: they were attached to Torpedo Squadron 8 on the carrier *Hornet* (which was still using Devastators) and had been delivered to the airfield on Midway just three days before the Japanese attacked the island. All six of the TBFs accompanied the rest of Midway's aircraft on a strike against the Japanese carriers: none scored any hits, and five of them were shot down with the remaining one heavily damaged.

It was an inauspicious beginning. But within a year the United States was launching *Essex*-class aircraft carriers at an astonishing rate, each supplied with a squadron of Avengers. The TBFs were also assigned vital roles on escort carriers which provided anti-submarine cover for supply convoys crossing the Atlantic, and also formed "hunter-killer" groups that sought out German U-boats and destroyed them. About 400 of the planes were given to the British, who used them for anti-submarine and shore patrol duty.

One pilot who flew the Avenger was future US President George HW Bush, who was based on the light carrier USS *San Jacinto* as the youngest aviator in the Navy. In September 1944 he was flying a mission over Chichi Jima when his plane was shot up by Japanese fighters. After nursing his crippled Avenger long enough to drop his bombs on target, Bush bailed out and was rescued by a submarine. He was awarded the Distinguished Flying Cross.

Grumman continued to make TBF Avengers for the rest of the war, but they were also committed to producing F6F Hellcats and were unable to keep up with the Navy's requests for TBFs, so the General Motors company retooled several of its plants to manufacture Avengers under license. These GM-made planes were designated TBM models. By the end of the war, GM had turned out over 7,500 Avengers out of the 10,000 total. The TBFs and TBMs had accounted for sinking 6 Japanese battleships, 11 carriers, and 10 heavy cruisers.

Douglas SBD Dauntless

The "dive bomber" was still a relatively new development in air warfare during World War Two, but it quickly demonstrated its usefulness in the Pacific War

Like so many of the basic concepts of air warfare, the idea of "dive bombing" appeared during the First World War. By 1918, the Entente had developed the Sopwith Salamander, a specialized ground-attack plane with heavy armor to protect the pilot from enemy fire. It was found that the most accurate way to hit a pinpoint target on the ground was to dive on it, using the nose of the airplane to aim and releasing the bomb at low altitude before pulling away. In experiments with naval bombers from aircraft carriers, this was found to be particularly useful against small moving targets such as ships. But the wooden-frame biplanes of that time were unable to withstand the massive g-forces and stresses that resulted from pulling out of a steep dive, and so the proposal was of limited practicality.

By the mid-1930s, metal-tube mono-wing airframes were becoming strong enough to withstand the necessary g-forces, and the invention of the automatic dive brake (which pulled the plane out of a dive even if the pilot passed out) finally made the idea of dive-bombing useful. Several air forces began experimenting. The most in-depth work was done in Nazi Germany, who was rebuilding its Luftwaffe. Dive-bombers appealed to them for several reasons: first, they were more accurate than high-level heavy bombers. Bombsights of the time were crude and were not capable of hitting pinpoint targets (and this remained true throughout the war, despite the claims made by the Americans for their Norden bombsight). Small single-engine dive bombers were also much cheaper than multi-engine heavies and could be deployed in greater numbers at lower cost. In strategic bombing, the dive bomber was not very useful, but Germany did not consider this to be a factor since they expected their air arm to serve as a tactical force supporting the troops on the ground, not as a long-distance strategic force. The Junkers Ju87 Stuka dive bomber encapsulated all of these approaches. Even the Junkers Ju88 medium bomber was built with a dive-bombing ability.

The Japanese also adopted most of this outlook, and the Imperial Navy developed the Aichi D3A carrier-based dive bomber, known to the Allies by the codename "Val". In Britain the concept was somewhat different: the RAF attempted to use the Blackburn Skua in multiple roles: it was designed to carry and deliver a bomb by diving, and then use its multiple front and rear machine guns as a fighter. As a result, the Skua did neither very well, and it was soon quietly dropped. Instead, the British turned the idea of a "bomber-fighter" into the "fighter-bomber", by equipping very capable fighters with supplementary ground-attack weapons like rockets or bombs. For the most part, both the UK and the US gave up the idea of dive-bombing land targets in favor of the four-engined heavy bomber, which did not need precise aiming but simply obliterated the target with a massive bomb load.

In the area of naval air attacks on enemy ships, however, the need for pinpoint accuracy remained. In 1935, the Northrop company had introduced the BT-1, a mono-wing dive bomber with automatic dive brakes, retractable landing gear, and a big 700-horsepower radial engine. The Navy adopted it for use, but once tested the plane proved to be difficult to handle at low speed, which made carrier landings hazardous. The Chance-Vought SB2U Vindicator became the standard carrier dive bomber instead.

When the Douglas company merged with Northrop, however, it inherited the BT-1 design and decided it could do better. After extensive modifications which included a bigger engine and new landing gear, it was re-designated as the SBD. The Navy began replacing its Vindicators in late 1940, and by 1941 the Dauntless was the standard Navy carrier dive bomber. The Marines were also using the SBD as a land-based bomber, and even the Army had adopted a handful of them, designating it the A-24 Banshee.

The Dauntless had a crew of two—a pilot and a rear gunner, armed with two .30-caliber machine guns. It could carry up to 2250 pounds of bombs, usually with one large 1600-pound bomb under the fuselage and two smaller ones on the wings. Although its primary mission was dive-bombing, carrier-based SBDs were also used as reconnaissance and patrol craft, and on some occasions flights of Dauntlesses flew "Combat Air Patrol" missions as fighters, circling the task force in search of approaching enemy airplanes.

The SBD had its greatest moment of glory in the Battle of Midway, when Dauntlesses sank three Japanese carriers in the span of less than five minutes and later helped sink a fourth, tearing the heart out of the Imperial Navy and altering the whole course of the Pacific War.

By this time, plans were already being made to replace the Dauntless with the newer Curtiss SB2C Helldiver. The Helldiver ran into design and production problems, however, and in the end it did not offer much substantial improvement over the SBD. So although the Dauntless was replaced on the Navy's fleet carriers, it remained in service in secondary roles throughout the war. Almost 6,000 were manufactured. SBDs accounted for sinking six Japanese carriers, fourteen cruisers, and six destroyers.

At the US Naval Aviation Museum in Pensacola FL, an SBD-2 with serial number 2106 is on exhibit. Built at the Douglas plant in Segundo CA in November 1940, it was sent to the San Diego Naval Air Station and flew patrol and training missions before being assigned to the carrier USS *Lexington*.

In November 1941, the *Lexington* left California for Pearl Harbor, and upon arrival in the first week of December was ordered to deliver a flight of aircraft to the Marines on Midway Island. The carrier offloaded several of her own planes (including number 2106) at Pearl to make room. Thus, this SBD was parked at Ford Island when the Japanese attack came on December 7. It emerged undamaged.

After once again rejoining the *Lexington* and carrying out combat missions at New Guinea, number 2106 was re-assigned to the Marine unit on Midway Island, and was delivered there in May 1942. When the Battle of Midway began on June 4, number 2106 was one of 18 SBDs launched from the island to attack the Japanese carriers: only 8 came back, and number 2106 was heavily damaged, landing on one wheel. The pilot, First Lieutenant David Iverson, was awarded the Navy Cross.

Number 2106 was repaired and returned to the US, where it was assigned to the Great Lakes. Here, on merchant ships that had been hastily fitted with flight decks, pilot trainees were taught how to make carrier takeoffs and landings. In June 1943, while being flown by a student pilot, this SBD missed the landing and crashed into the lake. It was recovered in 1994 and restored in 2001, and is now on exhibit.

Ilyushin Il-2 Shturmovik

The most widely-produced aircraft of the war, the Soviet Shturmovik functioned as an "aerial tank" and was extremely effective against German armored Panzer columns.

When the Nazi Panzer columns poured into the Soviet Union in June 1941, the Russian air force had only recently deployed the Ilyushin Il-2 "Shturmovik" ground attack aircraft, though early versions had seen combat in the Spanish Civil War and the 1939 Nomonhan Incident with Japan. A single-seater with a liquid-cooled inline engine, the Il-2 carried a load of 1,000 pounds of bombs and two 20mm cannons which, though not capable of penetrating the front armor of a tank, could do damage against the thinner armor at the top, and was also effective against softer targets like armored cars and convoy trucks. Rather than installing armor by adding plates to an aluminum skin, the Ilyushin design bureau simply fashioned the forward part of the skin itself out of plate armor to protect the engine, cooling system, gas tanks, and pilot from all directions: the tail and wings were left unarmored and were made from plywood. The resulting aircraft weighed five tons.

But the Russians (and the German fighter pilots) soon learned that the Shturmovik had a serious flaw—it was undefended to the rear, and was a sitting duck for Me-109s if it was caught without fighter cover. In desperation, the Soviets began cutting a door into the unarmored wooden side of the tail where someone could enter with a handheld machine gun and sit on a wicker chair to shoot at enemy attackers. These improvised rear gunners were often forced into service from the gulag detention camps or from Red Army "discipline brigades".

The Ilyushin Bureau acted quickly, however, and made major modifications. The most vital of these was an expanded armored cockpit carrying a rear gunner to provide all-around protection from fighters. To deal with the extra weight, the 1,680 horsepower AM-38 engine was replaced by the 1,750 horsepower AM-38F, and to counter the shifted center of gravity, the wings were swept back by 15 degrees. The 20mm ShVAK wing cannons were upgraded to 23mm Vya autocannons, and the bomb racks and rocket rails were strengthened and expanded. The new version, dubbed the Il-2M3, began reaching the frontline in August 1942.

The Shturmovik became the most important combat airplane on the Eastern Front. Stalin himself, in a letter to factory managers, declared, "Our Red Army now needs Il-2 aircraft like the air it breathes, like the bread it eats." Over 36,000 Il-2s were churned out in just five years, in a bewildering variety of configurations—making it the most widely-produced military airplane in history. Before the war ended, the Soviets also introduced an improved all-metal version designated Il-10.

Unlike the air war in the European theater, which centered mainly around strategic bombers and took place at high altitude, the Eastern Front was mostly a tank war, and air combat here was at low altitude, often below 100 feet. Although the Shturmovik is often popularly pictured as a tank-buster, that was not really its role: the Russians had their T-34 tank to take on the Panzers, and the Ilyushin's armament was not capable of penetrating the front armor of a main battle tank. Instead, the IL-2 acted as a sort of aerial artillery, and was most often used in low-level sweeps that closed in suddenly on troop columns, light armored vehicles, truck convoys, artillery batteries, airfields, and other softer targets, which could be hit with rockets, bombs and cannon fire. The Shturmovik's speed made it a difficult target for anti-aircraft gunners, and its heavy armor and rugged construction meant it could take a considerable amount of damage: Il-2s would often return to base with chunks shot out of them. Nevertheless, losses were high, especially in the early years of the war when the Germans had air superiority: the average life expectancy for a Shturmovik pilot was nine missions. More than 12,000 Il-2s were shot down.

The heavily-armed plane also played an anti-shipping role. A few experimental models carried torpedoes, but even the standard 23mm cannons were capable of sinking small ships, and the Shturmovik's bombs could handle larger targets. In all, some 100 German cargo and merchant vessels in the Baltic were sunk by Il-2 air attacks.

After the war, Shturmoviks, particularly the Il-10 model, continued in service with the air forces of the USSR and its satellites until the 1950s. At least 6,000 Il-10s were produced, and some of these saw combat in the Korean War flying with the Chinese and the North Koreans.

Today, despite the fact that the Shturmovik was produced in greater numbers than any other military plane ever (and is the second most numerous airplane of any type, exceeded only by the civilian Cessna 172), only around a dozen remain, most in Russia. Nearly all of these are restorations from recovered crashed wartime aircraft. One of these was restored at the Pima Air and Space Museum in Arizona and is now on display.

Messerschmitt Bf-109

Although it became one of the most famous aircraft of the Second World War, the Messerschmitt Bf-109 (also referred to as the Me-109) was almost not built at all.

In 1933, the new Hitler regime was already planning for a war in Europe, and the secretly-rebuilding Luftwaffe was already seeking new high-performance aircraft—in violation of the Versailles Treaty. The Bayerische Flugzeug Werke (BFW), run by Willy Messerschmitt, was anxious to get in on the action, but Messerschmitt didn't get along with the Nazi official in charge of procurement, Erhard Milch, and was blocked from bidding on military contracts. Desperate to keep the company financially afloat, BFW accepted an order to build cargo planes for Romania. This irked the hyper-nationalist Nazis, and when Messerschmitt complained that he had no choice but to accept foreign contracts unless he was allowed to bid on German orders, Herman Goering intervened and Milch relented.

As it happened, the Air Ministry had just issued a set of requirements for a modern mono-wing all-metal fighter with two machine guns, to use the new V-12 engine being secretly developed by Daimler and Jumo. (To hide the project from the Allies, the Germans designated it as a "courier aircraft".) Messerschmitt's proposal was designated the Bf-109. The first prototype was tested in September 1935, with two .30-caliber machine guns in the nose. Because the Daimler V-12 was not ready yet, the prototype flew with the smaller Rolls-Royce Kestrel engine from Britain. In 1936, the British began work on the Hurricane and Spitfire fighters, which would carry at least four machine guns in the wings. The Bf-109A had been designed with a thin wing which had no room for guns, so to keep up with the British a third machine gun was added to the Messerschmitt, firing through the propeller hub, and in later prototypes this was upgraded to a 20mm cannon. The new version was dubbed the Bf-109B ("Bertha"). In November 1937 a modified 109B set a new speed record of 379.38mph.

In April 1937, the first batch of production Messerschmitts were sent to Spain, where Germany was backing the regime of Francisco Franco in the Civil War. At first, biplane pilots found the new monoplane difficult to fly. The Bf-109's strong propeller torque, combined with the narrow landing gear, made takeoffs and landings difficult, and several pilots died in wrecks. But once this transition was made, the new fighters proved themselves to be superior to the Soviet-made Polikarpov I-16's flown by the Spanish Republicans. The Messerschmitt's first air combat victories came on July 8, when two Bf-109's shot down two Tupolev bombers.

In the fighting that followed over the next two years, Messerschmitt ace Werner Molders developed new tactics that took advantage of the plane's speed and maneuverability. At this time, most fighter forces were using a flight formation called a "vic", which was a V-shaped pattern of three aircraft. The theory was that the lead plane would search for and shoot down the enemy while the two wingmen would protect the leader. In reality, however, the vic formation was difficult to maintain and required a lot of attention, which made the whole flight vulnerable. Molders instead organized his formations into two pairs, with each wingman covering his partner and the flight set into a loose formation he called a "finger four". Molders would go on to score 115 air victories in Spain, France, and England before being killed in a transport crash in 1941.

Messerschmitt, meanwhile, was also learning the lessons from the Spanish Civil War. The 109B model was followed in quick succession by the 109C ("Clara") and the 109D ("Dora"), each with better armament and more powerful engines.

By 1939, the Messerschmitt was undergoing more radical improvements. Daimler had a new fuel-injected V-12 DB601 engine, producing 1,050 horsepower, and this was fitted to the 109's airframe to push the speed to 350mph. The bigger engine required additional radiators, and these were placed in new redesigned thicker wings — which were also adapted to hold two 20mm cannons. The plane also got a name change, as the "Bayerische Flugzeug Werke" was renamed "Messerschmitt AG". The new version was designated the Me-109E "Emil". It began entering service in 1939. Almost 1,000 of them were produced, with a number being sold to Switzerland and Yugoslavia. Three were sent to Japan for testing, but the Japanese ultimately decided to go with their own Zero and Oscar designs instead.

When World War II broke out, the Emil was Germany's frontline fighter. In Poland, it quickly cleared the skies of obsolete Polish PZL fighters. In France, it proved itself more than a match for the French MS.406 and the British Hurricane. And by August 1940 it was poised to take on England's best fighter, the Spitfire.

On paper, the Messerschmitt and the Spitfire were a pretty even match, with each having both advantages and disadvantages over the other. But in the end the Me-109E was severely crippled by its limited fuel supply and its short range. Flying across the English Channel from bases in France and tied to the slow bombers they were escorting, the Emils had only 10-15 minutes to engage the British Spitfires in combat before they ran low on fuel and had to turn and fly for home. Many Messerschmitt pilots waited too long, ran out of gas on the way back, and had to ditch in the Channel.

Even as the Germans were losing the Battle of Britain, however, Messerschmitt was working on a new version. The Bf-109's short range, he decided, made it more suited for the role of defensive fighter, and the next version, the Me-109F "Friedrich", was optimized for that task. The engine was a larger 1200 horsepower, the airframe was streamlined for more speed, and the armament was reduced to two .30-cal machine guns in the cowling and one 20mm cannon in the propeller hub. Although the pilots were unhappy with the reduced armament, the Me-109F regained the parity that the Emil had lost to the latest-model Spitfire, the Mk V. In North Africa, "Trop" versions of the Friedrich, with filters and screens to protect against sand, were fitted with bomb racks and used for ground attack.

In the summer of 1942, the best variant of the Messerschmitt was introduced, the Me-109G "Gustav". The 1475-horsepower DB 605A engine could drive it at almost 390mph, and a methanol injector was added which gave a temporary boost of power to over 420mph. The two .30-cal machine guns were replaced by .50-cals, giving it greater punch. In 1943 there were 6,500 109G's produced, followed by 14,000 in 1944. To help with production, the Messerschmitt was also produced by the Fieseler company under license. Although the Gustav was outclassed by later Allied fighters like the Spitfire Mk IX, the P-51D, and the Yak-9, it remained in production till the end of the war. Some 109G's were fitted with unguided 210mm rockets to attack Allied bombers.

In 1945, a new Me-109K "Konrad" version was fitted with two 20mm cannons in the cowling and one 30mm cannon in the propeller hub, but by this time Germany was already near defeat and few of them were built.

In total, the Nazis produced over 33,000 Messerschmitts in various models, making it the second most-produced military airplane in history (behind the Soviet Il-2 Shturmovik). Me-109's shot down more aircraft than any other fighter, and most of the top aces of the war, some with more than 300 air victories, flew Messerschmitts.

After Germany's surrender in 1945, the Messerschmitt flew on for a few decades. License-built versions of the Konrad were produced in Spain and in Czechoslovakia in the 1950's and flew until 1967. (When the classic movie "The Battle of Britain" was filmed in 1969, it was Spanish-made Messerschmitts that were used by the production crew as stand-ins for Me-109E's.) Around two dozen of the Czech Messerschmitts made their way to Israel in 1948, where they flew for a few years before being replaced by British Spitfires.

Today, around two dozen wartime Messerschmitts still survive, including E, F and G models.

In July 1944, a Frenchman named Rene Darbois climbed into his German Me-109G fighter on his first combat mission—and promptly flew to Italy and landed at an Allied airfield to defect, claiming that the Nazis had forced him to fly for the Luftwaffe. His plane was sent to the US for evaluation, and was donated to the Smithsonian in 1948. It remains on display.

Mikoyan-Guryevich MiG-3

The Soviet MiG-3 was designed as a fast high-altitude interceptor, but this was not the type of war it ended up fighting.

As with so much of Soviet aviation history, the story of the MiG-3 revolves around politics.

In the 1920s and 1930s, the Soviet Union, like many other countries, assumed that air combat in any future war would be much like air combat had been in the First World War: it would center around ground support for the infantry and would take place at low altitude. A few visionaries were touting the air power of the strategic bomber, but in Russia this was dismissed—planners believed that the vast distances inside the USSR made strategic bombing too difficult.

In the Spanish Civil War, however, the world saw firsthand the real potential of the long-distance high-altitude bomber, and now many countries, including the Soviet Union, scrambled to put together a defense. In 1939, the Polikarpov design bureau submitted a design for a fast interceptor that could climb quickly to great height and intercept incoming bombers. Polikarpov's previous fighter designs, the I-15 biplane and the I-16 monoplane, had used radial engines, but when the Soviet-built supercharged Mikulin AM-37 inline engine was introduced, he decided to build his new fighter around it, fitting the engine into the smallest possible airframe. To save weight, and also as part of Stalin's directive to use as little scarce aircraft aluminum as possible, the front of the fuselage was framed with steel tube, while the tail and wings were plywood. The result was the I-200, which he estimated could reach speeds of 410mph.

Then, in August, Polikarpov, who had already been arrested and confined in a prison labor camp a few years before, once again fell out of political favor with the regime. Stalin set up a new division inside Polikarpov's design bureau which was designated the Experimental Construction Section, headed by two promising young aircraft engineers named Artyem Mikoyan and Mikhail Guryevich. First the I-200 project was taken away from Polikarpov and reassigned to Mikoyan and Guryevich (and was renamed the MiG-1), and later in 1940 the pair were given control of the entire design bureau, which was then renamed Mikoyan-Guryevich.

Mikoyan and Guryevich would later go on to produce some of the best-known jet fighters of the Cold War, but for now they were stuck with the MiG-1 design that had been largely done by Polikarpov. The planned Mikulin AM-37 engine turned out to be unreliable and was never produced, so Mikoyan and Guryevich switched to the less powerful but available AM-35A V-12 engine instead. The prototype first flew in April 1940, and despite the smaller engine still reached over 400mph at altitude and could climb to 23,000 feet in 7 minutes. Test flights revealed a number of issues including poor visibility and a tendency to stall and spin, but

Stalin was anxious to defend against a potential German attack, and ordered the MiG-1 into production anyway.

Mikoyan and Guryevich, meanwhile, were already working on modifications. To improve stability, they moved the engine forward by four inches and increased the dihedral on the outer wings by one degree. The radiator was replaced by a more efficient design, and an additional gas tank was added to increase the range. Armor plate was added to the pilot's seat, and self-sealing coatings were added to the gas tanks.

All of this additional weight degraded the plane's performance somewhat, but it was still faster than the German Bf-109 and the British Spitfire, and was the best interceptor that was available. Stalin ordered that production of the MiG-1 end after just 100 planes, and that manufacture of the new MiG-3 begin. The planes began to enter service in 1941. By the time the Nazis invaded Russia in June, the Soviets had deployed almost 1,000 MiG-3s.

Most of these were destroyed on the ground at the beginning of the German attack. The ones which survived found that the bulk of their combat missions were taking place at low altitudes, and that was not what the fighter had been designed for. Low to the ground, the MiG was less maneuverable than the Germans. Its armament of two .30-caliber machine guns and one .50-caliber was inferior to the Bf-109 with its 20mm cannon. To add more firepower, the Soviets added another .50-cal under the wing in a pod, but this reduced the speed, so most pilots removed it. The gunsight was also found to be inaccurate, forcing pilots to get in close and fire from pointblank range. Over time the Russians tried a variety of different engines and armament on the airframe, but none of them could solve the basic problem—the MiG-3 was trying to do a job that it had not been intended to do.

By the end of 1942, the Yak-3 had become available, and the remaining MiG-3s were pulled from frontline squadrons and relegated to rear-area services. A number of MiGs were modified for photoreconnaissance, a role for which they could finally utilize the fast high-altitude performance that they had been designed for.

Virtually no MiG-3s survived the war. In 2005, however, a Russian company called Aircraft Restoration Department of Rusavia Ltd recovered the wreckage of five MiG-3s that had crashed in wartime, restored them to flying condition using over 50% of the original parts, and put them up for sale. One of these is now on display in the Military Aviation Museum in Virginia Beach VA.

Yakovlev Yak-3

Light, maneuverable, and fast, the Yak-3 was one of the best Soviet fighters of the Second World War.

In 1938 the Yakovlev design bureau submitted a design for a new fighter that was specifically intended to be made using as little scarce aluminum as possible, to be easy and cheap for unskilled factory workers to assemble in quantity, and to allow trouble-free patches and repairs in the field. The Yak-1 would be constructed of steel tube frame covered with plywood and fabric. The engine would be a Klimov M-105P V-12 water-cooled inline of 1100 horsepower, and it would be armed with a ShVAK 20mm cannon and two .30-caliber machine guns in the nose. Production began in 1940. A short time later, improvements were added such as a bigger engine, a bubble canopy with better visibility, and a single .50-cal gun instead of the twin .30-cals. This became the Yak-1B.

The Yak-1B did well in combat against the Germans, serving as an escort for Shturmoviks and as an air superiority fighter against the Me-109 and Fw-190. Almost 9,000 were manufactured during the war, remaining in service until 1944.

As early as 1941, the Yakovlev bureau was already considering a lighter and faster version of the Yak-1, christened the Yak-3, but the project was beset with delays caused by shortages of materials and the relocation of aircraft factories. Production finally began in early 1944, and 5,000 Yak-3s were turned out in the next two years.

A series of design changes lightened the Yak-3 by roughly 1,000 pounds. Combined with its better Klimov VK-107 engine, producing 1700 horsepower, it had a superb power-to-weight ratio and could reach speeds of over 400mph, with later models approaching 450mph. The cockpit in the Yak-3 was moved forward a bit to give the pilot better visibility and the wings were also set forward to help with handling. The Yak was armed with a 20mm cannon and two .50-cal machine guns, which was considered light by American standards but which fit well with the Soviet philosophy of having a small number of guns in the nose (the Russians didn't use wing guns) that could be accurately aimed at close range. And the fuel tank was reduced to save weight. This of course also reduced the flight time to just forty-five minutes, but since the fighter was flying from rough grass fields near the front (also in conformity to Soviet philosophy) and was being used only for point defense and sent directly into air-to-air combat, this was not considered to be a problem.

The Yak-3 was faster than the Messerschmitt and more maneuverable than the Spitfire, and it proved to be capable of absorbing considerable damage and still getting home. The first squadron to be equipped with the Yak-3, the 91st Fighter Aviation Regiment, flew 431 missions, shooting down 23 Luftwaffe aircraft and losing only two Yaks. Most consider it to be the best Soviet fighter of the war.

No original wartime Yak-3s survive today. But the Yakovlev company still exists, and in 1991 it began offering specially-built replicas of Yak-3, Yak-7 and Yak-9 fighters made from the original factory drawings and using the authentic dies. Designated Yak-3M, they use WW2-era Allison V-1710 or Pratt and Whitney Twin Wasp engines instead of the original Soviet Klimovs. Some of these replica Yaks appear regularly at air shows. One of the replica Yak-3Ms is on exhibit at the Cavanaugh Air Museum in Dallas TX. The Commemorative Air Force in southern California also exhibits a Yak-3M.

Mitsubishi A6M Zero

The Mitsubishi A6M Zero fighter is one of the most famous aircraft of the Second World War. For several years, it dominated the skies over the Pacific. But, like the island nation that built it, the Zero was unable to keep up with the industrial power and technological advances of its opponents.

The first aircraft carriers had been built by Britain in the last years of the First World War. The United States followed during the 1920's. But the tiny nation of Japan became the most enthusiastic proponent of naval air power, and built one of the largest carrier fleets in the world.

In 1937, Japan had been locked in a war with China for several years, and had already conquered most of the coastal areas. The Japanese Navy had just introduced a new fighter plane, the Mitsubishi A5M Type 96, a low-wing monoplane with fixed landing gear which was given the code name "Claude" by American intelligence. The Claude quickly established itself as a nimble fighter, capable of taking out anything the Chinese could put in the sky—including American and British designs.

But Japan had bigger ambitions and was already planning for new military conquests—either a move against the Soviet Union into Siberia, or a thrust into southeast Asia to seize the Dutch, British and American possessions there. Either move would, the Japanese knew, bring war with the British and American fleets, and that would require a fighter plane even better than the Claude.

So just a few months after the A5M took to the skies, the Japanese Navy released specifications for a new fighter to replace it, to be known as the A6M. The new plane had to have a speed of 310mph at 13,000 feet, it had to be capable of climbing to 9800 feet in 3.5 minutes, and it had to be able to fly for 6-8 hours at cruising speed, and at least 2 hours on normal power. Finally, it had to be at least as maneuverable as the Claude and carry the same armament—two .30-calibre machine guns and two 20mm cannon. It was a performance standard that no plane in the world at that time could match.

The Nakajima company kicked around some preliminary designs, but decided that such a plane was simply impossible with current technology. A design team at the Mitsubishi company, however, led by Jiro Horikoshi, concluded that these standards could be met, but only if the plane were exceptionally lightweight. Horikoshi's design therefore took every possible opportunity to save weight. The fixed landing gear of the Claude was replaced by retractable gear. The A6M's skin would be made from a new lightweight aluminum alloy, and flush-riveted together. A smaller air-cooled radial engine, the Zuisei-13, would be used to drive a two-bladed propeller. And, to save more weight, the plane would have no armor plating to protect the pilot; even the gas tanks would have their self-sealing rubber coatings dropped from the design.

Two prototypes were completed in 1939. The test flights revealed some problems with vibration, so the two-blade prop was replaced with a three-blade, and the Mitsubishi Zuisei engine was replaced by the slightly more powerful Sakae-12, which was manufactured by the Nakajima company. The resulting aircraft was designated the Mitsubishi A6M2, and was adopted by the Japanese Navy as the Type Zero Carrier Fighter, or Reisen. The Allies gave it the codename "Zeke", but it was always known to British and American pilots as the Zero.

The Zero had been developed in complete secrecy, and when it first appeared in the skies over China in 1940, it was a total surprise. The British and Americans, in a fit of silly racism, had dismissed the Japanese as nearsighted inferiors who could neither build nor fly a credible airplane. The Zero demonstrated how wrong they were. Not only were the Japanese Navy pilots some of the best-trained in the world, but their Zero fighter could outmaneuver anything else in the sky. The first Zero squadron in China shot down 99 Allied planes with the loss of only two of their own. One flight of 27 Soviet-built I-16 fighters had been completely destroyed. When Claire Chennault, commander of the American "Flying Tiger" volunteers in China, sent reports to the US describing the performance of the new Japanese fighter, American intelligence simply did not believe him, concluding that such an airplane could not exist. The Japanese Navy, meanwhile, ordered both the Mitsubishi and Nakajima companies to begin manufacturing carrier-based Zeros.

By the time the Japanese launched their carrier attack on Pearl Harbor in December 1941, they considered the Zero fighter to be the combat equivalent of at least 4 or 5 Allied P-36, P-39 or P-40s. Although the Imperial Japanese Navy carriers had over 400 A6M2 Zeros available, they elected to use less than 100 of them in the attack, figuring that would be enough to handle the entire American fighter force in Hawaii. In the event, nearly all the American fighters were destroyed on the ground, and only 8 Zeros were lost in the raid, mostly to anti-aircraft fire.

Over the next six months, the Zero established unquestioned Japanese air superiority. In the Philippines and the Dutch East Indies, the A6M2 took on everything from Brewster Buffalos to British Hurricanes. At Coral Sea, it demonstrated its dogfighting superiority to the US Navy F4F Wildcat. By the middle of 1942, however, the Americans began to develop effective tactics to deal with the Zero, by exploiting the plane's weaknesses and avoiding its strengths. Chennault's P-40s in China found that they could fly above the Zeros, dive down on them to make a rapid pass, then continue diving to run away and climb back up for another pass. The Navy adopted the "Thach Weave", in which a pair of Wildcats would fly back and forth to cover each other's tails.

In June 1942, the Japanese Navy lost four carriers and hundreds of planes and pilots at Midway, a blow which crippled it for the rest of the war. During the battle, a Zero fighter crash-landed in one of the Aleutian Islands and was found by the Americans, giving them their first close look at the fabled fighter. Within months, new fighters like the F6F Hellcat and F4U Corsair appeared, which were specifically designed to beat the Zero. Although the Japanese made some improvements in the A6M5 model, and designed a number of very capable fighter planes to replace the Zero, their inferior industrial base was never able to keep up with the war's demands, especially after B-29s began their systematic bombing campaign. Though outclassed, the Zero remained in production until the end of the war, with almost 11,000 built in various models—over half of these by the Nakajima company. Its final role was as the favored plane for *kamikaze* suicide attacks on American carriers.

Nearly all of the remaining Japanese Zeros were destroyed by the occupying Allies after the end of the war. Today only a little over a dozen survive, many of them being crashed airplanes that were recovered and restored.

In April 1944, US Marines captured a group of 12 intact A6M5 Zeros on Saipan. They were shipped back to the US for technical evaluation. One of them was sent to the test facility at Eglin, Florida, for assessment flights, then to Wright Airfield in Dayton, Ohio. In 1974 the Zero was restored by the Smithsonian, painted in the markings of the 261st Naval Air Corps stationed at Saipan, and is now on display at the Air and Space Museum.

Nakajima Ki-43 Oscar

The Nakajima Ki-43 "Oscar" was the standard Japanese Army fighter during the Pacific War. Although overshadowed by the more famous Zero used by the Japanese Navy, the Army's Oscar was actually more maneuverable and shot down more Allied aircraft in total than the Zero did.

In the years leading up to the Second World War, the Japanese government became dominated by militarists who sought to use a policy of conquest to build up a Japan-dominated "Co-Prosperity Sphere" in Asia. Within the military, however, the Japanese Imperial Army and Navy found that they couldn't get along with each other. Strategically, they had entirely different ideas about Japan's expansion and how it should be accomplished. The Army wanted to make a massive thrust up through China and into Russia to capture the untapped mineral resources in Siberia. Not coincidentally, this would involve a series of land campaigns in which the Army would play the central role. The Navy, on the other hand, favored a move into southeast Asia towards Australia, which would capture the oil and rubber areas in Indochina and the East Indies. Not coincidentally, this series of island conquests would leave the Navy as the key player. As a result, both branches simply began preparing for the kind of war it wanted to fight and viewed the other merely as a rival for resources and support. In the course of the war, the Navy therefore recruited and trained its own ground troops, while the Army would go so far as to build its own helicopter-aircraft carriers; in places like New Guinea and Iwo Jima where both branches had forces, they operated independently of each other, with their own separate chains of command.

One area in which the two branches flatly disagreed was air power. In the 1930s, air power was still a new concept, unproven in combat. The Japanese Navy, under the leadership of Admiral Isoroku Yamamoto, was an early proponent, and built up a powerful force of carriers and planes as well as long-range land-based bombers. The Japanese Army, however, influenced by its experiences in the invasion of China, viewed air power as simply a tactical force whose primary role was to support troops on the ground. This was reflected in the standard Army fighter of the time, the Nakajima Ki-27 "Nate" — a lightly-armed fighter/bomber.

In 1939, however, the Japanese Army got a shock. A border incident at the Mongolian village of Nomonhan led to a full-scale battle with the Soviet Union, and the Japanese Nates suffered huge losses to Russian I-16 fighters. The Japanese Generals realized that they needed a new fighter. The new design was designated the Nakajima Ki-43.

By this time, most fighters around the world were being built with 6 or even 8 heavy .50-caliber machine guns. The Japanese Army, however, still wanted an aircraft built for the war in China: the Chinese did not have much of an effective air force, so the primary role of the new fighter would be tactical support rather than air superiority. Like the Nate, the Ki-43 would be armed with two 500-pound bombs for ground attack and just two .303-caliber machine guns in the cowl for air combat (it was assumed that the superior training and marksmanship of the Japanese pilot would make up for this relative lack of firepower). What the Army *did* want, however, was long range: airfields in China were primitive and far apart, and the Japanese had also learned the lessons from the Nazi experience in the Battle of Britain, when the short range of the Messerschmitt fighter limited its ability to carry out operations over England.

So, the new fighter/bomber was, essentially, a long-range version of the Nate. The Ki-43 replaced the fixed landing gear of the Ki-27 with retractable wheels, added new internal gas tanks, and an Ha-25 radial engine with 950 horsepower. Top speed was a little over 300mph. A pair of "butterfly flaps" supplemented the ailerons and gave the plane phenomenal maneuverability, while its forgiving handling characteristics made it easy to fly.

The first combat models, the Ki-43-I, were introduced in 1941, with 40 planes in service by the time of the Pearl Harbor attack. Because one of the first Japanese Army units to receive the new fighter was the 64th Fighter Wing, known as the "Peregrine Falcons" from their insignia, the plane became known as the "Hayabusa", the Japanese word for "falcon". Although the new Hayabusa was the subject of much press fanfare in Japan and even had a propaganda movie and a song made about it, it took a while for intelligence services in the US to recognize it: most pilots who encountered it in China thought it was a Navy Zero. Eventually the Ki-43 received the Allied designation "Oscar".

The Japanese Generals had, however, chosen poorly. Although its lightweight construction gave it incredible range for the time and it was the most maneuverable plane anywhere in the sky (capable of out-turning even the Zero), the Oscar had not been designed for air-to-air combat, and it was slow, unarmored, and too vulnerable to the multiple .50-calibre machine guns carried by Allied fighters, while its own twin guns were woefully insufficient. Compared to the P-40 Warhawk fighters being flown by American volunteers in China, the Ki-43 was already outgunned.

New versions followed. In late 1942 the Ki-43-II was introduced: the engine was upgraded to the supercharged 1150 horsepower Ha-115 with a three-bladed prop, the wings were slightly shortened, and one of the .30 caliber guns was replaced with a .50-caliber, or sometimes a 20mm cannon. This was followed a year later by the Ki-43-III, with two .50-cals or 20mm on a longer nose, and a more powerful engine with a top speed of 360mph. In 1944, plans were made to replace the Oscar with the new Ki-84 Frank, but American bombing made this impossible.

In all, about 6,000 Oscars were produced during the war. They were the most common Japanese Army fighter, and saw more combat (and shot down more Allied aircraft) than the Japanese Navy's much more famous Zero. By the end of the war, a large fleet of Oscars had been assembled in Japan, where they were intended to be used in suicide attacks against the American invasion fleet. After the war, a number of captured Oscars continued to fly with the Chinese Communists until 1949.

Today, only one complete WW2 era Oscar survives. During the war, a captured Ki-43 was sent to the US, where it ended up as a gate display at a US Air National Guard base in New Mexico through the 50s. It was given to the Smithsonian in 1959, then loaned to the Experimental Aircraft Association's museum in Oshkosh WI, where it was restored and put on display for a time. In 2004 the Oscar was sent to the Museum of Flight in Seattle, where it remained on exhibit for four years before being moved to the Pima Air and Space Museum. It remains there, on loan from the Smithsonian.

Macchi C.202 Folgore

The C.202 Folgore ("Lightning Bolt") was the best Italian fighter plane to be produced during the Second World War. It was fast and maneuverable, and was the plane of choice for the Italian fighter aces on both sides of the war. Its one crippling flaw was its weak armament.

When World War Two began in 1939, the best fighter plane in the Italian Regia Aeronautica was the Macchi C.200 "Saetta", one of the first all-metal retractable-gear monoplanes designed by Mario Castoldi in 1935. The Saetta however quickly proved itself no match for the more modern British fighters. (And the Italian Air Force was still largely dependent on biplane fighters like the Fiat CR.42 "Falco".)

In 1939, Castoldi began planning improvements to the Saetta design. To maintain the plane's impressive maneuverability, he kept the same tail, undercarriage and wings as the Saetta (which also allowed much of the same production equipment to be utilized). The major improvement would be to replace the radial engine with a slimmer more aerodynamic inline to increase the speed. The new plane was dubbed the C.202 Folgore.

But the only existing Italian inline engine was the Isotta-Fraschini Delta IV, which at only 840 horsepower was far too small, and efforts to produce a more powerful inline engine, the Fiat A.38, were not a success. The Italians did not have much experience in producing inline aircraft engines, and the A.38 engine was continually delayed and could not meet its specifications.

To get around this problem, Mussolini negotiated an agreement with Hitler for Italy to produce the Daimler Benz DB 601A inline V-12 with 1,175 horsepower, the engine used in the Bf-109 Messerschmitt fighter, in Italy. Four complete Daimler-Benz engines were sent to Italy, with two going to the Macchi design factory and two going to Reggiane. The German engines were produced by the Alfa Romeo company as the Model Ra 1000R.C.41.

At Macchi, the new engine was immediately mated to the planned C.202. As had been done with the earlier C.200, to make the plane easier to handle, the designers deliberately lengthened the right wing over the left by about eight inches, producing more lift on that side to counter the torque from the propeller.

Production of the Folgore began in 1940, and it first entered combat in Northern Africa in 1941. And a crippling problem immediately became apparent. The British Hurricanes had eight .303-caliber machine guns mounted in the wings, and the American P-40 had four .50-caliber; the Folgore had only two .50-caliber machine guns mounted in the nose, and was far outgunned by the Allied aircraft. In early 1942, two more .50-caliber machine guns were added to the Folgore, one on each wing. The C.202's speed and maneuverability outclassed the Hurricane and the Warhawk and was an even match for the early model Spitfires, and along with the German Bf-109's it gave the Axis forces air superiority for the first years of the North Africa campaign. But the Folgore was always hampered by its relative lack of firepower. In later years, the Italians modified a small number of planes to add two underwing hardpoints to attach external fuel tanks, or light bombs for ground attack.

To increase production, the Regia Aeronautica assigned the C.202 design to the Breda company, which eventually ended up producing far more of the fighters than the Macchi company did. Around 1200 Folgores were produced during the war. Four of Italy's top five scoring aces during the war flew the Folgore.

By 1943, the Folgore was beginning to be outclassed by Allied fighters, especially the new model Spitfires and the American P-51. By the time Sicily was invaded in July 1943, only 100 Folgores remained in flying shape. A new version of the C.202 was planned which would add two 20mm cannon to increase its firepower, especially against bombers, but Allied bombing of the Italian aircraft factories crippled the program, and it never entered service. Another new airplane, the C.205 Veltro ("Greyhound"), was planned to use the C.202 airframe with added cannons and a newer German DB 605 engine, but it too was hampered by Allied bombing and only 6 ever reached service.

When the Italian government surrendered to the Allies in September 1943, the Italian Regia Aeronautica became split into two; the air bases in the southern part of Italy, occupied by the Allies, became the Co-Belligerent Air Force, and the air bases in northern Italy occupied by the Nazis became the Italian Social Republic Air Force. Neither of them flew Folgores in combat: the Allied forces replaced them with Spitfires, and the Fascists used the C.202 only as trainers.

After the war, C.205 Veltro versions of the Folgore continued to fly with the Egyptian Air Force until 1949. A number of C.202s were also shipped to the US for evaluation. In 1975, the Smithsonian found a crated Folgore in storage with the US Air Force and restored it. This plane is now on display at the Air and Space Museum in Washington DC.

F4U Corsair

With its long nose and bent wings, the F4U Corsair was one of the most distinctive fighters of the Second World War – and a TV series also made it one of the most famous.

In 1940, the Pratt and Whitney company unveiled the XR-2800 Double Wasp engine, which used 18 radial cylinders arranged in two banks to produce 1850 horsepower, making it the most powerful engine in the world. Designers at the Vought Aircraft Company began work on a new carrier-based fighter plane that would be built around the new engine. It was designated the V-166-B.

The design was mostly determined by the engine. The Double Wasp's two banks of cylinders required a very long nose to fit it inside. The enormous horsepower would also need a very large propeller to efficiently transfer thrust—Vought settled on a three-bladed prop (later changed to a four-blade) with a diameter of over 13 feet. This was much larger than any other fighter plane's propeller, and it presented an awkward problem: in a normal plane, the prop was too long and would dig into the ground. One solution would be to make the landing gear longer to hold the prop higher off the ground. But the V-166-B was intended as a carrier-based airplane, which required short but stout landing gear to absorb the impacts of rough carrier landings. So the Vought designers came up with a different solution—the "inverted gull" wings would descend sharply downwards at the fuselage, to hold the nose high off the ground, then would bend outwards.

For maximum speed, the rest of the airframe would be made as clean as possible. The landing gear was designed to rotate flat before being tucked inside the wings and covered with hydraulic doors. The oil coolers and the intakes for the supercharger were fitted into the front of the wing roots. The fuselage was built with a round cross-section to give it the smallest possible weight and surface area, and the panels were spot-welded together rather than riveted. When the prototype was flown in May 1940, it reached speeds of 405 mph, making it the fastest fighter in the world. The Navy adopted it as the F4U Corsair and in June 1941 placed an order for 584 planes. Production began in 1942.

But the Corsair immediately ran into problems. Although it was a formidable fighter, fast and maneuverable and tough, the long nose made visibility during carrier landings almost impossible (this was compounded by an annoying tendency for the engine to leak oil and smear up the windshield). The shock absorbers were also unsuitable: Corsairs often bounced hard upon landing, causing them to miss the carrier deck's arresting wires. And the plane had some dicey stall characteristics that made low-speed landing hazardous. The Navy decided to look for another carrier fighter (which turned out to be the F6F Hellcat) and kept the Corsair as a ground-based fighter for the Marine Corps. The plane was also used by Britain, Australia and New Zealand in the Pacific. In early 1943, the Corsair entered combat in the Solomon Islands campaign. To speed production, the Goodyear company also manufactured F4U's under a license from Vought.

As a fighter, the Corsair proved to be more than a match for the Japanese Zero. F4U pilots shot down 2,140 Japanese aircraft with a loss of only 189 Corsairs in combat. Almost half of all the fighter missions in the Pacific theater were flown by F4U's.

Later versions of the Corsair were modified to carry bomb loads and unguided rockets for ground attack, and the fighter-bomber versions became one of the primary close-support aircraft during the island fighting in Guadalcanal and then across the Pacific. During ground-attack runs the wind would often scream into the Corsair's wing-edge inlets, leading the Japanese troops to dub it "Whistling Death".

By 1944, the British had made some modifications to the Corsair and worked out procedures (including a long curving landing approach) that allowed them to operate F4U's successfully from aircraft carriers, and the US Navy immediately followed suit.

After the end of the Second World War, the US Navy adopted the F8F Bearcat as its primary carrier fighter, later replaced by the F9F Panther jet fighter. But the F4U Corsair was kept as a fighter-bomber. When the Korean War broke out in 1950, the Corsairs saw heavy action. Although the F4U had some early success against Soviet-supplied North Korean Yakovlev fighters (and one Corsair pilot even managed to shoot down a MiG-15 jet), it was used mostly in the ground-attack role. In 1952, the last F4U rolled off the assembly line. It had been in production for ten years. By the end of the war, the Corsair had been replaced by newer jet attack fighters.

The F4U, however, wasn't finished quite yet. In the 1950's, Corsairs were flown by French pilots in Indochina in the war against the Viet Minh guerrillas. After the French withdrew, many of these were sold to air forces in South America. When the "Soccer War" briefly broke out between El Salvador and Honduras in 1969, both sides were equipped with vintage F4U Corsairs.

But the Corsair probably reached the peak of its fame long after the last one had flown in combat. In 1976 the TV series "Baa Baa Black Sheep" (later renamed "Black Sheep Squadron") premiered on NBC. Starring Robert Conrad, the series was loosely based on the exploits of Corsair ace Gregory "Pappy" Boyington during the 1943 Solomon Islands campaigns, and although it ran for only three seasons, it made both Boyington and the Corsair famous. The series used seven airworthy F4U's, all privately owned, to film its aerial combat scenes: the Japanese "Zeros" were AT-6 Texan trainers painted to look Japanese, some of which had also been used to film the movie "Tora! Tora! Tora!".

Today about 80 Corsairs of different models still survive, of which about half are airworthy.

The Sacred Cow

Nowadays, air travel around the globe by a US President is routine, and "Air Force One" is as familiar a part of the office as is the White House. But the history of Presidential aircraft goes back only to the 1940's.

By 1943, the Second World War had finally reached a turning point. The Allies decided that they needed to meet, to plan out the rest of the war and to draw up a set of firm goals. The place they chose to hold their conference was Casablanca, a port city in Morocco. At the Casablanca Conference, the Allies would agree to an invasion of Europe at the earliest opportunity, to open up a second front and relieve the pressure on Stalin's Red Army. They also agreed that none of them would seek a separate peace with the Axis, and they would accept nothing less than "unconditional surrender" to end the war.

For US President Franklin D Roosevelt, however, the biggest difficulty about the Casablanca Conference was how to get there. A victim of polio that had left him unable to walk, Roosevelt made every effort to hide his disability in public. Previous meetings with Churchill had taken place at sea, aboard an American cruiser, but traveling to Morocco by Navy ship would take far too long. FDR, therefore, decided to do something no sitting US President had ever done before—he would travel by air. At that time, air travel was viewed as exotic and a little bit dangerous, but Roosevelt thought it would project the image of the United States (and himself) as being willing to take risks and endure hardships in order to overcome any challenges.

On January 11, 1943, Roosevelt arrived by car at the Dinner Key Seaplane Base in Miami FL and boarded the "Dixie Clipper". The Boeing 314 "Flying Boat" was operated by the Pan Am airline as part of its "Pan American Clipper" service. The flight took FDR from Miami to Brazil and then across the Atlantic to Gambia, where he boarded a C-54 transport operated by TWA and went on to Casablanca. On the way back after the conference, Roosevelt celebrated his 61st birthday.

After FDR's return to the United States, the Army Air Force began talks with the Secret Service. It was apparent that air travel would soon become a necessary part of a President's duties, and plans needed to be made for it. The Secret Service was interested in insuring the safety of the President during air travel: the Army was interested in having the President use an Army Air Force aircraft rather than a Navy seaplane. Together, the two agencies made plans to convert an Army C-87A transport plane, named "Guess Where II", for the President's use. But the Secret Service became concerned about the C-87's rather spotty safety record, and there were some difficulties adapting the airplane for use with FDR's wheelchair. So in late 1943 it was decided to purpose-build a transport plane for the President from scratch, and the Douglas Company was given the job. It was codenamed "Project 51".

The basic plan for the "Flying White House", as it was officially named, was to take the fuselage from a standard C-54A Skymaster transport plane and add the wings from the C-54B model, which were bigger and had larger fuel tanks for greater range. The one-of-a-kind model was designated the VC-54C. The cargo bay was converted into a series of rooms, connected by an extra-wide hallway that would accommodate FDR's wheelchair. There was a large conference room for meetings, with a bulletproof glass window to the outside. At the back of the fuselage was Roosevelt's private stateroom, with a leather chair, a fold-out bed, and a private bathroom. The galley was equipped with a stove and an electric refrigerator. And a battery-powered elevator lift was added at a doorway, allowing the President to easily board the plane.

There were, of course, technological limitations. The plane was unpressurized, which kept it at low altitudes. Since there was no air conditioning, each room was provided with electric fans. And although there was a phone connecting the conference room and FDR's cabin to the cockpit, the only communication between the aircraft and the ground was through the cockpit radio.

The "Flying White House" was delivered to Washington DC from the Douglas factory in California on June 12, 1944. Because of the heavy security that surrounded it, newspaper reporters began to refer to the new plane as the "Sacred Cow", and, despite repeated complaints from the White House staff that it was "undignified", the moniker stuck.

By February 1945, it was apparent that Nazi Germany would soon be defeated and the European War would be over. So it was decided that another conference was needed to plan out the Allied occupation of Germany, and to focus the war effort on Japan. This conference was to be held in Yalta, a resort town in the Crimea. At Yalta, Stalin agreed that he would enter the war against Japan six months after Germany surrendered. The Sacred Cow carried FDR to the Soviet city and back. It would be the only time he ever flew aboard the plane. Two months after Yalta, Roosevelt suddenly died from a stroke. The Presidency fell to VP Harry Truman.

President Truman used the Sacred Cow extensively. When he signed the National Security Act of 1947, which established the CIA and NSA as well as separating the US Air Force from the Army, he was traveling aboard the Sacred Cow. Later, Truman received his own specially-built Presidential airplane, the "Independence". The Sacred Cow continued to be used as a VIP transport by the White House until she was retired in 1961.

In 1983 the Sacred Cow was donated to the Air Force Museum in Dayton OH, and after ten years of restoration work was put on display along with other Presidential aircraft. In 2015, a new building was completed on the Museum grounds to display all the Presidential planes.

De Havilland DH98 Mosquito

The "Mozzie" was the most versatile aircraft of the war, fast and lightweight. Different variations served as interceptors, photoreconnaissance, light bombers, and ground attack.

When the war broke out, it was apparent that every military in the world would need a lot of aircraft. In England, designer Geoffrey De Havilland, who had built airplanes in the First World War, also realized that the materials used to make them, especially aluminum, would also become scarce, as would the engineers and skilled metal-workers who knew how to assemble parts from these materials.

And so De Havilland went off in a different direction. He proposed a design for a twin-engined bomber that would be made entirely of plywood. This would help save on scarce aluminum, and could also be assembled quickly using cabinet-makers and carpenters as workers. And then De Havilland became even more radical. Unlike conventional bombers like the Lancaster, which were big and slow and depended on heavy armor and machine guns for protection, De Havilland's bomber would be small, light, and have no armor or guns at all—it would depend entirely on speed for protection. The DH98 Mosquito would be able to reach occupied Europe, come in fast and low to evade and outrun enemy fighters, and drop its 1,000-pounds of bombs on a pinpoint target.

It was a unique vision, but it was too unorthodox for the British Air Ministry, and they turned him down. De Havilland, undeterred, used his own money to continue work on the project, remarking to a colleague, "They may not want it now, but they will."

And he was correct. After the Battle of Britain, the English began to look for some way to strike back against Germany. There were not enough heavy bombers yet to begin the nightly air raids that would begin devastating the Nazis in 1943, but there was a small fast bomber that could reach targets in Europe: the Mosquito. In November 1940, De Havilland was commissioned to build 40 of his twin-engined bombers. In their first flights, they reached speeds of over 400mph—and remained the fastest bombers in the world until the jet age. It quickly became known as "The Wooden Wonder". Soon, woodworkers at 400 locations in Britain would be gluing and screwing Mosquito parts together from birch wood, to be assembled at the De Havilland factory.

It was its low-level precision that made the Mosquito so useful as a bomber. While the Lancaster was good for area-bombing, dropping large bomb loads over an entire city from height, De Havilland's bomber could come in low under German radar and pinpoint a specific target. Although the plane was designed to be unarmed, it was found that it could indeed carry a variety of rockets and guns, all the way up to an immense 57mm cannon, for attacking ground targets (this version was known as the "Tsetse").

This opened up an option that had never existed before: unlike the heavy bombers, the Mosquitoes had the capability to go in and target a single building, destroying it while minimizing any damage to its surroundings. One of the first of these types of raids was against the Nazi Gestapo headquarters in Oslo, Norway, where members of the anti-Nazi Resistance were being held. Other similar raids followed against the Jail in Amiens, France, the Shell House in Copenhagen, Denmark, and the Central Registry Building in Holland. The first British raids on Berlin took place in January 1943—and they were made by Mosquitoes. That morning, Goering was scheduled to give a speech at a Berlin parade bragging that Allied aircraft would never be able to reach Berlin, which was disrupted by a flight of Mosquitos roaring in at rooftop level. Later that same afternoon, the performance was repeated at another rally where Goebbels was speaking. Throughout the war, Mosquitoes would be sent in for pinpoint attacks on small targets like power stations and V-2 launch sites. They were also one of the few British aircraft that were fast enough to reach V-1 buzzbombs in the air and shoot them down.

Once the Mosquito was flying, it also did not take long for the British to realize the tremendous versatility that their light fast long-distance airframe offered. The most obvious adaptation was for photoreconnaissance: the bomb load was replaced with up to five cameras, and with its superior speed the Mozzie could streak over a desired target at treetop level, snapping clear closeup 3D stereoscopic photos the entire way.

Other adaptations soon followed. The planes were used to deliver weapons and supplies to Resistance fighters in Europe, and also functioned as light cargo planes and VIP transports. Mosquitoes became "Pathfinders" which went in at low level ahead of the heavy bomber raids and accurately marked the target; these long-range bombing missions became test platforms for various electronic navigation systems such as "Oboe". By 1944, small flights of Mosquitoes were flying diversionary raids over Germany which used electronic devices to make them appear as a much larger force on radar, luring German fighters away from the actual bombers—a practice known as "spoofing".

Fitted with torpedoes or depth charges, the plane also proved to be effective as shore patrols and submarine hunters, and some were modified to drop anti-ship mines into harbors. When small radar sets became available, the Mosquito was converted into a formidable night fighter, armed with four 20mm cannons.

Even after the war, the Mosquito was still useful. The RAF continued to use it as a reconnaissance platform until 1953, when it was replaced by the jet-engined Canberra. Of the 7700 total De Havillands that were manufactured, around 1,000 came after 1945.

The United States obtained around 160 Mosquitoes from Canada and the UK, using them for photoreconnaissance, advance weather planes, and as light bombers. After the war ended they were used to tow target drones for gunnery practice. One of these Mosquitoes, delivered to the US in 1946, is on display at the US Air Force Museum in Dayton OH.

Junkers Ju-88

The Ju-88 proved to be enormously adaptable for the Luftwaffe. After flying in the Battle of Britain as a medium bomber, it went on to become a submarine hunter, a torpedo bomber, a ground-attack tank-buster, and a night fighter.

When the Nazis began to rebuild their Luftwaffe in preparation for their planned European war, one of the first things they needed was a bomber. The Heinkel He-111 and Dornier Do-17 models were rushed into production in 1934, but, while effective against biplane fighters, they were already vulnerable to the new monoplanes that were beginning to appear on drawing boards. The Germans needed something better.

In 1935, the Nazis released a requirement for a *Schnellbomber* — an all-metal medium bomber that could deliver a 2,000-pound bomb load at 300mph, fast enough to outrun any of the existing biplane fighters of the time. Further, since the bombsights of the day were inaccurate, the *Schnellbomber* was required to have the capability to perform dive-bombing on pinpoint targets. It was a tall demand.

The Heinkel and Dornier factories were already committed to other projects, so they did not submit a proposal. Messerschmitt also withdrew a proposal, saying they would concentrate on new fighters. Focke-Wulf's offer was called the Fw-57, but the company was inexperienced with large metal airframes, and could not keep the weight under control. So the job went to the Junkers company almost by default.

The Junkers bomber was designated Ju-88. In a historical irony, it had been produced by two designers named Alfred Gassner and W. H. Evers, both of whom who had lived and worked in the United States for a time and still held American citizenship. They in turn based much of their design on an earlier bomber, the Junkers Ju-86, which had been originally produced as a two-engined airliner to hide its real purpose from the Allies. (The Ju-86P model, with a pressurized cabin allowing altitudes up to 40,000 feet, found service in the early part of World War Two as a reconnaissance platform.)

The new Ju-88 design envisioned a twin-engined bomber powered by two water-cooled inline Daimler Benz DB 600 engines (though the wing nacelles were intentionally made round in shape to accommodate radial engines as well). The landing gear consisted of single rugged struts that were able to absorb the impact of landings and allowed the plane to operate from rough grass airstrips close to the frontlines. The Junkers was also intended to absorb a lot of damage while still flying, and to be easy to repair in the field.

After the first prototype was destroyed in a crash, new variants were produced. By March 1939, test versions of the Ju-88, equipped with two Jumo 211B-1 engines, had a range of 1500 miles and were exceeding 300mph, faster than any biplane fighter and not much slower than the new German Me-109 and British Hurricane monoplanes. The original design had not carried any defensive machine guns, it being presumed that the *Schnellbomber* would be fast enough to outrun enemy fighters. But the air wars in Spain and

Libya were already demonstrating that an unarmed bomber would be a sitting duck for modern monoplane fighters, so three machine gun positions were added to the nose and fuselage. Combat versions of the Junkers began reaching the frontline in September 1939, just as the war was breaking out.

Most models had a crew of four. The pilot flew the plane himself—there was no co-pilot. The bombardier in the nose also operated the forward machine gun when necessary. Likewise, the radio operator and the navigator both also doubled as machine gunners.

During the Battle of Britain in 1940, the Junkers proved itself to be superior to the He-111 and Do-17 and the only German bomber to have a fighting chance against the new British fighters, but there were not enough of them in service. It was quickly discovered that dive-bombing with such a large aircraft was not really practical, and the Ju-88 was only rarely used in that task, but the requirement itself had an unexpected side benefit: the airframe was so sturdy that it easily lent itself to modifications for other assignments that it had not been originally intended for.

So after the Battle of Britain the Ju-88 not only became the Luftwaffe's primary frontline medium bomber, but was adapted into a bewildering range of different versions, using a wide selection of engines and armament. Fitted with a torpedo or depth charges, it did well as a submarine hunter and coastal patrol for use against shipping, and some planes were used to drop naval mines in enemy waters. When Allied raiders began appearing over Germany in 1943, the Junkers was provided with radar to find enemy bombers, and also armed with upwards-aiming machine guns in a turret, which allowed it to fire from below at the unprotected belly of an American or British bomber—making it one of the most effective night fighters of the war. Night fighters were sometimes sent to circle around British and American bomber bases, hoping to catch bombers on their way in or out. The "destroyer" daytime interceptor version was armed with 20mm cannons in the nose for use against heavy bombers, and ground-attack models were fitted with rockets as well as cannons.

The final use of the Junkers was as part of the experimental "*Mistel*" project. In its initial form, this consisted of a Focke-Wulf fighter mounted to the top of a Ju-88 that had been packed with explosives. Known as the "Piggyback", the whole contraption would be flown by a pilot inside the fighter, who would release the unmanned bomber and fly it into the target using radio remote-control. Later versions were planned to use jet-engine fighters mounted to rocket-powered bomb-carriers.

Roughly 15,000 Ju-88s were produced during its nine years of service. Today, only two remain intact. One of these, built in 1942 as a bomber and later converted into a fighter, was flown by its German crew to Scotland in 1943, where they defected. British technicians were able to examine the intact airplane, including its new FuG 202 Liechtenstein BC A.I radar unit—and develop counter-measures. This aircraft is now on exhibit at the Royal Air Force Museum in England.

Another wartime Ju-88 is at the US Air Force Museum in Dayton OH. This is a D-1 "Tropicalized" version that was fitted with special filters for use in the Mediterranean and North African deserts. Built in 1942, it was in service with the Romanian Air Force as a photoreconnaissance plane when it was flown to Cyprus by a defecting Romanian pilot. The British turned it over to the Americans, who took it back to Wright-Patterson airfield in Ohio for evaluation, then placed it into storage. It was given to the Museum in 1960, and is today displayed in its Romanian markings.

A small number of wartime crash sites have also been found in various places, and the remains of these wrecked Ju-88s are undergoing restoration for exhibit.

Lockheed P-38 Lightning

The P-38 was tough, heavily-armed, and had exceptional range. Many of the highest-scoring American aces of the war won their victories in Lightnings.

In 1937, the US issued a request for something that most aviation engineers considered to be impossible: a design for a high-altitude fighter that could quickly intercept long-range bombers before they could reach their targets. There was a list of requirements: the new fighter had to be able to climb to 20,000 feet within six minutes; it had to be capable of a level speed of 290mph at sea level and 360mph at 20,000 feet; it had to be capable of cruising at full power for one hour at altitude; it had to be capable of taking off and landing from a runway no longer than 2200 feet. And it had to be armed with at least one 20mm cannon.

At Lockheed, chief engineer Hall Hibbard and his assistant Clarence "Kelly" Johnson looked over the specs. In the future, Johnson would be the head of the top secret "Skunkworks" team at Lockheed, which would produce the U-2 and SR-71 spy planes. At this time, though, he was just a young aeronautical engineer. But he already had a talent for the unorthodox. As the two talked, they decided that no single aircraft engine then in existence, or even still on paper, could produce that level of performance—but *two* engines might.

Together they roughed out a sketch. Two liquid-cooled Allison engines on twin booms, one on each side, with superchargers and their inlets behind them. The cockpit in a nacelle in the middle, with 20mm cannon and four .50-cal machine guns in front where the propellers would not interfere—saving the weight of synchronizing gears. The landing gear would also fit into the nacelles, giving a nice wide stance for stability. The rear of the booms would be joined by a crosspiece where the tail controls would be, and the tailwheel would be moved to the nose of the nacelle to form a tricycle.

It was a radical leap, and in peacetime it would certainly have been shelved. But war was approaching, and nobody else had any better ideas to offer. The "P-38 Lightning" was approved for development. The prototype was built in the strictest of secrecy, and first flew in January 1939. It reached 400mph. It also encountered problems with vibration and tail flutter, though. More adjustments were made, and the problem seemed to have been solved.

And now, the Army decided that perhaps their fast new plane might be able to generate some friendly publicity, by breaking the transcontinental speed record that Howard Hughes had set back in 1935. Setting out from March Field in California, the prototype plane refueled in Texas and Ohio before approaching Mitchell Field in New York. Unfortunately, the plane crashed (investigation determined that there had been ice in the carburetor), and while the pilot survived, the plane did not.

When the P-38 began flying again in 1941, it encountered new problems. There were mechanical issues with the engines. The tail would still flutter under some conditions. The supercharger regulators would sometimes freeze at high altitude. Most serious was a problem known as "compressability", when an airplane in a high speed dive causes shock waves on the control surfaces, locking them and making it impossible to pull out.

By the time the US entered the war in December 1941, the entire P-38 program had been delayed by several years. Britain received three of the fighters, but for some reason specified that they didn't want superchargers on the engines, which made the Lightnings useless at high altitudes.

In mid-1943, the various production issues had been fixed and the P-38 began reaching frontline units in force. Immediately it was found that the twin-engined plane was not very maneuverable and was limited in dogfighting. It had, of course, been designed to intercept high-altitude bombers, but by this time in Europe there were barely any Luftwaffe bombers left. So the P-38 was stripped of guns and armor, fitted with a camera, and used for photo-reconnaissance—the counter-rotating props made it a very stable camera platform. For a time, P-38's also escorted American bombers on long-distance raids into Germany, until they were replaced by the more nimble Mustangs.

In the Pacific, the Lightning's extended range made it useful for covering the long distances between islands. Certainly the most famous mission carried out by the P-38 was the shootdown of Japanese Admiral Isoroku Yamamoto in April 1943: after decrypted radio messages revealed Yamamoto's schedule, a flight of Lightnings were sent over 1,000 miles to intercept his plane.

The top two American aces of the Second World War were both P-38 pilots in the Pacific. Major Richard Bong had 40 air victories, and Major Tommy McGuire had 38. Neither survived the war: McGuire was shot down over the Philippines in January 1945, and Bong was killed in August 1945 when the P-80 jet fighter he was flight-testing crashed on takeoff.

At its Udvar-Hazy Center, the Smithsonian Air and Space Museum has a P-38J on exhibit. Records show that it was made in November 1943 and was converted into a two-seat trainer, intended to teach test pilots how to fly the planes for evaluation purposes. Converted back to single seat, it was then used for various tests, at one point being briefly flown by Richard Bong, who cut his experimental flight short when one of the engines malfunctioned.

In 1946, the P-38 was given, along with several other planes, to the Smithsonian, which put it into storage. It was later restored and placed on display. The Museum's P-38 is one of roughly 25 surviving Lightnings.

Grumman F6F Hellcat

The Hellcat was specifically designed as a "Zero Killer", and it won back the air superiority in the Pacific that the Japanese had enjoyed since the beginning of the war.

Even before the US entered the war, the British experience with the F4F Wildcat in 1940 had shown that the plane was limited in its performance against German planes, and engineers at Grumman were already working on a new version. The most likely opponent for the new American carrier fighter, however, would be the Japanese Zero fighter. The new F6F would be designed from the start as a "Zero killer".

The core of the new fighter would be the new 2000-horsepower version of the Pratt and Whitney R-2800 Double Wasp engine. To accommodate the bigger engine, the airframe needed to be completely remodeled. In the end, although they looked similar, the F4F and F6F shared no parts in common. The Hellcat fuselage would be thicker and longer, about 33.5 feet, and the wings proportionately bigger with a span of almost 43 feet. The F6F would be about 60 percent heavier than the Wildcat, with an empty weight of 9150 pounds. This necessitated new sturdier landing gear that could withstand carrier landings on rough seas, and the hydraulic struts were moved from the nose to the wings to give a wider track and more stability. The Navy, meanwhile, was already making plans to produce a new and much larger aircraft carrier, the *Essex* class, which would be able to handle the bigger and more powerful fighter.

The Navy adopted the new Grumman design in June 1941, dubbing it the F6F Hellcat. The prototype was first flown a year later in June 1942.

The Hellcat's development was then inadvertently aided by the Japanese. During the fighting which took place in the Aleutian Islands of Alaska as part of the Battle of Midway, a Japanese Zero crash-landed on the tiny island of Akutan, killing the pilot. The US was able to recover the Zero, which was virtually intact, and return it to the mainland for testing and evaluation. It provided invaluable information about the Japanese plane's abilities, strengths and weaknesses, and allowed the design and tactics of the new Hellcat to be adjusted to take advantage.

Production began in November 1942. To speed things up, Grumman turned over production of its Wildcat fighters and TBF Avenger torpedo bomber to General Motors, and devoted its entire Bethpage NY factory to producing F6Fs. By April 1943 the plant was turning out 130 Hellcats per month. A short time later it was 500 a month. Some 12,250 were produced during the war.

The Hellcat was a vast improvement over the F4F, and more than a match for the Zero. It was some 60mph faster than the Japanese fighter, could match its climb rate as well as outdive it, and carried enough armor around the pilot and the engine to absorb a lot of damage and still get home. It also had bullet-resistant glass in the cockpit canopy. Originally armed with six .50-caliber machine guns, later models replaced the two inner guns with 20mm cannon. The Hellcat could also haul two 1,000-pound bombs and six powerful 5-inch unguided rockets (known as HVAR—High Velocity Aircraft Rockets) for ground attack. Later versions carried two even larger rockets, almost 12-inches in diameter, known as Tiny Tim—each equivalent to the explosive power of a heavy cruiser's main gun shell.

The Hellcat began reaching frontline units in August 1943, in time for the bombing campaign on Japanese-held Wake Island carried out by four Navy aircraft carriers. Hellcats also played a large role in the destruction of the Japanese naval base at Rabaul. During the subsequent island-hopping campaigns from Tarawa to Okinawa, the Hellcats had a kill ration of 19 to 1. In all, the F6Fs accounted for three-fourths of all the Japanese planes shot down by American fighters in the Pacific War.

In early 1942, the Navy also began experiments to equip some carrier fighters as radar-guided night fighters. At first, these tests were carried out with new F4U Corsairs, but the Hellcat proved to be more suitable: it was more stable in flight, and it was much easier to land at night. Soon Hellcats began to appear that carried primitive but effective radar-intercept sets that had been hastily put together at MIT. The more capable APS-6 radar system, which fit into a pod carried under the wing, had a range of five miles and made the Hellcat an effective night fighter. Some 1800 radar-equipped models were produced.

The UK would receive over 1200 Hellcats under Lend-Lease, dubbing it the Gannet. They shot down a total of 52 enemy aircraft in Norway, the Mediterranean, and the Pacific, including a number of German Messerschmitts and Focke-Wulfs. Production of the Hellcat did not stop until November 1945, and late-model F6Fs remained in service with the US Navy—some as photo-reconnaissance planes—until 1953. (When the US Navy Blue Angels flight demonstration team was formed in 1946, they flew F6Fs.) In 1952, during the Korean War, a number of old radio-controlled Hellcat drones were packed with bombs and used as guided missiles to destroy bridges. A small number of F6Fs also served with the French during the Indochina War in the 1950s. The Uruguayan Navy flew a handful of Hellcats as patrol planes until 1960.

Today, around ten World War II vintage F6F Hellcats still exist. One is in the USS *Intrepid* Museum in New York City; another is in the New England Air Museum in Connecticut. The Planes of Fame Museum in Chino CA has a Hellcat, as does the US Naval Aviation Museum and the Smithsonian Udvar-Hazy.

The Smithsonian's Hellcat was manufactured at Bethpage in February 1944 and originally assigned to the carrier USS *Hornet*, but was instead damaged in a crash-landing and was sent to a ground unit and used for training. After the war it was converted to an unmanned radio-controlled drone, and served as an instrument plane during the Operation Crossroads nuclear test in 1946. It was given to the Smithsonian in 1948, and was loaned for a time to the USS *Yorktown* Museum in Charleston before being returned to DC, restored, and put on display.

Focke-Wulf 190

Though overshadowed by its much more famous Me-109 contemporary, the Focke-Wulf 190 was arguably the better fighter, scoring a 60:1 kill ratio compared to 20:1 for the Messerschmitt.

The Albatros aircraft company, which had made some of the best German fighters of the First World War, went bankrupt and in 1931 merged with the Focke-Wulf company. In the run-up to the Second World War, Focke-Wulf was best-known as the maker of the Fw-44 biplane trainer, and in 1937 began producing the Fw-200 Condor, a four-engine civilian trans-Atlantic airliner that was, when the war broke out, converted into a long-range marine patrol and anti-ship bomber.

So when Focke-Wulf submitted a design for a new fighter in 1937, the Nazis, knowing that the company had never made a production fighter before, were skeptical. But Focke-Wulf had inherited the design expertise of the Albatros team, and when they began flying the prototype for the Fw-190 fighter using the BMW 139 radial engine, it was a winner. A short time later, another prototype was fitted with the newer 1600-horsepower BMW 801, and the Nazis ordered it into production. They called it the *Wurger* ("Butcher Bird").

The radial engine, Focke-Wulf's designers thought, offered several advantages over the water-cooled inline used in the Me-109. Radial engines were more reliable and easier to repair in the field. The big chunk of metal in front of the cockpit offered protection to the pilot from enemy fire, and when the radial engine was shot up, it could absorb an impressive amount of damage and still bring the pilot back. Also, it would be easier to manufacture in large numbers than the more complex inline engines. The German Air Ministry, on the other hand, liked the radial engine design because it would not cut into the availability of inline engines for the Messerschmitt.

Radial engines did of course produce more drag than the slimmer inlines, but Focke-Wulf figured they could plan around that, and added a streamlined hub to the propeller and a tight-fitting aerodynamic cowl around the engine which pulled air inside and increased the air-cooling effect. The big engine also blocked the pilot's forward view while on the ground, so pilots took to having a ground crewman sit on the wing and guide them while taxiing.

The Focke-Wulf's wider and sturdier landing gear, however, gave better ground handling than the Me-109, which made takeoffs and landings easier for less-experienced pilots — especially on rough field airstrips. And with its two machine guns and two 20mm cannons (later upgraded to four 20mm cannons), the Focke-Wulf was better-armed. The Fw-190 design also had a bubbletop canopy which gave the pilot better visibility in combat than the Messerschmitt.

The first combat models entered service in September 1941, and quickly demonstrated that they outclassed the latest Mark V Spitfires. For much of the rest of the war, new versions of the Fw-190 were introduced that put it ahead of Allied fighters, leading to a game of "catch-up". The basic Focke-Wulf airframe was fitted with a wide variety of engines and weaponry for different roles. The ground-attack version, with bomb racks, rockets, and a 30mm cannon in the propeller hub, replaced the Ju-87 dive bomber as the primary Luftwaffe close-combat support weapon, and heavily-gunned variants were used as bomber interceptors. Radar-equipped models were used as night fighters. As an air superiority fighter, the Fw-190 was fast and maneuverable. The final version, the Fw-190D "Dora", dropped the radial engine in favor of the more powerful turbosupercharged inline Junkers Jumo 213, which gave a much better performance at high altitudes. This returned much of the speed and maneuverability advantages that the Luftwaffe had lost, but it was hampered by shortages and manufacturing difficulties.

When the German ace Adolf Galland flew the Fw-190, he considered it superior to the Messerschmitt, and recommended that the German aircraft industry focus solely on producing Focke-Wulfs. Allied pilots found the Fw-190 to be a formidable adversary, until the constant air attacks on Luftwaffe bases began to reduce the number of German fighter planes, and the loss of experienced pilots and the abbreviated training regimen meant that the quality of Luftwaffe pilots declined steadily over time. By the end of 1944 the Allies had complete control of the sky, and the Luftwaffe was virtually spent as a significant force.

In June 1942, moreover, a German pilot accidentally landed his Focke-Wulf 190A at an Allied airfield, an enormous intelligence coup that gave the British and Americans their first good look at the aircraft. After testing and evaluation, the British specifically designed the Hawker Fury to defeat it, while also influencing American designs. The Allies began fielding planes like the P-51 and Mark XIV Spitfires that could deal with the German fighters.

The Germans produced about 20,000 Focke-Wulf fighters during the war, in at least 40 different designated versions. About two dozen planes still survive, some in private hands. Five of these are Fw-190A models that flew with the JG5 fighter group at a base in Herdla, Norway.

The Imperial War Museum in London has a Focke-Wulf 190A on exhibit. The early history of this plane is unknown, but at some time it was used as a test airplane for the German *"Mistral"* program, which attempted to attach an Fw-190 to a Junkers Ju-88 and use the bomber as a radio-guided missile. The War Museum's 190 still has the rack which would have attached it to the bomber. It was captured in 1945 and brought back to England.

The RAF Museum also has a Focke-Wulf, built under license by the Arado factory and later converted to a two-seat trainer. It was captured in May 1945 in Schleswig-Holstein.

The Air and Space Museum in Washington DC exhibits a Focke-Wulf 190A that was manufactured in 1943, was damaged in combat and then remodeled into a ground-attack version. In 1944 it was based in Hungary and was captured in 1945. It was given to the Smithsonian in 1949 and underwent restoration in 1980, and is now on display at the Udvar-Hazy Center.

The US Air Force Museum in Dayton OH has a "Dora" model that flew with the JG3 unit before being captured and brought to the US for flight testing. It was given to the Smithsonian by the Pentagon, and is now displayed in the Air Force Museum under loan.

In 1997, a German company called FlugWerk began producing modern reproductions of the Fw-190, using Chinese copies of the Russian Shvetsov ASh-82 radial engine.

Republic P-47 Thunderbolt

Unlike the sleek and graceful German and Japanese fighters that it opposed, the "Jug" was big, heavy and ugly. But it was one of the most numerous and effective fighters that the Allies had.

As the Seversky Aircraft Company, Republic had already built the P-35 fighter for the US Army Air Corps, which became the Army's frontline fighter in the years just before World War Two. The all-metal monoplane (the first American fighter with retractable landing gear) had been powered by a huge radial engine, a design preference that continued when the Seversky company was taken over in 1939 by new management in a corporate coup and was renamed Republic Aircraft. So when the Army asked for a new bomber interceptor design with good armor protection and lots of firepower, Republic stuck with what was familiar to them.

It was not merely an aesthetic choice, however. Several fighter planes had already been built with liquid-cooled inline engines, and they had demonstrated teething problems that took some time to work out. Radial engines, on the other hand, had been in use for years: all the kinks had already been removed, and they were dependable, durable, and easy to work with. And the most powerful radial yet had just appeared, the turbo-supercharged 2,500 horsepower R-2800 Double Wasp. The new fighter design was literally planned around this engine and the ductwork needed for its turbo-supercharger.

For maximum efficiency, the engine would require a four-bladed propeller to convert its power into thrust. This, however, meant that the landing gear had to be longer, which in turn would take up space inside the wings that could be used for guns and ammunition. So the P-47 had a telescoping landing gear which extended upon landing and retracted on takeoff.

Early pilots did not like the visibility from the cockpit. The initial production models had a "razorback" with a hump behind the pilot, blocking his ability to see to the rear. This was fixed in the P-47D model by removing the hump and installing a bubble canopy, which gave the pilot good all-around vision.

All this power and reliability came at a cost, however: at five tons even when empty, the P-47 Thunderbolt was massive for a fighter, weighing almost twice as much as its contemporaries. It quickly earned the nickname "Jug"—some say because it looked like a milk bottle lying on its side, while others say it was short for "Juggernaut" for a plane that could not be stopped.

But when the first test flights took place in May 1941, the Thunderbolt was impressive. With a top speed of 430mph, it was faster than almost anything in the sky, and with its eight .50-caliber machine guns it packed enormous firepower. And with its capacious fuel tanks it also had significantly longer range. That would become important, since the mission that the Thunderbolt was given was not the mission it had been designed for: it had been conceived as a bomber interceptor, but what the Allies really needed was a bomber *escort*—one with as much range as possible. This was the job that the P-38 Lightning had been pressed into use for, but it had run into problems and was behind schedule. The P-47 was to be the stopgap. Though even with external fuel tanks they could not follow the B-17s all the way to Germany and back, they could at least escort them partway.

The P-47s flew their first escort mission—a short hop to France—in April 1943. They continued their escorts for the next year or so, accompanying the B-17s as far as they could, then turning back without them.

On the way back, however, those Thunderbolts that still had ammo left would often use it up on railways or airfields or any other tempting target that they found themselves flying over—and it was in these ground-attack strafings that the P-47 really came into its element. With its eight machine guns, the plane could chew up a ground target, while the Thunderbolt's speed made it harder for anti-aircraft fire to hit it, and all that bulk not only protected the pilot but was able to absorb an amazing amount of damage and still keep flying. By the time the P-51 Mustangs had taken over the bomber-escort duties in 1944, the Thunderbolt had become a superb ground attack fighter-bomber, able to strafe with machine guns, drop half a ton of bombs, and fire unguided rockets from racks under the wings.

In all, the US made around 15,500 P-47s between 1941 and 1945. The Thunderbolt was also flown by the British, the Free French, and the USSR, and finished the war with an 8:1 kill ratio. As the war ended, a new version of the Jug was already being planned, which would use two counter-rotating props on the same engine to give as much thrust as it was possible to get from a piston engine.

About 60 wartime Thunderbolts still exist, and are on display around the world. The US Air Force Museum in Dayton OH has two P-47s, both D models; one is a razorback and one is a bubble canopy. Another USAF Museum D model is on loan to the New England Air Museum in Connecticut. The Smithsonian has a D model on exhibit in its Udvar-Hazy Center, while the Planes of Fame Museum in Chino CA has a P-47G model.

North American P-51 Mustang

Widely regarded as the best fighter of the war, the long-range P-51 had a shaky start, but proved to be the key to success in the European strategic bombing campaign.

After the Battle of Britain in 1940, the British needed fighters in a hurry. The RAF had the Spitfire, but there were some production problems and it was feared that they would not be available in large enough numbers. So the English Government contacted the North American Aircraft Company to inquire about obtaining a contract for the factory to build licensed versions of the P-40 Warhawk (at that time the best fighter in the USAAF) for export to the UK. Instead, North American offered to design and produce an entirely new fighter for the British. It was known by the code name NA-73X until the British RAF dubbed it the Mustang.

The prototype was built in less than four months. The Mustang Mark I had twice the range of the Spitfire, and was also faster, at 380mph. The American Allison V-1710 engine, however, had poor performance at high altitude, and the plane also suffered from a slow climb rate. It would not do the job as a bomber escort or interceptor. But the British thought it could do well as a low-altitude fighter and ground-attack aircraft, and the RAF ordered 600 of them. By 1941, fifteen squadrons of British Mustangs were carrying out strafing and bombing attacks on targets in occupied France. The Mustang scored its first air victory while flying with the British during the disastrous raid on the German-held port of Dieppe in August 1942. The Americans, meanwhile, had adopted the P-51 Mustang as well, using 60 of them for low-level photo-reconnaissance and 500 more as A-36 Apache close-support light attack craft, armed with bombs and 20mm cannons. These were fitted with aerial brakes to allow dive-bombing.

After the United States entered the war, a strategy of round-the-clock strategic bombing was mapped out that would systematically destroy German industry. But the industrial centers in Germany were some 600 miles away from the airfields in England, too far for any Allied fighter to go. At first, the Americans believed that their heavily-armed B-17s would be able to defend themselves from Luftwaffe fighters using their own defensive fields of machine-gun fire, but during the initial raids in early 1943, losses were so severe that large-scale daylight bombing raids were suspended, and it became obvious that the Allies needed a new fighter that could fly with the bombers and protect them. The new P-47 Thunderbolt was assigned to bomber-escort duty—it was tough and rugged, but, crucially, its huge engine drank fuel at the rate of two gallons a minute, and even with external fuel tanks the fighter only had enough range to stay with the B-17s about halfway before it had to turn back, leaving the bombers unprotected over the targets. What was desperately needed was a fighter that was as maneuverable and powerful as the Nazi Messerschmitts and Focke-Wulfs, but had enough range to defend the bombers through the entire mission.

So, attention turned back to the P-51 Mustang being produced for the English: it had enough range, it was fast, and it was nimble enough to deal with German fighters. What it did not have was sufficient engine power. It was the British RAF who came up with the answer: by replacing the American-built Allison engines with the more powerful British-made Rolls-Royce Merlin, already in heavy production, the Mustang was transformed from a low-altitude ground-attack plane into the premiere fighter of the war. Both the US and Britain began placing orders for Mustangs, and both countries agreed that the Packard Automobile Company in Ohio would be assigned the task of mass-producing American copies of the Merlin engine for use in the P-51. The first Packard-engined Mustang P-51B rolled off the line in November 1942. It could reach 440mph. While the British versions of the P-51 had been fitted with the standard RAF armament of six .303-caliber machine guns, the American models carried four .50-calibers.

The effort culminated in May 1944 when production began on the P-51D model. It had a new bubble canopy which gave the pilot a better view of his surroundings, and a narrower fuselage which increased the speed. Six .50-caliber machine guns in the wing gave it better firepower, and though it was not as maneuverable as the Spitfire, the P-51D's square-tipped laminar-flow wings allowed it to out-fly anything the Axis could put up against it. And with three internal fuel tanks and two extras under the wings, the Mustang could fly over 2000 miles — enough range to not only reach targets in Germany, but to loiter and fight for a time before running low on fuel.

The P-51D changed the air war. It did this not through any major innovation or technical breakthrough, but instead by distilling all of the best aspects of conventional fighter design and incorporating them into one airframe.

Within a short time, the German Luftwaffe was suffering. The Mustang outclassed both the Me-109 and the Focke-Wulf, and Nazi pilot losses were heavy. By 1944, the Mustangs were facing inexperienced German pilots with little training, and shot them down in droves.

On the way back from escorting a raid, once the bombers had peeled off, the Mustangs were also authorized to use any remaining ammunition on "targets of opportunity" and carried out low-level strafing attacks on German airbases, locomotives, ammo dumps, or road convoys. These proved to be more dangerous than the escort missions: five times as many P-51s were lost to ground fire during strafing than to Luftwaffe fighters during escort missions. But the Mustangs helped to destroy the Nazi logistical system. In the weeks before D-Day, the fighters were unleashed in a wave of ground attacks and sweeps that cut off German reinforcements and supplies. By the time the Allied troops landed in Normandy, the Mustangs and Spitfires had established complete air superiority. P-51s shot down about 5,000 enemy fighters—more than any other Allied fighter.

In the Pacific, the P-51's long-range was particularly useful. A few P-51A models were deployed along with A-36 versions to Burma in 1942 where they saw limited action, and in 1943 P-51s began replacing the P-40s in China. But during the island-hopping campaigns of 1943 and 1944, the P-51s found their role. Mustangs based at Iwo Jima and Okinawa were able to fly escort missions for B-29s over Japan, and also carry out their own raids on Japanese bases and airfields using wing-mounted bombs and rockets.

The final model of the war, the P-51H, was lighter and faster, able to reach 490mph, but the war ended before it could be deployed. Production continued until 1947, and Mustangs saw action during the Korean War as close-support fighter/bombers, often operating from bases in Japan where their longer range allowed them to reach areas that the jet-engined P-80 Shooting Star and P-84 Thunderjet could not. In all, around 15,000 P-51s of various models were produced, with 8,000 of these being the D model. Many Mustangs were sold as "surplus" where they were flown as air racers or as civilian general aviation aircraft.

Because so many P-51s were manufactured during the war, a large number still remain, many of them airworthy. Nearly every major air museum has a Mustang on display, including the Smithsonian, the USAF Museum, Pima Air and Space, and others.

Boeing B-17 Flying Fortress

The iconic bomber of the Second World War, the B-17 flew in every theater, but was most active in the air war over Europe.

By 1933, the US Army Air Force realized that long-range strategic bombing capability would be crucial in any modern war, and the United States, after introducing its revolutionary B-10 design, was falling behind. So a Request for Proposals was issued seeking a new bomber. The Boeing company responded with a large four-engined design known as the XB-15. While the C-105 transport version was adopted in 1937, and the XB-15's wing design was used by Boeing in its huge Pan-Am Clipper flying boats, the bomber never entered production and remained "experimental".

The Navy, meanwhile, was working on a larger version of the Martin B-10, dubbed the B-12. This led to a political conflict, as both the Navy and the Army argued that they should be in charge of developing and deploying long-range strategic bombers.

Nevertheless, in August 1934, the Army issued another request for designs, specifying a bomber with at least twice the payload and range of the old B-10—it had to be capable of carrying 2000 pounds of bombs at 250mph and 10,000 feet altitude over a range of 2000 miles. Douglas Aircraft offered a design based on the twin-engine DC-2 passenger airliner. Boeing's design mated the wings of the XB-15 design to its 247 passenger plane, resulting in the B-17. It was a daring concept: not only were four-engine planes more expensive to build and operate, but they were widely considered to be more difficult to fly. But Boeing responded by scaling down the size of its XB-15/247 airframe while keeping the same engines, thereby increasing the power-to-weight ratio and producing a better-handling design.

The first B-17 prototype flew in July 1935, and was an immediate sensation. On one of its first flights, the new bomber flew 2100 miles nonstop from the Boeing plant in Seattle to Wright airfield in Dayton OH, averaging 238mph—faster than any American fighter of the time. Not only could the B-17 carry 2500 pounds of bombs, but it also bristled with five machine guns to defend against enemy fighters. It quickly became dubbed the "Flying Fortress". But when the B-17 prototype crashed during a test flight, the Army, worried about the delay this might cause, as well as the Flying Fortress's expense, ordered production of the twin-engine Douglas B-18 Bolo bomber instead.

But the Army had liked the Boeing design, and ordered a small number anyway just to keep it available, and as it became more and more apparent that the US and Nazi Germany would inevitably have to face each other, the Air Corps continued to demand a long-range strategic bomber, and the underpowered and already near-obsolescent B-18 was not up to the job. So in January 1939 Congress approved money to begin producing B-17s.

By the time of the Battle of Britain in 1940, the US had manufactured a total of 38 B-17C models and had sent 20 of them to England as Lend-Lease supplies, where they were evaluated by the RAF. Now sporting a supercharged engine, the speed in the C model had climbed to over 320mph and range expanded to 2800 miles. But the bombers were a disappointment. The B-17 was unpressurized and open to the air, and while the crews wore electrically-heated suits, the machine guns got so cold at altitude that they froze and became inoperable. The plane had insufficient firepower to the rear. There were also issues with the in-flight oxygen mask system and the bombsight, and the plane's tail structure was weak.

Some of these problems were corrected with the B-17D model, and then the plane was heavily modified with the B-17E model, known irreverently as the "Big Ass". A tail turret was added, the tail fin was greatly expanded and strengthened, which helped with stability, and the armament increased to nine machine guns and 4,000 pounds of bombs. When the United States entered the war in 1941, production of the E model was ramped up. The F model followed shortly after—it had expanded to 11 machine guns and had better engines and better armor. But these later models paid a price in performance for their added weight.

The first B-17 raid in Europe was in August 1942 when eighteen B-17Es struck the railroad yards in Rouen, in France. There was no fighter opposition. On January 27, 1943, B-17F bombers based in England made their first attack on Germany, bombing the port at Wilhelmshaven. Subsequent missions, however, flown without fighter escort, highlighted problems with the bomber and also with American strategic doctrine. The Americans and the British had been arguing over bombing strategy since the beginning. The British favored high-altitude night-bombing with incendiaries that would burn out and destroy large areas inside each city: the Americans preferred lower-altitude daylight raids with precision-dropped high explosive bombs that would target and cripple specific factories and manufacturing plants.

But although it had been hoped that the heavy armament on the Flying Fortress would allow it to fend off enemy attackers, the B-17 was not up to this task. Flying in daylight without fighter escort, the Flying Fortresses suffered horrendous losses from Luftwaffe fighters. The Messerschmitts took advantage of the relatively weak forward fire of the B-17F by making head-on attacks. In March 1943 the P-47 Thunderbolt fighter became available and was immediately assigned to escort B-17s to Germany, but they did not have sufficient range to accompany the bombers the entire distance, and losses continued to be heavy. The average lifetime of a B-17 was 14 missions.

But by the end of 1943, the B-17G model had been introduced, which contained two additional machine guns in a chin turret, and with more powerful engines that could carry a load of up to 17,000 pounds of bombs. At the same time, the P-51 Mustang arrived in large numbers, and it had the range to escort the bombers all the way to Germany and back. Now, the Americans began bombing the Nazis almost daily. In the "Big Week" in February 1944, the Americans massed over 3,000 B-17s to carry out a systematic attack on Germany's aircraft manufacturing ability, targeting plants in Leipzig, Augsburg, Regensburg, Schweinfurt, and Stuttgart.

In the Pacific, meanwhile, the B-17's were based in Hawaii, the Philippines and Midway, and were heavily used in China and Burma. By the time the US had obtained suitable bomber bases within range of Japan itself, the B-17s were being replaced by the B-29 Superfortress. But the Flying Fortress's long range made it useful for reconnaissance and antisubmarine patrols, and the Navy also operated the aircraft under the designation PB-1W.

In all, some 12,725 B-17s were produced during the war — 8600 of them G models. At its peak, the US was turning out 130 B-17s each week. Today about 100, of various models but mostly B-17G, still survive. Of these, around a dozen are airworthy.

The B-17G "Shoo Shoo Shoo Baby" flew 24 missions with the 91st Bomb Group in 1944. On its last mission, over Poland, the airplane developed engine trouble and was forced to land in neutral Sweden, where the crew and the B-17 were interned for the rest of the war. Somehow the plane made its way to France, where it was found in 1968, brought back to the United States, and restored by the US Air Force Museum, where it is now on display.

Another B-17G, "Aluminum Overcast", was delivered to the Army Air Corps in May 1945 — too late to have flown in the war. She was sold as surplus and used as a cargo hauler before being obtained by the Experimental Aircraft Association in 1983, restored, and placed on display.

Avro Lancaster

The Lancaster would be the frontline heavy bomber of the RAF during World War Two, and would drop, in total, more tons of bombs than the American B-17.

By the late 1930s, England knew that a war with Hitler's Germany was looming. She also knew that the Royal Air Force was not prepared for it: the new and more modern Nazi bombers and fighters outclassed everything the British could put up against them. And so the RAF made desperate attempts to catch up.

In 1936, the UK requested proposals for a new two-engined medium bomber that could deliver 4 tons of bombs to a radius of 1,000 miles. At the Avro company, designer Roy Chadwick took up the challenge, and within a few months had drawn up plans for the Manchester. By mid-1937, the British Air Ministry ordered 200 of the bombers, to be fitted with the still-in-development Rolls-Royce Vulture engines, before a prototype had even been built.

But when the Manchester began entering service in November 1940, it proved to be a disappointment. The Vulture engine was simply not powerful enough, and the Manchester struggled to keep up speed or to gain altitude. The engine was also mechanically unreliable. Once the initial order of 200 had been delivered, the RAF stopped procuring the planes. Other two-engined bombers were rushed into production—the Whitley, the Wellington, the Blenheim—but they were also inadequate. What was needed was a heavy four-engine bomber that could take the fight into Germany.

At Avro, Chadwick recognized that the Manchester's problems came not from his airframe, but from the underpowered Vulture engines. So he redesigned the aircraft, turning it into a heavy bomber with four less-powerful but more reliable Rolls-Royce Merlin engines, mounted onto bigger wings. The Merlin had already been put into service with the Hurricane and Spitfire fighters, had been proven to be dependable, and was already being produced in large numbers. Many would dub it the best aircraft engine of the war.

And so, with more fuel tanks added to increase the range, the Manchester airframe became transformed into the Lancaster heavy bomber. The first prototype flew in January 1941, and a second test model appeared in May, using the most powerful Merlin XX engine available. The second prototype also altered the original triple-tailfin design to a twin tailfin, to allow for a better field of fire for the turret guns. The Air Ministry immediately began placing orders—1,000 planes in October, and more to follow. Avro couldn't keep up, and licensed Lancaster Model B Is were soon being produced by other British companies. At one point there was a shortage of Merlin engines: to keep up continuous production of both fighters and bombers, a new Lancaster B II model was introduced as a stopgap, using the Bristol Hercules engine instead. Only 300 of these were made. Another version was produced by the Victory Aircraft Company in Canada, using American-built Merlin engines from the

Packard automobile manufacturer, and the British began producing Model B III "Lancs" which also used American-built Merlin engines.

The Lanc had a crew of seven. The pilot flew the plane, and the flight engineer sitting next to him monitored the mechanical systems and controlled the fuel tanks (he was not a co-pilot—he had no flight controls). Behind them, the navigator kept the plane on course, and further back was the wireless radio operator who maintained communications. In the nose, the bomb-aimer took control of the aircraft once over the target and dropped the bombs; he also manned the forward-facing machine guns. And there were two additional gunners, one in the upper turret and one in the tail turret (with four guns), to defend against enemy fighters. In all, the Lancaster had 8 .303-caliber machine guns. Early designs had a gun turret in the belly, but this was later removed.

Air Marshall Sir Arthur Harris, who had been appointed in early 1942 to head the RAF's Bomber Command, immediately recognized the potential of the big bomber. The Lancaster could deliver a huge bomb load, and it could do it over long distances. After the Battle of Britain and the Blitz, it would become the weapon that England would use to carry the war into Germany's heartland. "Bomber" Harris began to plan a relentless air campaign that would, he hoped, bring the Nazis to their knees.

A controversy quickly broke out with the Americans, however, on the best tactics to use. The Americans wanted to wage a bombing campaign that would specifically target key areas of German industry and hit them with "precision strikes". That would require bombing from relatively low altitudes during day, since even the best bombsights of the time were barely able to give any accuracy. The RAF, however, had already tried precise daylight raids early in the war, and had suffered heavy losses from Luftwaffe fighters. So Harris argued that the Allies should launch "area strikes" that would saturate entire German cities with bombs, which would fly at night and at high altitude to escape the Nazi defenses. In the end, there was no agreement, and each side began to plan and carry out the type of raids that it wanted to do. The B-17s and B-24s went in during the day, and the Lancasters and Halifaxes went in at night. Germany would be bombed round the clock.

Although it had over 50,000 separate parts, the Lancaster had been designed to be constructed in five sections which could then be fitted together, making it easier to mass-produce. British factories were soon churning them out at the rate of five a day. But losses were heavy too: by the end of the war, over half of the 7,377 Lancasters that had been built were lost to enemy fire or to accidents. The average lifetime of a bomber crew was seven and a half missions.

Bomber Harris's night-bombing campaign went into action in 1943. A series of electronic navigation systems were introduced and continuously improved to help the bombers reach their targets. Particular airplanes were fitted with radar sets and radio direction finders and their crews trained as "Pathfinders". Their job was to go in first and drop their bombs as accurately as they could: the rest of the bombers behind them would then drop their own loads onto that marked aiming point. One by one, German industrial cities were targeted and destroyed.

Other crews were trained for their own special missions. The Lancaster could carry the biggest payload of any Allied bomber, an advantage that was often useful. The 11-ton "Grand Slam" bomb was designed to take out hardened targets like submarine pens, while specially-built "skip bombs" were used to destroy the hydroelectric dams in the Ruhr Valley. In all, Lancasters flew 156,000 wartime sorties and delivered 608,000 tons of high-explosive bombs and 51 million incendiary bomblets.

After the war ended, the Lanc continued as a long-range anti-submarine patrol and as a photo reconnaissance platform. The airframe was also modified into the Lancastrian, a civilian trans-Atlantic passenger plane. In March 1946, a Lancastrian became the first aircraft to fly out of London's new Heathrow Airport.

Today, there are about 17 surviving Lancaster bombers, two of them in flying condition. Most are on display in the UK, with several in Canada, including "Bazalgette" at the Bomber Command Museum of Canada in Nanton, Alberta, and a post-war version on exhibit at the National Air Force Museum of Canada in Trenton, Ontario.

Consolidated B-24 Liberator

Over 19,000 B-24 Liberator bombers were manufactured by the US during the Second World War, making it the most widely-produced American aircraft of the period.

In 1938, in response to the deteriorating political conditions in Europe and the Pacific, the US decided to ramp up production of its B-17 bomber. As part of this effort, the Army Air Force contacted the Consolidated Aircraft Corporation to ask them to produce Flying Fortresses under a license from Boeing. But Consolidated did not want to manufacture a design which was then already four years old (and it especially did not want to license a design that had been made by another company). So instead, Consolidated offered to design and make a new heavy bomber to the Army's specifications.

The project was given the working name Model 31. It would be a long-range four-engine heavy bomber with a longer range, faster speed, and heavier bomb load than the B-17. Much of the design, including the high-aspect-ratio wings and the distinctive tail, was based on the company's earlier Model 31 flying-boat seaplane. The fuselage was drawn up with two bomb bays. The first prototype flew in December 1939.

The US immediately ordered a number of the new B-24A bombers for the Army and additional YB-24 patrol bombers for the Navy. But with the war in Europe already raging, the first production runs were for the LB-30 export model. Orders came in from France for 120 bombers and Britain for 160. Many of these were used for coastal and anti-submarine patrols, and one of them was modified to serve as Winston Churchill's personal transport aircraft. When France surrendered to Germany in May 1940, its LB-30s had not yet been delivered, and they were subsequently diverted to England. The US Army Air Corps received its first operational B-24D models in May 1942.

Improvements quickly followed. The original production B-24A used Pratt & Whitney R-1830-33 Twin Wasp engines, which were then upgraded with a supercharger. These were themselves soon replaced by the new turbo-supercharged 14-cylinder R-1830-41, which gave a top speed of 310 mph. Throughout the war the Liberator was constantly modified, with each new model introducing a change in armament or configuration. Gun blisters were added to the sides of the fuselage, and ball turrets to the belly and chin. The number of guns grew from six to eleven, and the bomb load expanded from 8,800 pounds to 10,800 (using external bomb racks). The unique bomb bay doors rolled up into the fuselage, preventing the drag that resulted from open "barn doors". Some ground-attack versions were fitted with four 20mm cannon in the nose.

As the war progressed, older models were sent back to the factory to be refitted and upgraded. At some points in time the factories were unable to keep up with all the changes and bombers were already obsolete as they were produced, and ended up being sent directly from the assembly line to be upgraded.

Unarmed versions were used as C-87 cargo aircraft and as C-109 fuel tankers, and cameras were fitted for reconnaissance flights. Naval patrol versions, designated PB4Y and used for anti-submarine work, were equipped to carry depth charges and, towards the end of the war, were modified to carry an experimental radar-guided anti-ship missile known as the "Bat".

To keep up with the heavy demand, Consolidated produced new B-24s at both of its aircraft plants, and also licensed their production to other plants run by Douglas Aircraft, North American Aircraft, and the Ford Motor Company. By the spring of 1944, the Ford plant alone was churning out a finished B-24 every 100 minutes, running 24 hours every day. In all, a total of 19,200 Liberators of various models were produced.

The B-24 saw service in virtually every theater. In Europe, although it was faster than the B-17 it could not reach as high an altitude, and it often flew in below the Flying Fortresses. One notable raid carried out by the B-24s was on the Ploesti oilfields in Rumania. In the Pacific, the B-24's high speed and long range were an advantage, and as the B-17s were diverted to Europe, the B-24 became the principal heavy bomber used by the Allies against Japanese-held islands. In all, B-24 bombers dropped a total of 630,000 tons of bombs in all theaters.

But many aircrews did not like the Liberator. It was not as rugged as the B-17 and could not withstand as much battle damage. It was also not an easy plane to fly, and many were lost in crashes and training accidents. The gas tanks had a tendency to leak, sometimes producing mid-air explosions.

After the war, a number of B-24s remained in service with the Coast Guard as patrol aircraft. The Indian Air Force also inherited a number of B-24s from the British, which continued to fly for a number of years (a number of them flew in the Berlin Airlift in 1948).

Today, around a dozen WW2 B-24 Liberators still survive, in museums in the US, UK, Canada, Australia, and India. Many of these are from the group of 36 that was abandoned in India at the end of the war and restored by the IAF. One of these is on display at the Pima Air and Space Museum in Arizona, where it was obtained from the Poona Air Force Base. This B-24J was manufactured in Ft Worth TX and sent to the RAF's Southeast Asia Command. The US Air Force Museum in Dayton OH has a B-24D that was built in San Diego and flew 56 missions in Italy from 1943 to 1944. After the war it was returned to the US and placed in storage. The Museum acquired it in 1959. There are two airworthy examples surviving, in Massachusetts and Texas, which often travel to air shows.

North American B-25 Mitchell

The B-25 medium bomber is most famous for its part in the Doolittle raid over Tokyo. But it was an extremely versatile aircraft that carried out multiple roles in every theater of the war, for the US Army, Navy and Marines as well as for the British and Soviet air forces.

As it became more and more apparent in the late 1930s that the world was heading towards war and the US was not equipped to face it, the United States Army Air Corps was in the midst of a frantic expansion. In virtually every aspect of modern war, America was far behind its potential enemies.

When the Army issued a request in March 1939 for new medium bomber designs, it wanted a capability to deliver 2400 pounds of bombs over 1200 miles at an average speed of at least 300mph, one of the companies that submitted a proposal was North American Aviation. North American had submitted proposals in previous years and none had ever been selected, but now they learned from those earlier designs and pushed them ahead.

The new design was labeled "NA-62". It called for a twin-engine bomber powered by the Wright R-2600-9 radial engine, with two vertical tail fins, powered gun turrets with five machine guns, and a bomb load of 3600 pounds. The Martin aircraft company, meanwhile, had submitted a proposal of their own with similar capabilities. The Air Corps liked them both, and ordered both into production. The Martin bomber became the B-26 Marauder, and North American's bid became the B-25 Mitchell.

North American hurriedly built a new factory in Kansas City KS, and installed another B-25 production line in its main plant in Inglewood CA. By 1942, several changes had been made to improve the bomber, and the new B-25B model began rolling off the assembly lines. Modifications continued to be added throughout the war, and at one point North American was making different models at each of its assembly lines. By the time the final B-25J model appeared, the engines had become more powerful, there were more machine guns for defense, and the bomb load had gotten bigger. There were also photoreconnaissance, transport, and weather monitoring versions, and a specialized fire-support "gunship" variant that packed up to 14 .50-caliber machine guns into the nose and turrets for strafing ground targets, while another alternative mounted a huge 75mm cannon for use against bunkers or small ships. The Navy had its own model called the PBJ for anti-submarine duty and coastal patrol, which carried torpedoes or depth charges. Export versions were also sent to England, Canada, China and Holland, and a few were sent to the Soviet Union. In all, about 10,000 B-25s were manufactured, and they continued in use until the early 1950s.

Each bomber carried a crew of six. The pilot and co-pilot sat in the cockpit, with the bombardier (who doubled as the navigator) below them in the Plexiglas nose turret. The engineer sat behind the cockpit, and manned the upper gun turret when necessary, likewise, the radio operator also doubled as the waist gunner. And the tail gunner sat in the back by himself.

The Mitchells served in every theater of the war, but most were assigned to the Pacific, where their ability to use short runways was helpful on small airfields, and their range gave them enough reach to deliver bomb loads to Japanese-occupied islands. By the end of the war, B-25s based on Okinawa were flying missions against targets in Japan. The bomber had originally been designed with the intention that its defensive turrets would provide enough firepower to defend it against enemy fighters, but hard experience soon shattered that illusion, and the bombers were usually escorted by friendly fighters.

The most famous of the B-25's missions came in April 1942, when 16 B-25s, stripped of unnecessary equipment, took off from the US carrier *Hornet* and attacked Japan, dropping bombs on Tokyo. The actual damage was only slight, but the psychological impact was enormous: it gave a much-needed boost to American morale, and also scared the Japanese and led them into a final effort to lure out and destroy the American aircraft carriers—which ultimately led to the decisive Battle of Midway.

After the war, many B-25s were converted to civilian use as transports, cargo planes, or firefighters. Because of this, around 100 WW2-era Mitchells still survive, many of them in flyable condition.

Messerschmitt Me-262 Schwalbe

The world's first operational jet fighter, the German Me-262 was a technological breakthrough, but it came too late to affect the outcome of the war.

By the time the Second World War began, British engineer Frank Whittle had already been thinking about jet engines for almost ten years. What he lacked was money, and in the 1930s nobody was really interested in the concept. But when the war broke out in 1939, Whittle approached the British Government and told them about his idea for a turbine jet engine, which could be capable of driving an aircraft at speeds far higher than anything a conventional piston engine could do. The Air Ministry agreed to fund the experiments.

Whittle and the British Government were unaware that the Germans were also experimenting with jet engines, particularly at the Heinkel and Messerschmitt aircraft companies. By 1938, Heinkel was working on the prototype for the He-178, a turbojet-powered single-engine fighter. It made its first flight in August 1939. The Nazi regime, however, rejected Heinkel's proposal: it was decided that developing the technology into a practical frontline fighter would take several years, and since Germany seemed to be already winning its wars with conventional aircraft, there did not seem to be any good reason to focus resources on the jet. Heinkel's project was put on the back burner, and although Messerchmitt had not produced a working prototype yet, his work was put on hold as well.

In England, Whittle had a working jet engine by April 1941 and made his first test flight in May in an airframe produced for him by the Gloster company, called the E-28. One of the people who heard about the successful flight was US Army Air Corps Major General Hap Arnold, who immediately asked the British for details. In turn, the RAF sent one of Whittle's engines to a General Electric plant in the United States, and in October 1942, the US made their first successful flight with the experimental P-59 Airacomet twin-engined jet fighter, using improved versions of Whittle's basic design. Gloster meanwhile encountered a series of issues and did not get into the air with their first jet fighter, the Meteor, until 1944.

The Germans were having their own difficulties. Both Heinkel and Messerschmitt had continued their work on jets, using their own funding and resources. Heinkel tested another airplane, the twin-engined He-280, in March 1941, reaching over 500mph. Messerschmitt continued to work on the experimental Me-262, making a test flight of the airframe in April 1941 using a conventional piston engine because his jets were not yet reliable enough. But Messerschmitt was already delving into areas that were far in advance of everyone else, such as using swept wings for aerodynamic efficiency at high speeds. Finally, in July 1942, he was able to get a test version of his Me-262 in the air under jet power. It reached a speed of 450mph. After some adjusting, this swelled to 550mph.

And now a conflict broke out between Messerschmitt and the Nazi hierarchy. Messerschmitt had intended the jet to be used as a fighter, able to climb rapidly to high altitude, destroy British Lancasters and American B-17s with its four 30mm cannons (or with wing-mounted air-to-air missiles that were then under development), then use its blazing speed to escape escorting fighters. Hitler, however, wanted to turn the jet into a "wonder weapon", a superfast bomber that could wreak havoc on Allied cities, and ordered that one-third of all the jets produced be bomber versions. It wasted precious resources that Germany could not spare.

But although Germany, England and the United States all now had flyable jet fighter designs, each would find that getting them into practical frontline service was not easy. The United States, like Germany before it, decided that its priority was winning the war, and jet aircraft were viewed as a long-range project and given a low priority. In the UK, the Meteor was deployed in 1944 but was plagued by technical issues and never saw combat over Germany.

The first Me-262s began to enter service in April 1944. But German efforts continued to be hampered by the circumstances caused by losing the war. There were shortages of critical materials which delayed production. There were also shortages of pilots to fly them: at first, the jet had been reserved only for the most experienced pilots, high-scoring aces who had flown hundreds of missions in Europe or Russia. But soon Germany was drafting young recruits and putting them into cockpits with a bare minimum of training. Over 200 of these were killed in training accidents. The jets themselves were delicate, and even if they did not break down they required a lot of routine maintenance just to keep them flying. Each engine had to be replaced and refurbished after around 20 hours of flight.

By the end of the war, the Germans had managed to complete assembly of almost 1500 Me-262 jets. Another 500 had been destroyed in air raids, and Germany's transport network was so badly shot up that only 300 fighters ever actually reached their airfields. The airfields themselves were under constant attack, and the jets were soon forced to shelter inside railroad tunnels and under highway bridges. Despite its technological superiority, the Me-262 was not numerous enough to make any difference in the war: one or two dozen jet fighters were often sent against formations of over 1,000 bombers. Even this "wonder weapon" was not enough to stave off Nazi Germany's defeat.

At the end of the war, the Me-262 was the target of intelligence services from the US, UK, and USSR, all of whom wanted to use its technological advances in their own jet fighters. Dozens of planes, crates full of parts, and captured technicians and designers were all sent to the United States for testing and evaluation. Today, one of these, originally flown by the Luftwaffe's JG7 squadron, is on display at the Smithsonian's Air and Space Museum. The US Air Force Museum in Dayton's Me-262 was brought to the US in July 1945, while the Messerschmitt on exhibit in the Naval Aviation Museum in Pensacola FL is a two-seat training version.

Bell P-59 Airacomet

Although America's first jet fighter began its life near the beginning of the war, a series of difficulties prevented it from seeing combat.

The American jet fighter program is a direct outgrowth of the British efforts led by Frank Whittle. Until Whittle's W.1 turbojet engine made its first successful flight in May 1941, virtually no work had been done in the US on jet engines. So when Army Air Corps Major General Hap Arnold was invited by the British to observe the flight, he was stunned.

The US had not yet entered the war, but was already deeply committed to England as an ally and was providing aid in the form of Lend-Lease, so the British felt comfortable in sharing the super-secret discovery with the Americans. Copies of both the engine and the design drawings were dispatched to the US onboard a B-24 and, under the strictest secrecy, the General Electric Company was assigned to produce their own version of the Whittle engine (known as the I-A) under the codename of "Type I Supercharger", and Bell Aircraft was given the task of producing an airframe to be used as a testbed for it. (Bell was selected mostly because its P-39 fighter was no longer in production, so the company did not have the previous commitment of resources that the other aircraft manufacturers had.) The result was the Bell P-59 Airacomet program. The airframe was a hastily-upgraded version of a previous design for a twin-engined prop fighter: Bell enlarged the airframe, strengthened it, and moved the engines to the wing roots, running alongside the fuselage. It was given the codename "Model 27".

The first flight tests with Whittle's design, in October 1942, did not meet expectations. So GE went back to the lab and made some modifications that increased the thrust of the I-A engine by 15% to 1250 pounds. This new version was called the I-16, and was eventually designated the J-33. But when the J-33 was flight-tested in the summer of 1943, it was still not meeting its planned specs.

The National Advisory Committee on Aeronautics (one of the forerunners of what would decades later become NASA) had already set up a committee to study possible new technologies in aircraft propulsion, and had begun construction of a lab next to the Cleveland Municipal Airport to be called the Aircraft Engine Research Laboratory (AERL). For reasons of military secrecy, NACA had not been told about the Whittle jet engine, but now the Army Air Corps decided that it needed their help, and in July 1943 a selected team of NACA researchers were briefed about the top-secret device and provided with engineering drawings. It was decided that the AERL would be dedicated solely to jet experiments as soon as it was completed, and in September the newly-finished lab was given the established cover name of the "Supercharger Building" to disguise the true nature of its secret research.

Testing of the I-A and J-33 engines began immediately: there were test runs over a wide range of temperatures and air pressures to simulate different altitudes, and tinkering produced some changes in the design that resulted in gains in thrust. Within a few months, GE had produced the I-40 engine. When the lab's fullsize wind tunnel began operations in January 1944, Bell engineers began experiments on models of the P-59 to test various shapes and configurations.

The US Navy, meanwhile, was also interested in jet engines, but was far more cautious than the Army due to the stringent requirements for taking off and landing from carriers. So in 1943 the Navy tasked the Ryan Aircraft Company to design an airplane that could utilize both a standard piston-propeller engine and a turbojet. This resulted in the XFR-1, an experimental plane that was able to take off and land from a carrier using a Wright R-1820 radial engine in the nose, but which could also switch in flight to an I-16 jet engine in the tail when it needed a burst of speed. The Navy hoped to get a carrier-based interceptor that would be fast enough to catch Japanese *Kamikaze* planes before they could reach their targets.

Test flights of the "Ryan Fireball" began in June 1944. The first three prototypes were all lost in crashes, which were determined to have been cause by wing rivets that were too weak to withstand the stress. These were doubled in strength, and the Navy officially ordered 700 FR-1 Fireball fighters, to be delivered beginning in March 1945. As it turned out, only 66 had been sent to the Navy before the war ended in August, and none of those were ever deployed.

The Army, meanwhile, was flying nine test versions of the P-59. The original designs were now designated P-59A, and the newer versions, with engines of 2000 pounds thrust, were P-59B. Most of the test flights were carried out at the remote Muroc dry lakebed in Death Valley. Whenever the planes were near people, they wore fake propellers on their nose to disguise them.

While GE had at last gotten the jet engines working up to specs, the rather simple airframe, combined with the low thrust-to-weight ratio of the engines, led to aerodynamic problems, and the P-59 had trouble reaching 400mph, a speed that piston-engined fighters like the P-47 were already routinely exceeding. As a result, plans to equip the P-59 with 20mm cannons and put it into production were shelved, and it became treated as simply an engine testbed. By the time the war ended in August 1945, Bell had produced 66 of the experimental aircraft in total. One of these was traded to the UK for a Gloster Meteor fighter, but after flying it a few times the British realized that it was far inferior to the Gloster and sent it back to the US.

Six P-59 Airacomets are on display. One of these is a P-59A in the Smithsonian Air and Space Museum, and the US Air Force

Museum exhibits a P-59B. There is also a P-59B at the Planes of Fame Museum in Chino CA.

Messerschmitt Me-163 Komet

The liquid rocket-powered Me-163 was the last gasp of the defeated Luftwaffe in its efforts to stop the Allied air forces from devastating German cities.

The Treaty of Versailles which ended the First World War banned Germany from developing propeller-driven warplanes, but it did not mention rockets. As a result, Germany invested heavily in rocket engines, ultimately leading to the V-2 "vengeance weapon" which indiscriminately blasted London.

But while Wernher von Braun and his ballistic missile crew were the most famous of Nazi Germany's rocket researchers, he was not the only one. In 1936, the Reich Air Ministry began supporting the work of Hellmuth Walter, who was working on a liquid-fueled rocket engine that, it was hoped, might find a use as a potential aircraft powerplant. Walter's engine contained two fuel tanks, one holding *T-Stoff* (80% hydrogen peroxide) and the other filled with *Z-Stoff* (calcium permanganate in water). When the two were mixed in a combustion chamber, they ignited and burned furiously, ejecting a stream of superheated gases from the rocket nozzle.

To provide a testbed flying vehicle for a possible aerial engine, the German Research Institute for Gliding Flight, known by the German initials DFS, was to produce working models of a design that had been put forward by glider engineer Alexander Lippisch. The tiny little airplane, designated Project X, was a tailless single-seat plane with swept wings. Initial versions would be powered by a conventional propeller engine to test the aerodynamics: later versions would, it was hoped, be powered by a derivative of Walter's rocket engine. DFS would produce the plane's wings and engineers at the Heinkel company would produce the body. The whole project would be under Lippisch's direction.

When DFS submitted its proposal for the wings, however, disagreement arose. DFS was planning to control the plane solely with moveable fins at the wingtips; Lippisch thought this would cause too much instability, and wanted a central fin containing a standard rudder instead. It provoked much argument, and in the end Lippisch, with the permission of the Reich Air Ministry, left DFS and moved to the Messerschmitt company, taking his Project X with him. Here he produced a design he liked, with a large central stabilizing fin and rudder, which received the designation Messerschmitt Me-163. It was January 1939.

When the initial test airframe arrived from DFS in 1940, it was fitted with an early version of the Walter rocket engine designated RI-203, and launched in a series of test flights. These proved to be successful, with the rocket plane reaching a speed of 342mph. Encouraged, Lippisch assembled another airframe for the Me-163 and tested it with a propeller engine, then sent it to the rocket research center at Peenemunde to be fitted out with a more powerful Walter RII-203 rocket motor. Some of the tests exploded on launch, but one flight reached 620mph. Once again, Lippisch made modifications to his aircraft and planned for an even bigger rocket motor.

By the autumn of 1942, Walter was using a new fuel mixture that provided more thrust. Now, he was mixing his hydrogen peroxide *T-Stoff* with *C-Stoff*, a solution of methyl alcohol and hydrazine hydrate. He had also found a way to ignite the oxygen that was escaping from the rocket nozzle, increasing the thrust.

It made the manned testflights even more dangerous. Not only would the fuels explode if even the tiniest amounts were mixed together, but the fuel was highly caustic and would dissolve exposed flesh. Ground technicians and pilots had to wear full rubber anti-contamination equipment.

The test flights were limited by the tiny amount of fuel that the rocket plane could carry. The Me-163 would take off from a ramp using a wooden dolly with wheels which were jettisoned once the plane was airborne. The rocket motor would burn for only eight minutes, but it was enough to push the little plane to an altitude of 25-30,000 feet and make a brief powered horizontal flight before running out of fuel. From there, the Messerschmitt would fly using only its momentum, until gravity inevitably began pulling it down. The pilot would then extend a wooden skid from the belly and glide down to a landing.

There were numerous difficulties. The engines would occasionally develop bubbles in the fuel and explode. If the landing dive was too steep, the controls would lock up, leading to a fatal crash. The landing skid sometimes did not extend, and even when it worked properly the pilot had to make an unpowered landing at high speed, and he only had one chance. If he tipped the plane over upon landing, the fuel residues could mix and cause an explosion or fire, or the pilot could be burned by the corrosive fuel spraying out all over him.

So far, this was all in the realm of basic research and testing. But by 1944, with massive Allied air raids laying waste to one German city after another, the Nazis were desperate for some way to stop them, and they settled on the Me-163. The little plane would be packed with two 30mm cannons and ammo to enable it to shoot down enemy bombers during its brief flight. Pilots were recruited and trained, and in May 1944 the I/JG400 fighter group was organized, with a complement of Me-163s. In all, the Nazis managed to produce just 279 rocket-fighters, deploying only a few dozen in three groups before the end of the war.

Despite the great dangers involved, the rocket fighters barely had any effect. Only nine bombers were attributed to the little Messerschmitt's cannons, and in exchange they lost fourteen of their own planes, most due to crashes and accidents. A larger version, with tricycle landing gear and a powered flight time of twelve minutes, perhaps armed with air-to-air rockets, was already in the works, but would not reach production before the war ended.

The Japanese, meanwhile, purchased licensing rights from Messerschmitt and were planning their own version of the Me-163, designated as the Mitsubishi Ki-200 (*Shusui*, after the sound of a swishing samurai sword). Their first test model crashed in July 1945, and the Japanese were not able to produce any combat-ready versions before they too surrendered unconditionally to the Allies.

When the Allies reached Husum, the operational base of the JG400, they captured 48 intact Me-163s. Half of those were shipped to the UK for examination, and one was test-flown by being dropped, unpowered, from a bomber. Today around ten of those Messerschmitts still survive and are on display in various museums in England, Canada, Australia. Five of them were sent to the US, where two of them are now on display, and one is in private hands.

The Me-163 displayed at the US Air Force Museum is interesting because there are indications it may have been sabotaged by some of the French forced-laborers who worked in the plant where it was assembled. On the inside of the aircraft's skin somebody has written, in French, *"Manufacture ferme"* ("Factory closed") and *"Mon coeur est en chomage"* ("My heart is unemployed"). There is also a contaminant in the glue holding the wings together, and a pebble forced between one of the fuel tanks and a holding strap, which may have been able to puncture the tank in flight and cause a fatal fuel leak.

Kawanishi N1K2-J Shiden Kai

The Shiden Kai (known to the Allies by the codename "George") was a marked improvement over the Japanese Zero, but came too late in the war to have any effect.

In December 1941, the Japanese looked unbeatable. The US Navy in Hawaii had been crippled, and Imperial Army troops were swarming across the Pacific. To the Kawanishi company in Japan, it looked like the military advance might soon outrun the ability of the Japanese to construct new airfields to keep up, and it seemed likely that there would be a need for fighter aircraft that could operate from water, without any landing strips.

The Imperial Navy already had a floatplane version of its famed Zero fighter, known as the Rufe, but Kawanishi, who specialized in seaplanes and flying boats, thought they could do better. The design they came up with was based on the Mitsubishi MK4C Kasei 13 engine, driving an 11-foot four-bladed propeller. It would be faster than the Rufe, and, equipped with the company's new automatic flap system, it would be more maneuverable as well. Large floats would allow it to take off and land in water. And with two machine guns and two 20mm cannons, it would carry the same armament as the Zero. It was designated the N1K1.

But only six months later, as production of the new floatplane was just beginning to come together, the situation was entirely different. Japan was in retreat, and there was no need for forward-based floatplanes that could operate without airfields: instead, Japan needed fighters that could effectively defend its existing bases.

Kawanishi now thought that their seaplane could still provide a solution. With the floats removed, the N1K1 would still be a formidable fighter and an improvement over the Zero. The modification was pretty simple, although the large propeller blades presented a difficulty: they required long landing gear to hold the prop off the ground, and this would make the gear too weak for rough carrier landings. Kawanishi's solution was to make telescoping landing gear. They also upgraded the engine to use the Nakajima NK9A Homare 11. The resulting fighter was designated the N1K1-J (the "J" indicating that it was a modified seaplane) and named the *Shiden* ("Purple Lightning").

But when the first prototypes flew in December 1942, there were problems with the engine and with the landing gear, and within a week Kawanishi decided to make major modifications. The two machine guns were replaced with two additional 20mm cannons, making four in all—enough firepower to bring down a B-29. The wings were lowered from mid-body to the bottom of the fuselage, which allowed for shorter and sturdier landing gear. The engine was also upgraded yet again to the more reliable 18-cylinder Nakajima Homare NK9H model with 2,000 horsepower, and the overall weight was decreased by about 500 pounds, producing speeds up to 370mph. The new version was designated N1K2-J, and became known as the *Shiden Kai* ("Purple Lightning—Improved"). After it was deployed in May 1944, the Allies gave both of the N1K type fighters the codename "George".

The *Shiden Kai* was a formidable fighter. It was as fast as a Mustang or Hellcat, more maneuverable, and packed heavy firepower. For the first time since 1942, Japanese pilots had an aircraft that could take on the Americans on equal terms, and in the hands of a trained and experienced pilot, it was lethal. But by this time in the war, Japan had very few experienced pilots left: they had been steadily worn away by years of war. Unlike the Americans, who had their flyers serve a fixed tour of duty and then sent them home to help train new pilots, the Japanese kept flying until they were wounded, captured or killed. So although the George was a superb fighter plane, there were no longer enough suitable pilots to fly them.

Nor were there ever planes in sufficient numbers. By this time, the Japanese merchant fleet had been destroyed by American submarines, and Japanese industry was at a virtual standstill because of raw materials shortages and constant B-29 raids. In the end, then, the George was simply a case of too little, too late. Less than 1500 were produced, and most of these were the inferior Model N1K1-J *Shiden*. Only 400 *Shiden Kais* were made, and most of them never got to the frontlines.

Only four *Shiden Kai* fighters survive today. One is on display at Miho Park in Tokyo. After the war, the US sent four captured Georges to the US for flight testing: three of these are now on display. One is at the US Naval Aviation Museum in Pensacola FL, another is at the Smithsonian's Udvar-Hazy Center, and the third is at the US Air Force Museum in Dayton.

Yokosuka MXY7 Ohka

The Ohka human-guided bomb was a last desperate effort by the Japanese to stave off defeat.

By 1944, it was becoming clear to the military leaders of Japan that the war was lost, unless there was a miracle. So, they decided to create a miracle—or, more accurately, to *re*-create one. In the 13th century, Mongol invasions of Japan were thwarted when a fierce typhoon struck and destroyed the Mongol fleet. In late 1944, the Japanese military turned to suicide air attacks to help beat back the US forces that were approaching Japan. The result was the *Kamikaze* ("Divine Wind") forces. And the pinnacle of the *Kamikaze* forces was the MXY-7 "Ohka" piloted bomb, the only plane in the world that was deliberately designed to kill its pilot.

The Samurai spirit that was inculcated into the Japanese military emphasized that death in battle in the service of the Emperor was the highest honor. As a result, suicide attacks were common on the Pacific battlefields. On land, waves of Japanese troops would make "*banzai* charges", only to be mowed down by US machine guns. The first air suicide attack happened on the very first day of the war, at Pearl Harbor, when Lt Fusata Iita's Zero fighter was hit in the fuel line. Unable to return to his carrier, Iita intentionally crash-dived his Zero into the American hangar at Kaneohe Field.

By 1944, however, Japan's naval and air forces had been largely destroyed, making large-scale conventional attacks on US fleets impossible. In response, Japanese officers asked air crews in the Philippines to volunteer to intentionally crash-dive their planes into the American carriers. The "special attacks" began in October 1944 during the battle for Leyte Gulf. Forty American ships were hit by *Kamikazes*, sinking 5 and heavily damaging 23. By 1945, *Kamikaze* attacks were being made by Japanese squadrons all over the Pacific. (The Americans had all sorts of stories about how the *Kamikaze* pilots had been chained inside their airplanes, or how they had been taught how to take off but not how to land—the reality was that all of the *Kamikaze* pilots were regular pilots who volunteered for "special attacks".)

The idea for a purpose-built suicide plane came from Ensign Mitsuo Ohta, a transport pilot, who submitted rough plans for a rocket-engine piloted bomb with a 2,000-pound warhead. The Japanese Navy tested ten different models, all of which were unsuitable, before settling on a feasible design. The Navy Technical Arsenal (Kushigo) drew up blueprints for the craft and began production by the end of February 1945. Called the MXY-7 Model 11 "*Ohka*" ("Cherry Blossom"), it was 20 feet long with a wingspan of almost 17 feet, and carried a 1200 kg (2646 lb) warhead in the nose section. It was powered by three solid-fuel rocket engines, which drove it at a top speed of 500 mph in level flight, or almost 650 mph in a dive. Basic flight controls allowed the pilot to steer the craft, and a crude metal gunsight at the front of the cockpit allowed him to aim at a ship. About 750 Model 11 *Ohkas* were built. The *Ohka* pilots were named the "Thunder Gods". The Americans took to calling it the "*Baka*" bomb—the Japanese word for "idiot".

The *Ohka's* rocket engines only burned for a little over one minute, giving it a range of less than 25 miles. In combat, the *Ohka* had to be carried close to the US fleet by a "mother ship", the twin-engine "Betty" bomber, then released to fly to its target. This turned out to be the Ohka's most crippling defect. The Betty bomber itself was very vulnerable to American fighters, and most *Ohkas* were shot down along with their mother ship before they could even be released. Sometimes the threatened Betty crews would release the *Ohka* too soon, and the suicide pilot would crash ineffectually into the sea short of his target.

The most heavy use of the *Ohka* came during the Okinawa campaign in April 1945. The Japanese launched almost 1500 *Kamikaze* planes against the US/British fleet at Okinawa, and sank or heavily damaged about 30 ships. *Ohka* piloted bombs struck the US destroyers *Abele, Stanly, Hadley, Jeffers,* and *Gayety,* and the minesweeper *Shea.* The *Abele* was sunk, and the *Hadley* damaged beyond repair.

To correct the problem of limited range, engineers at Kushigo developed a more powerful set of engines. Instead of using solid rocket motors, the new Model 22 *Ohka* would use an Ishikawajima Tsu-11 "thermojet" engine, in which a four-cylinder conventional piston engine was used to drive a compressor, and the compressed air, along with injected fuel, was driven into the combustion chamber and ignited. Distinctive air intakes were added to the rear sides of the Model 22 *Ohka.* The new engine gave the Model 22 a much greater range, but because the engine itself was bigger, it reduced the size of the warhead that the *Ohka* could carry, from 1200 kg to just 600 kg (1320 lb). The new *Ohkas* could be carried aloft by twin-engine "Frances" bombers, or launched from ramps in concealed caves. The Japanese planned to produce hundreds of the Model 22 *Ohkas* and deploy them at the coasts to attack the US invasion fleet, but the war ended before production could begin. Only 3 functional Tsu-11 thermojet engines and 50 Model 22 airframes were completed before Japan surrendered.

Another version, the Model 33, was planned to use the same Nakajima Ne-20 turbojet engine as the *Kikka* jet fighter (the Japanese version of the German Me-262 jet fighter), but this engine never went into production and no Model 33's were ever built.

One of the surviving Model 22 *Ohkas,* along with its Tsu-11 jet engine, is on display at the Smithsonian's Udvar-Hazy Center in Washington DC. The US Air Force Museum exhibits a training version of the Model 11, fitted with a landing skid.

Boeing B-29 Superfortress

Although the design was already in the works before Pearl Harbor, the B-29 was one of the most technologically advanced aircraft to be produced during the war.

In 1940, things were looking bleak for the United States. England had barely survived the Battle of Britain and was being pounded by the Blitz, and soon Hitler's troops would be driving deep into Russia. It looked increasingly possible that the United States might be the only remaining democracy, and with the loss of France, Britain and Russia as allies, the US may have been forced to wage a long-distance war. The Army Air Force had just deployed the new B-17 Flying Fortress and B-24 Liberator heavy bombers, but neither of these had anything near the capability to strike across the vast expanses of the oceans.

In response the United States considered two new strategic bomber designs. The four-engined Consolidated B-32 concept offered gains in speed, range and payload over the B-17 and B-24, and featured a pressurized crew compartment. But the B-29 proposal by Boeing was a radical leap forward: it too had pressurized crew compartments, but also promised remote-controlled guns operated by analogue computers, and a radar-guided bomb-aiming system that gave all-weather accuracy.

In April 1941, the Army placed an order for 250 B-29s before the prototype had even been built (this was soon increased to 1,500). And, as an insurance policy in case the Boeing ran into difficulties and didn't work as advertised, the Air Corps also placed an order for Consolidated's B-32, which became known as the "Dominator". Around 100 were built, but only 15 ever entered service.

After the attack on Pearl Harbor near the end of 1941, Japanese forces quickly overran much of southeast Asia, and now the US needed a heavy strategic bomber which could handle the extreme long ranges in the Pacific, and needed it quickly. The B-29 "Superfortress", with a speed of 359mph and a range over 4,000 miles, fit the bill. The first B-29 prototype flew in September 1942.

The Superfort could deliver 10,000 pounds of bombs: these were carried in two bomb bays fore and aft of the center of gravity, and the bombs were released alternately from each bay. There were ten .50-caliber machine guns in five turrets, which were operated remotely by gunners inside the pressurized crew compartments. Each gunner could control several turrets at once to concentrate his fire. The tail turret also carried a 20mm cannon.

The plane had a crew of ten. In the Plexiglas nose sat the bombardier, who used the AN/APQ-7 Eagle radar set to find his target even under cloud cover. Above him in the cockpit were the pilot and co-pilot, behind them were the navigator and flight engineer, and the radio operator sat further aft. In the tail compartment, connected to the crew compartment by a pressurized tunnel, was the turret gunner, two side gunners, and the tail gunner.

Even as the prototypes were undergoing flight testing, the companies who would manufacture the new plane—Boeing, Bell, and Martin—were constructing huge new factories for the assembly lines. Curtiss-Wright and Dodge Auto Company, meanwhile, had already begun making 2200-horsepower Wright R-3350 Duplex Cyclone turbo-supercharged radial engines for the big bombers. They were the most powerful piston engines produced during the war.

Even as assembly lines went into action, constant new changes and modifications were being made to the design. Smaller satellite factories were set up where updates could be made to planes after they had left the main factory, so as not to interfere with production.

By 1943, the war in the Pacific had been turned around, and the War Department made plans to begin bombing the cities of Japan with B-29 bombers based in China. But there were difficulties with the B-29 assembly lines, and production at first was slow. Then, Chinese forces under Chiang Kai-shek proved unable to deal with the Japanese, and when the planned locations for the bomber bases were overrun by a Japanese offensive, it appeared that, with China unavailable, the US would need to bomb Japanese cities from bases in the Pacific Islands.

The first operational B-29 squadrons were in place in Calcutta, India, by May 1944. They were too far away to hit Japan, but they were able to bomb targets in China and Burma. In June, B-29s were based at a handful of airfields in Chengdu, China, that were just barely in range of a few targets on the southern tip of the Japanese islands. Logistically, this turned out to be enormously difficult. All of the fuel, ammo and supplies needed to keep the B-29s going had to be flown over the Himalayan "hump"—and it took three gallons of fuel to deliver one gallon to the Superforts.

It wasn't until the capture of the Marianas in August 1944 that the B-29s were finally able to begin striking Japanese cities in force, from airbases that were hastily built on Tinian, Saipan and Guam. The first raids, in December 1944, were carried out at high altitude to avoid enemy fighters and anti-aircraft fire. But the pilots encountered an unexpected difficulty—the jet stream winds over Japan were so strong that the bomb-aiming computers could not accurately compensate for it. After several raids with mediocre results, Major General Curtis LeMay, placed in charge of the bombing campaign, switched tactics to low-altitude night attacks using incendiary bomblets. The Japanese had virtually no night-fighter capability, and their anti-aircraft guns were also of limited effect in the dark. So LeMay had all the gunners and turrets removed except the tail gunner, which allowed a bigger load of incendiaries. One by one, virtually all of Japan's major cities were firebombed by over 100 B-29s at a time. The devastation was massive. In just one night raid on Tokyo, the bombers wiped out 15 square miles and killed 150,000 people.

On five separate occasions during these raids in 1944 and 1945, B-29s that had suffered battle damage or mechanical failure were forced to land in Soviet territory, near Vladivostok. As Russia was officially neutral in the Pacific War, these planes were interned, and while their crews were eventually released, the B-29s were kept by Stalin. Soviet technicians from the Tupolev design bureau took the Superforts apart and examined them in minute detail, then built their own versions using Soviet Shvetsov ASh-73 engines, designating them the Tupolev T-4 (with the NATO code name "Bull"). It became the USSR's first strategic nuclear bomber, and it remained in Soviet service until the 1950s, with some 1200 built.

The US ceased production of the B-29 in May 1946, but the Superfortress continued to serve as the only nuclear-capable American bomber until the development of the B-50. B-29s also served in the Korean War in 1950.

There are about 25 surviving B-29s on display at museums, nearly all in the United States—though the Imperial War Museum in England has one. Two B-29s are still airworthy: "Fifi" is owned and operated by the Commemorative Air Force, and "Doc" is flown by a nonprofit group in Wichita, Kansas. The B-29A "Jack's Hack" is on exhibit at the New England Air Museum in Connecticut, and the Castle Air Museum in California also has a B-29A. There are B-29s at the Museum of Flight in Seattle, the Barksdale Museum in Louisiana, the Museum of Nuclear History in Albuquerque, and the Pima Air and Space Museum.

Enola Gay and Bockscar

In late July 1945, after the successful Trinity test of an atomic bomb in New Mexico, the US began to plan the combat use of its new weapons.

When the initial list of potential targets for atomic bombs was drawn up, the city of Nagasaki was not on it. (The original list was Yokohama, Kyoto, Hiroshima and Kokura, with Niigata as an alternate.) During the wave of nightly fire-bombings that wrenched Japan in 1945, Nagasaki was mostly spared—only four small-scale raids were sent against the city. This was not because the city was unimportant: Nagasaki was a port and a shipbuilding center, and also had a large steel mill, an arsenal, and a torpedo factory. But the city presented a difficult target for aerial bombing. Unlike most Japanese cities, which were built on flat plains, Nagasaki was in a bowl-shaped depression, surrounded by hills and separated into sections by tongues of water—all of which made it difficult to bomb at night using radar, and would also limit any damage produced by firebombing. In addition, there was no defined industrial area that could easily be targeted: instead, small factories were scattered randomly all across the city. Nagasaki was also known to have an Allied POW camp nearby, which nobody wanted to hit by accident.

Within days, though, the initial atomic target list was altered. The ancient capitol of Kyoto, though the second-largest city in Japan, was a cultural, religious, and historical center with little military significance, and the political fallout the US would receive from destroying it was not worth the gains. So Kyoto was placed on the "reserved" list: it would not be designated as a target for either atomic or conventional firebombing.

Yokohama was an important industrial center, but it had already been the target of several B-29 firebombings, and the US military wanted an intact untouched city as a target for the atomic bombs, so they could better judge the damage levels that the bomb produced. Yokohama was removed from the list of atomic targets as well.

That left Hiroshima, Kokura, and Niigata, and on July 24, 1945, these cities were placed with Kyoto on the "reserved" list of cities that would not be hit by the firebomb raids. They would be the atomic targets, "in the priority listed".

But shortly after that, it was decided that Niigata was too far away from Tinian for a safe delivery of the heavy atomic bomb, and Niigata was dropped from the target list. It was apparently at this time that Nagasaki was added, likely because it was the largest city still available. The targets for the first two atomic missions were now set: for the first mission, the primary target would be Hiroshima with Kokura as secondary, and for the second mission, the primary target would be Kokura with Nagasaki as secondary.

On August 6, the first atomic bombing mission was carried out. On the airfield at Tinian, the uranium bomb "Little Boy" had already been loaded into the bomb bay of a specially-modified B-29 from the

509th Composite Group, commanded by Colonel Paul Tibbets, which had been practicing the mission for months at its training base in Utah.

As commander of the group, Tibbets assigned himself as pilot for the mission, and commandeered one of the still-unnamed B-29s that was normally flown by Robert Lewis. He also exercised his prerogative to name his aircraft, and the day before, Tibbets had ordered one of the group's ground crew to paint the name "Enola Gay" onto the nose, naming it after his mother.

It was still dark out when three B-29s took off from the runway at Tinian. "Enola Gay" carried the atomic bomb, and went first. Shortly later came "The Great Artiste", carrying scientific instruments to measure the explosion, and an unnamed B-29 (later dubbed "Necessary Evil") which carried film cameras and photographic equipment. After takeoff the three planes followed separate routes to Iwo Jima where they rendezvoused at about sunrise and headed for Japan.

About half an hour before they would reach the target city of Hiroshima, Captain William "Deak" Parsons and Second Lieutenant Morris Jeppson crawled into the "Enola Gay's" bomb bay. As a safety precaution for takeoff, the Little Boy bomb had been "safed" by having its propellant charge and electrical plugs removed, and now Parsons, who as the representative from Los Alamos was technically in command of the mission, was assisted by Jeppson in opening a panel on the bomb casing and inserting the live charges to arm the weapon.

Tibbets arrived over Hiroshima at a few minutes past 8am, and "Enola Gay" began her bomb run. Bombardier Thomas Ferebee dropped the Little Boy away at 8:15 and it exploded 43 seconds later. Between 70,000 and 90,000 people were killed by the blast, fire, and radiation — about one-third of the city's population.

"Enola Gay" landed back at Tinian just before 3pm, after 12 hours in the air. There, she was greeted by a crowd of reporters and photographers: General Leslie Groves, who had commanded the Manhattan Project, wanted to be sure the mission received wide press coverage. Colonel Tibbets was the first crew member off the aircraft, and was awarded with the Distinguished Service Cross right there on the tarmac. The mission had gone almost exactly as planned.

The second atomic mission, to Kokura, would not go so well.

Originally, the mission was planned for August 11. But when weather forecasts called for bad conditions, the schedule was moved up two days to August 9. The plutonium bomb "Fat Man" would be carried by the B-29 "Bockscar", piloted on this mission by Major Charles Sweeney, who had flown "The Great Artiste" during the

Hiroshima mission. "Bockscar's" regular pilot, Capt Frederick Bock, would now be flying Sweeney's B-29, which would once again be carrying instruments to measure the bomb blast. A B-29 called "Big Stink" would be carrying photographic and film equipment. The "Enola Gay", now piloted by Capt George Marquardt, would serve as an advance weather plane over Kokura, while another B-29, "Laggin Dragon", would fly weather reconnaissance over Nagasaki.

The difficulties began right from the start. On August 8, during routine firebomb raids, four B-29s in a row had crashed on the runways at Tinian during takeoff. The accidents had reinforced an uncomfortable fact: the runways at Tinian were only just barely big enough for a fully-laden B-29 to get airborne. When the "Enola Gay" had taken off for Hiroshima, the Little Boy bomb had been electrically "safed" and the internal cordite charge that set off the bomb had been removed, to prevent an accidental nuclear explosion if the B-29 had crashed on takeoff. The Fat Man bomb aboard "Bockscar" would also be electrically "safed", but the implosion system used to set off the bomb contained 2.5 tons of explosives. If the plane crashed on takeoff, there would be no nuclear explosion, but the conventional detonation would be enough to cause massive destruction.

Late that night, technicians from Los Alamos began preparing the bomb. Fat Man was shaped like an egg, five feet in diameter and eleven feet long, with a large box fin at the tail. It was painted bright yellow-orange, with black rubberized paint sealing all the seams. On the nose was the stenciled initials JANCFU, a joke from somebody on the crew: it stood for "Joint Army Navy Civilian Fuck Up".

"Bockscar" was scheduled for a 3:30 AM takeoff on August 9, but a problem appeared: one of the fuel pumps in a reserve tank was not working. It was too late to fix the pump or drain the tank, so 640 gallons of fuel now became unusable dead weight. "Bockscar" took off 17 minutes late, at 3:47 AM.

The mission plan called for "Bockscar" to make the six-hour flight to Japan alone, then rendezvous with the instrument planes "The Great Artiste" and "Big Stink" over the tiny island of Yakushima. When Sweeney got there, "The Great Artiste" was waiting for him, but "Big Stink" was nowhere in sight. The two B-29s circled over Yakushima for 45 minutes, but "Big Stink" never showed. (It turned out that her pilot had been flying at the wrong altitude and course.) Already an hour late, "Bockscar" and "The Great Artiste" flew on to Kokura, half an hour away.

The delay was crucial. "Enola Gay", circling over Kokura, had reported the weather clear. But over the next hour, as "Bockscar" waited unsuccessfully for its rendezvous, the clouds had begun to thicken, and smoke began blowing in from the nearby city of Yahata, which had been firebombed the night before and was still burning. By the time "Bockscar" and "The Great Artiste" reached Kokura, the city was socked in. Sweeney had been given strict orders that he was only to drop the bomb visually, and was not to carry out a radar approach. For nearly an hour, the two B-29's circled the city, but could see nothing.

Now Sweeney and his weaponeer, Navy Commander Frederick Ashworth (who was in actual command of the mission) had to make a crucial decision. It was 10:45 AM and "Bockscar" had already been in the air for seven hours. Fuel was beginning to get low (and the 640-gallons in the reserve tank remained unavailable because of the broken pump). Anti-aircraft bursts began appearing near them, and they could not see enough of the city for a visual bomb run. The decision was made to leave Kokura and head to the secondary target, Nagasaki, 15 minutes away.

Now their problems worsened. Calculations made on the way indicated that they already did not have enough fuel to reach the designated emergency landing field at Iwo Jima, and would have to land at Okinawa instead. When they got to Nagasaki, they found that it too was covered by clouds. As they circled, Sweeney and Ashworth first decided that they would scrub the mission and return to Okinawa, jettisoning the Fat Man into the Pacific. Then Ashworth decided to make just one bomb run over Nagasaki and to, despite their orders, aim the bomb by radar if they could not carry out a visual drop. At the last second, he reported, the bombardier spotted the city through a break in the clouds, and dropped the bomb at 11:02 AM. Fat Man exploded about a mile off-target. Estimates of the deaths ranged from 35,000 to 87,000. At least eight Allied POWs are known to have died in the explosion.

The B-29s could not stay to watch. "Bockscar" now had less than two hours of fuel remaining, and turned for Okinawa. When the plane reached the airfield at 1:20 PM, Sweeney found that his radio was not working and he was unable to contact the control tower for landing instructions—just as one of his four engines cut out for lack of fuel. While his crew fired emergency flares as a warning, Sweeney came in for a landing anyway. Turning hard to miss a group of parked B-24s at the end of the runway, "Bockscar" skidded to a stop just as a second engine ran out of gas. Exhausted, Sweeney and his crew piled out of the plane. When they finally returned to Tinian at 10 PM that night, there were, in contrast to the "Enola Gay's" flight three days before, no film crews and no celebration. In the United States, the lead news story that day was the Soviet Union's declaration of war against Japan.

The final screw-up of the second atomic mission, though, was still to come. After the bombing of Hiroshima, the Army Air Force had decided to wage psychological warfare against the Japanese civilians by dropping leaflets on several Japanese cities, including Kokura and Nagasaki, warning them that their city was a potential A-bomb target. But in the confusion that accompanied the rescheduling of the second atomic mission from August 11 to August 9, nobody had informed the PsyOps officers of the change. The leaflets warning of a possible atomic attack were, therefore, dutifully dropped over Nagasaki on August 10, the day after Fat Man had destroyed the city.

After the war ended, "Bockscar" suffered another indignity. In some of the press accounts of the mission, confusion over which pilot was flying what plane led to mistaken reports that it was "The Great Artiste" that carried Fat Man to Nagasaki, an error that would be repeated in published histories for years afterwards.

Today, the B-29 "Enola Gay" is on exhibit at the Smithsonian's Udvar-Hazy Center, and "Bockscar" is on display at the US Air Force Museum in Dayton OH.